A DISEASE of ONE'S OWN

Psychotherapy,
Addiction, and
the Emergence
of Co-Dependency

A DISEASE of ONE'S OWN

JOHN
STEADMAN
RICE

Transaction Publishers
New Brunswick (U.S.A.) and London (U.K.)

Copyright © 1996 by Transaction Publishers, New Brunswick, New Jersey 08903.

This book is printed on acid-free paper that meets the American National Standard for Permanence of Paper for Printed Library Materials.

Library of Congress Catalog Number: 95-37866
ISBN: 1-56000-241-7
Printed in the United States of America

Library of Congress Cataloging-in-Publication Data

Rice, John Steadman.
    A disease of one's own : psychotherapy, addiction, and the emergence of co-dependency / John Steadman Rice.
        p. cm.
    Includes bibliographical references and index.
    ISBN 1-56000-241-7 (alk. paper)
    1. Codependency—Social aspects—United States. 2. Popular culture—United States—History—20th century. 3. United States—Civilization—1970-
4. Self-actualization (Psychology)—Social aspects—United States. I. Title.
RC569.5.C63R5   1995
616.86—dc20   95-37866
                                                                                    CIP

Contents

Acknowledgments

This book began as a doctoral dissertation in the Department of Sociology at the University of Virginia. In the course of researching and writing that dissertation, I was at least doubly blessed to have worked with a group of first-rate sociologists who, as members of my advisory committee, accorded me the best possible combination of freedom and necessary guidance: James Davison Hunter, Gianfranco Poggi, and Mark Lupher from the University of Virginia and Robert Wuthnow from Princeton University.

My fellow graduate students at the University of Virginia were also consistent stalwarts, both as friends and as colleagues. Although all of the members of my cohort demonstrated a laudable interest in one another's works, five in particular—James Hawdon, Robert Shea, James Tucker, Randy Atkins, and Daniel Stuhlsatz—repeatedly engaged me in challenging intellectual exchanges, playing devil's advocate and critic at crucial moments and offering needed encouragement along the way. That, and their friendship, made both my time in Charlottesville and the work for this study immeasurably more enjoyable than it might otherwise have been.

I would also like to thank Jules Levine and Randy Canterbury, of the University of Virginia's Medical Center and Addiction Sciences Center, respectively. Thanks are also due to Rick Gressard, Walter Mason, Marian Kyner, Steve Sayre, Mary Lynn Applegate, Sandy McKown, Nancy Evans, Sarah MacDonald, and Penny Norford.

Finally, but most important, I wish to thank the only people who lived through the entire project with me: my wife, Marla, and my daughter, Jesse Simone. Their love, patience, and support more than once made all the difference.

While all of the above made invaluable contributions to this research, I alone, of course, am responsible for this final version of it, and any oversights must be my responsibility.

The author gratefully acknowledges JAI Press for permisssion to reprint material previously published [in revised versions].

Sociological Quarterly, "Discursive Formation, Life Stories, and the Emergence of Co-Dependency, vol.33, no.3, 1992:337–64.

Religion and the Social Order, "The Therapeutic God: Transcendence and Identity in Two Twelve-Step Quasi-Religions." vol.4 (1994):151–64.

Introduction

March 1991, 8:00 in the evening. In a small meeting room just off the administrative offices of the drug and alcohol treatment wing of a private hospital in suburban Los Angeles, a group of people sits in a circle listening to a man named Ken talk about himself.

> My dad was just emotionally unavailable, and he was pretty much an abusive s.o.b. So, I'm still pretty angry with him for his abusiveness and for not protecting me from other members of the family who were abusive. But, as a result I was overly-invested in mom, and that's shown up in my relationships with women. I'm *very* co-dependent on women. But things have really started to improve with this program. I've been in AA [Alcoholics Anonymous], too, for quite awhile, and in CoDA [Co-Dependents Anonymous] for a couple of years, and I've been seeing a woman for awhile, now. She's in AA, and working the program, and she says she loves me, which I believe is true.

Ken went on to explain to the group that, despite the positive changes in his life, he had recently fallen into old patterns of behavior. As he put it:

> I got into some real co-dependent shit this week. My ex-wife called me a while back and left a message. One of those "just wanted to be sure you're okay" calls. And she left me her phone number on a piece of paper some time before that, which, characteristically, I hadn't thrown away, "just in case"—which isn't too surprising, because I think I still love her. Anyway, I was going to return her call, and then I just decided that I had to go find her. Drove all the way up to where she's taking classes—a couple of hours, I guess—and I go running into the bursar's office and tell them I have to find this student, and the lady said, "well, we can't give that out." And I said, "why? What do I look like?" and she said, "well, we've got all kinds of things, like ex-husbands, coming here, and we have to protect the students." I just felt so ashamed, and I kind of shrank down, shoved my hands in my pockets, mumbled a few words, and got the hell out of there. Never have called her back. But, even though that happened, I'm still doing better than I was, and I can see that I still need to get some closure on these things, and get on with my life. Anyway, it's good. This is good. I see a lot of recovery going on in here tonight, and I'm just happy to be here. Thanks.

The other members of the group applauded, and one or two added, "Thanks for sharing, Ken." The applause died down, and another person began to talk.

* * * * *

Before the mid-1980s, neither the category of "co-dependent" nor Co-Dependents Anonymous (CoDA) groups like the one to which Ken told his story existed. But by the latter half of the 1980s and the early 1990s, Ken and his fellow co-dependents across the United States had engendered a veritable social movement, marked by hundreds of millions of dollars in book sales, frequent media attention, and the rapid formation of a wave of self-help groups styled after Alcoholics Anonymous.

The confessional talk show circuit—*Oprah, Donahue, Geraldo,* and the like—played an important role in these events, helping to spread word of this new discovery, co-dependency, across the popular cultural landscape. Throughout the latter 1980s, a handful of co-dependency experts made repeated appearances on such programs, touting their ideas and books, and offering commentary on the testimonials of the "average" Americans who usually appeared on the shows with them, serving as examples of co-dependent selves.

By providing a broad audience, programs such as *Oprah* can fan the flames of popular culture phenomena, but such shows in the main chronicle already existing cultural trends. Co-dependency's featured status on such programs followed on the heels of remarkable book sales and thus coincided with what all the evidence already suggested was a burgeoning popular interest. The first indication of this widespread public interest in co-dependency books was the dramatic success of Melody Beattie, an alcohol- and drug-addiction counselor and recovering alcoholic. Beattie's *Codependent No More*, first published in 1987, went on to spend almost three years (154 weeks) among *Publishers Weekly*'s top ten best-selling trade paperbacks, eventually selling well over 2 million copies. During that title's extended run, two more of Beattie's books also reached the ranks of best-sellers. Her 1990 reader *The Language of Letting Go* spent ten weeks on best-seller lists alongside *Codependent No More,* and *Beyond Codependency and Getting Better All the Time,* the 1989 sequel to her first book, was a best-seller for twenty-three weeks, going on to register sales of over half a million copies.

The successes of Beattie's books confirmed that the solid sales of titles by Anne Wilson Schaef were no fluke. Schaef's 1986 tome, *Co-*

Dependence: Misunderstood—Mistreated sold over 300,000 copies, as had her earlier work, *Women's Reality: An Emerging Female System in a White Male Society.* Another of Schaef's books, *Meditations for Women Who Do Too Much,* published in 1990, reportedly had sales of over 400,000.[1] Schaef, a psychotherapist and organizational consultant with Fortune 500 companies, also reported in 1990 that she had been approached by a major branch of the U.S. government about the possibility of developing personnel programs to address the problems of co-dependency and addiction. In spring 1989, the Soviet Peace Commission also sought Schaef's counsel on the problems of addiction, inviting her to lecture on that topic in the then–Soviet Union.

Sharon Wegscheider-Cruse, one of the pioneers in the Adult Children of Alcoholics movement (from which, as we will see, co-dependency was derived), also played an important role in the emergence of co-dependency. In addition to writing several popular treatises on addiction-related themes and making frequent appearances on the daytime talk shows, Wegscheider-Cruse was also a leader in efforts to secure co-dependency's status as a legitimate medical and psychological category. Onsite Training & Consulting, Inc., a Rapid City, South Dakota, firm run by Wegscheider-Cruse and her husband, Joseph Cruse (one of the founders of the Betty Ford Center), sponsored the first National Institute for Physicians Specializing in Co-Dependency during fall 1990. At that time, Wegscheider-Cruse estimated that several hundred physicians throughout the country recognized and treated co-dependency and said she expected that the medical establishment as a whole would soon recognize such treatment as a certifiable professional specialty.[2]

John Bradshaw, a former candidate for religious ministry and a recovering alcoholic active in addiction treatment, has been by far the most visible of co-dependency's founders—a visibility born of his successful use of a multimedia approach to disseminate his works and ideas. Each of his books has also been the basis for a Public Broadcasting System (PBS) presentation, each program more ambitious than the last. As of 1989, *Bradshaw On: The Family* (based on the book of that title published in 1988), the first of his efforts, had been carried by at least fifty stations nationwide, reportedly generating 140,000 viewer letters. In the same year, the book by that name was selling at the furious clip of 40,000 copies per month, as was his 1989 title (which was also made into a PBS special), *Healing the Shame That Binds You.* By

1992, each of these works had sold over 800,000 copies. On 2 and 8 December 1990, Bradshaw unveiled yet another program, based upon his then-new book, *Homecoming: Reclaiming and Championing Your Inner Child.* This therapeutic miniseries, which ran for six hours each day that it aired, featured an overview of the causes and symptoms of co-dependency and its diverse behavioral manifestations, interspersed with dramatic video footage of people engaged in various recovery strategies (besides, or in addition to, twelve-step group membership) that Bradshaw has adapted for his purposes. The book went on to spend all of 1991 on *Publishers Weekly*'s best-selling nonfiction hardcover list. Bradshaw's long-standing affiliation with PBS recently bore more fruit. *Bradshaw on Divorce*, another all-day affair, aired twice in the Boston area in the last two months of 1992, as did another program on *Creating Love.* In keeping with his multimedia approach, *Creating Love: The Next Great Stage of Growth,* the first installment of a four-book contract with Bantam Books, recently hit the bookstores. Bradshaw also lately reported that he had entered into discussions with Steven Spielberg about the possibility of hosting his own talk show; if the details could be ironed out, Spielberg would produce the program. Of Spielberg, Bradshaw said:

> Steven just gets this stuff instinctively.... Oprah [Winfrey] first sent him my 'Homecoming' tapes, which he loved. I wondered if this was a passing fascination for him, but after about 10 hours of one-on-one conversation, I could tell he really *gets* it. Plus, Steven understands that I've got to do what I do best. I can't be curtailed by this show-biz stuff."[3]

Not surprisingly, in light of the apparent windfall that co-dependency represented, several major publishers picked up these "recovery books" or started "recovery lines." In at least one case, publishing recovery-oriented titles pushed a small company into the ranks of relatively big-time publishers. Sales for Health Communications, Inc., a Florida-based publisher,[4] grew from half a million dollars in 1983 to $14 million in 1988. "Health Comm," as it is known among industry insiders, now offers well over a hundred titles on co-dependency and related subjects.

Larger and more mainstream publishers also jumped headlong into the emerging co-dependency market. By 1990, Harper and Row, Melody Beattie's first publisher,[5] was offering about eighty different co-dependency-related titles. Harper also entered into a joint publication and distribution agreement with Hazelden Treatment Center in Minneapolis.

Books launched under the auspices of this agreement were distributed under the Harper/Hazelden imprint. Such joint ventures became increasingly common. A spokesperson for the publisher noted that "other major publishers are [also] starting to hook up with the educational divisions of treatment centers," under arrangements similar to the Harper/Hazelden agreement. For example, Prentice-Hall entered into a similar co-marketing arrangement with Parkside, a national chain of close to 100 rehabilitation centers. Elizabeth Perle, vice president and publisher of Prentice-Hall Press, commented that the affiliation with Parkside was intended "to combine our sales and marketing strength with their direct-mail and community-based resources.... [E]ach [Parkside treatment] center will contact the book-selling community around them, and each will have an expert available for the local media."[6] Nor was the publishing industry's ventures into recovery books limited to trade books. In May 1990, Ballantine Books started publishing Hazelden titles for the mass market, as part of their own ongoing recovery line.

On the retail end of the publishing world, in addition to solid sales in conventional bookstores, more than three hundred "recovery bookstores" opened for business nationwide. These stores are stocked solely with titles and products that have inspired and speak to what some have called—a bit too loosely—the "recovery movement,"[7] hawking T-shirts, coffee mugs, and bumper stickers with insider slogans such as "Let Go and Let God" and "Codependent No More." The books are shelved by subject, in traditional bookstore fashion, but the subjects are all specialized forms of psychological suffering and the representative works feature theories of causation, descriptions of symptoms, and techniques of recovery for incest issues, adult children of alcoholics, adult children of dysfunctional families, compulsive overeating, smoking addiction, gambling addiction, narcotics addiction, alcoholism, and so on, covering virtually all of the problems addressed by a spate of new twelve-step groups.

In part because of its advocates' aggressive promotional tactics, codependency attracted a large and steadily growing minority of the American population. One manifestation of this increased awareness was the exponential increase in Co-Dependents Anonymous groups and meetings. As of July 1990, roughly one year after the organization was founded, there were already 2,088 CoDA groups meeting weekly throughout the country. In addition, as of that same date, there were sixty-four international groups registered with the CoDA International

Service Office, and spokespersons for CoDA estimated that approximately twenty-five new CoDA groups are formed each day.[8] It has been estimated that "there are 15 million Americans in 500,000 recovery groups and [that] 100 million Americans are related to someone with some form of addictive behavior."[9] In addition to the usual caveats about self-reported membership data, the "100 million" figure underscores the need for caution: as we will see, co-dependency defines almost every form of mood-altering activity as a "form of addictive behavior." Still, even if these figures are inflated by half, the twelve-step phenomenon has in recent years taken on enormous proportions, and co-dependency, since it emerged on the scene, has been the catalyst for much of that growth. Something in the themes associated with co-dependency plainly resonates in the public imagination.

Although co-dependency itself has by and large now gone the inevitable route of virtually all popular cultural phenomena—to the graveyard of more or less benign media neglect—its status *as* a phenomenon is an important development, and one that has never been adequately explained. Despite the current lack of attention, CoDA groups still meet regularly and tens, perhaps hundreds, of thousands of people still identify themselves as co-dependents. Where, exactly, did this co-dependency "movement" come from? What did and do the participants understand themselves to be doing? Why did all of this happen? This book will offer answers to these and related questions at some length. But those answers will depend upon a clear understanding of co-dependency itself. Therefore, let us begin by taking a brief but closer look at where the term "co-dependency" came from and what it means.

A Brief History of Co-Dependency

The concept of co-dependency is to some extent the offspring of an older term that originated among those associated with Alcoholics Anonymous: "co-alcoholism." According to the original usage, the spouses and children of alcoholics developed psychological problems as the result of the difficulties built into loving a person who was addicted to alcohol; these problems came to be called co-alcoholism; their sufferers, co-alcoholics. This general notion led to the creation of groups such as Al-Anon and Ala-Teen, which were designed to provide alcoholics' loved ones with the same kinds of fellowship and social support that AA had made available to its members.

In the mid-1980s, co-alcoholism underwent a terminological change. As part of a nationwide surge in the number of addiction-treatment facilities, addiction counselors began to use the term "chemical dependency" in reference to the range of addictions, including alcoholism, that those facilities addressed. In keeping with this new and more general category, the term "co-dependent," signifying those who were in a close relationship with a chemical-dependent person, supplanted the older notion of the co-alcoholic.

But the conception of co-dependency that fueled a veritable social movement involved much more than a simple terminological change; the co-dependency movement was and is the product of a fundamental change in the meanings of both the concepts of co-dependency and addiction. The new meanings began to emerge in the mid-1980s in the writings of a core group of co-dependency advocates and activists— some of whom I have already mentioned—including John Bradshaw, Melody Beattie, Sharon Wegscheider-Cruse, Anne Wilson Schaef, Robert Subby, and Charles Whitfield.

Subsequent chapters will address themselves to these changing meanings in some detail. But a brief overview at this juncture will help to set the stage. At its core, the activists' redefinition of co-dependency entailed three changes in the logic surrounding the original concept of co-alcoholism. The first of these is the claim that co-dependency is a disease—and, in fact, an addiction—in and of itself, rather than a condition caused by intimacy with an addict. Thus, for example, Anne Wilson Schaef observes that

> we are beginning to recognize that co-dependence is a disease in its own right. It fits the disease concept in that it has an *onset* (a point at which the person's life is just not working, usually as a result of an addiction), a *definable course* (the person continues to deteriorate mentally, physically, psychologically, and spiritually), and, untreated, has a *predictable outcome* (death). (Emphasis in original)[10]

Schaef's references to co-dependency's "onset," "definable course," and "predictable outcome" highlight both her own connections with the addiction treatment profession and co-dependency's links with theories of addiction. The imagery of a progressive and fatal condition that she invokes has long been a staple of the disease model of alcoholism (which Schaef here calls the "disease concept"), a model that serves as the theoretical centerpiece both of AA's twelve-step program and of the thera-peutic regimens offered in many addiction treatment facilities. The dis-ease model, as the term suggests, holds that alcoholics suffer from some sort of physiological malfunction that makes it impossible for them to control their use of alcohol. In the just-quoted passage, then, Schaef is arguing that co-dependency is not caused by close relations with an addict but is itself a disease; indeed, it is an addiction, like alcoholism.

The redefinition of co-dependency also entailed reversing the causal relationship between co-dependency and addiction: Co-dependency, the advocates asserted, is the cause of all addictions, rather than—as earlier thinking had held—the product of intimacy with an addicted person. This new conception of causal order issued from the advocates' shared conviction that the core of all addictions is an unhealthy dependence upon, a pathological "relationship" with, persons, substances, or, as they put it, "processes external to the individual." This conviction fueled a proliferation of new Anonymous groups designed to deal with an all but limitless catalogue of behaviors, including sexual adventuring, love and romance, spending, shopping, religious faith and observance, child and spouse abuse, incest, relationships—all understood as forms of addic-tion. Those who exhibit an overreliance and dependence upon any of these "external factors" are co-dependents.

The advocates did more than reverse the causal order between co-dependency and addiction. They also introduced a third claim: that the disease of co-dependency, and hence addiction, is itself caused by re-pressive socialization practices that, they maintain, are grounded in and characteristic of American culture as a whole. These practices, they as-sert, issue from antiquated cultural beliefs about child-rearing—beliefs that demand that children learn to stifle their emotions, abide by estab-lished social rules, and generally submit to conventional standards of propriety. These demands engender the reliance upon things outside of oneself that is the essence of co-dependency.

All of these conceptual changes are apparent in the advocates' defi-nitions of the disease they call co-dependency. For example, one of the less-visible activists, a chemical-dependency counselor named Sondra Smalley, has defined co-dependency as "a pattern of learned behaviors, feelings, and beliefs that make life painful."[11] This pattern, Smalley as-serts, is found in a person who is "human-relationship dependent [and who] focuses her/his life around an addictive agent.... It is a dependence upon people and things outside of self, along with neglect of the self to the point of having little self-identity."[12]

Another chemical-dependency counselor, Robert Subby, emphasizes precisely the same themes, defining co-dependency as "an emotional, psychological, and behavioral condition that develops *as a result of an individual's prolonged exposure to a set of oppressive rules*—which prevent open expression of feelings as well as the direct discussion of personal and interpersonal problems.... [Co-dependency is] born of the rules of the family" (emphasis added).[13]

In a similar vein, Charles Whitfield, a physician active in the Adult Children of Alcoholics organization, argued that co-dependency is *"any suffering and/or dysfunction that is associated with or results from focusing on the needs and behaviors of others. Co-dependents become so focused upon or preoccupied with important people in their lives that they neglect their True Self"* (emphasis in original).[14]

Eventually, co-dependency's founders arrived at a single consensual definition of the disorder they were all trying to describe. Immediately prior to the opening proceedings of the First National Conference on Co-Dependency, held in Scottsdale, Arizona, in September 1989, twenty-two of the movement's leaders convened for this purpose, ultimately settling upon a definition of co-dependency as "a pattern of painful dependence on compulsive behaviors and on approval from others in an attempt to find safety, self-worth and identity." "Recovery," they added, "is possible."[15]

As the definitions suggest, the advocates saw co-dependency as a concept with all but limitless applicability, a way of explaining a wide variety of national problems. Schaef, for example, maintains that the United States exhibits all of the symptoms of what happens "when society becomes an addict."[16] Whitfield, echoing Schaef, asserts that co-dependency "affects not only individuals, but families, communities, businesses, and other institutions, and even whole societies."[17] John Bradshaw's assessment of contemporary conditions in the United States also exemplifies these far-reaching claims. "[S]omething's wrong," Bradshaw argues,

> in a society where 60 million are seriously affected by alcoholism; 60 million are sex abuse victims; 60% women [*sic*] and 50% of men have eating disorders; one out of eight is a battered woman; 51% of marriages end in divorce, and there is massive child abuse. We are an addicted society. We are severely co-dependent.[18]

These remarks not only highlight the advocates' convictions about co-dependency's wide applicability, they also illustrate their characteristic indifference toward evidentiary support for their claims and an accompanying penchant for hyperbole. There are simply no reliable data supporting Bradshaw's assertions about the magnitude of such problems as alcoholism, sexual abuse, or eating disorders. These same tendencies are evident in the advocates' estimates as to the prevalence of co-dependency itself. For example, Schaef uncritically states that, "[a]ccording to [Sharon] Wegscheider-Cruse," co-dependency affects "approximately 96 percent of the population."[19] Schaef also approvingly cites Earnie Larsen, another addiction counselor, according to whom "there are between ten and fifteen million alcoholics in this society and...each one directly and adversely affects between twenty and thirty persons." Carrying out the arithmetic, Schaef calculates that "[u]sing [Larsen's] figures, and not accounting for any overlap, we see that the number of co-dependents in the United States exceeds the total population."[20]

Not surprisingly, comments and claims such as these invited and elicited a wave of scathing critical response. I have deferred any detailed discussion of these criticisms until the final chapter, not least because they make entirely too much of the validity, or lack thereof, of co-dependency advocates' definitions and prevalence estimates for the problems to which they refer. Advocates of any cause tend to exaggerate the significance of their own efforts; this is a relatively minor, and understandable, offense. More important, the far-reaching claims contain a significant clue for understanding what the phenomenon of co-dependency is all about, and literal-minded rebuttals of those claims have consistently overlooked this clue: Assertions that virtually an entire nation suffers from a fundamental psychological defect need not, and really cannot, be taken seriously as a diagnosis of individual problems; rather, such a claim must be understood as a wholesale cultural critique, an indictment of "traditional" American values and the negative consequences of those values for the organization of personality.

This book takes as its starting point the view that co-dependency is not something one "has" but, rather, something one believes. The analysis will treat co-dependency as a discourse, a symbolic system, a set of beliefs, about the self in relation to society. The co-dependency movement, in turn, is the product of people *selecting* those beliefs as a way of conceiving of, talking about, and acting upon the problems they encounter in their lives.[21] By "having" (that is, selecting) co-dependency, Ken—the man whose words opened this chapter—has an explanation for his own actions, actions that he apparently otherwise finds mystifying. As a co-dependent, Ken's impulsive and, for him, embarrassing trek to find his ex-wife effectively becomes a relapse of his disease, a manifestation of his "dependence upon compulsive behaviors... in an effort to find safety, self-worth, and identity," as the experts' consensual definition of co-dependency would have it. Moreover, as someone who "has" co-dependency, Ken also knows how he got this way, knows that his condition is the product of poor treatment by his family when he was a child. Being co-dependent, then, entails holding very specific beliefs, and those beliefs provide a means of making sense of and organizing one's life.

Seeing co-dependency as a discourse that people select as a way of conceiving of and talking about their lives and of dealing with their problems raises the question of why so many Americans are receptive to and readily accept that discourse. Forthcoming chapters will explain co-dependency's public selection as a function of both its content (the ideas that its creators and advocates seek to convey, the arrangement of conceptual elements into a system of discourse) and the historical context (conditions in the larger social and cultural environment) in which it emerged and found a large and receptive audience. Drawing from field research notes taken at Co-Dependents Anonymous meetings, I will also examine, through the testimonials of CoDA members themselves, what it means to "be" co-dependent, focusing upon the commitments elicited from and taken on by those who adopted the discourse. There are, then, four general points of inquiry that have shaped this book: co-dependency's creation and public selection, its content, the larger social and cultural context in which it emerged, and the social consequences—both for those who believe and those who do not—of its selection. Each of the chapters to follow interweaves these points of inquiry.

The central argument of the book is that co-dependency is the product of and a response to a transformation, still underway, in U.S. culture. This transformation has entailed widespread public acceptance, over the past thirty years, of a particular type of psychotherapeutic discourse, a "revolutionary" discourse, which I will call "liberation psychotherapy." The significance of liberation psychotherapy as a popular discourse, as chapter 1 will explain, is twofold: On the one hand, it has supplanted older understandings and become a dominant symbolism in contemporary U.S. life for thinking about and organizing social relationships; on the other hand, it espouses a fundamentally anti-institutional orientation. The net effect of liberation psychotherapy's rise to a position of cultural authority, then, is that millions of Americans now live in something of a cultural and social limbo in which the ideals, identities, and institutions they inherited from the past have in many ways been repudiated, but alternative ideals capable of engendering new bases for relationships, new institutional forms and practices, and new social identities have not yet been assembled.[22]

It is only in relation to this societal, cultural, and historical context that co-dependency's emergence and public selection makes much sense. Co-dependency is an instance of what I call a "discourse of reform." As the term suggests, this type of discourse, which chapter 1 will discuss in more detail, does not seek wholesale cultural change but is instead directed toward bringing social relationships into line with a more encompassing symbolic–moral system. In essence, co-dependency offers a reformed version of liberation psychotherapy, one that strongly "articulates" with—that is, is entirely faithful to—the core premises of that therapeutic system and at the same time provides a way of constructing social alternatives to the relationships and institutions that it has supplanted but not replaced.

As chapter 2 shows, liberation psychotherapy's cultural and societal influence underlies and is evident in the profound differences between those twelve-step self-help groups created before the "triumph of the therapeutic"[23] and those created after that "triumph." Although co-dependency was initially created in what I will call the "twelve-step subculture," its central premises are derived from liberation psychotherapy, and, as such, contradict the conservative, adaptational orientation that has historically counted as truth in that subculture.

Chapter 3 provides a more detailed analysis of co-dependency's structure as a symbolic system—the arrangement of its central conceptual and symbolic elements into a discrete discourse. This closer analysis reveals co-dependency's full articulation with liberation psychotherapy's core logic; although using different terminology, the conceptions of psychological sickness and its causes underlying the discourse are interchangeable with those in liberation psychotherapy. Drawing upon and expressing the same logic and symbolism, co-dependency effectively provides a life story for its adherents, one that explains their life experiences in liberation therapy's terms, and reduces their experiences to those terms.

By fusing liberation psychotherapy's core truths with selected tenets from AA's disease model of addiction, as chapter 4 explains, co-dependency designed and articulated what I call a "new theory of addiction." This new theory of addiction represents two significant accomplishments: On the one hand, it preserves the essence of liberation psychotherapy's worldview, defining virtually all problems in living—problems, I will argue, ultimately grounded in the cultural and social instabilities that liberation psychotherapy itself brought to bear—as "process addictions" caused by cultural repression and social control of the self; on the other hand, and most important, this new theory of addiction goes beyond liberation psychotherapy's radical individualism, giving people access to new and relatively stable relationships and communities in the form of self-help groups modeled after Alcoholics Anonymous.

Chapter 5 discusses the pivotal importance that the concept of process addiction had in making the co-dependency movement; indeed, without that concept, there would have been no movement, for it is only through self-identification as a process addict that groups such as Co-Dependents Anonymous became possible. Process addiction provides a rhetorically constructed common ground among people whose experiences and problems are otherwise too diverse to lend themselves to group identification and action. In addition, because of cultural meanings associated with addiction in general, being a process addict effectively requires membership in an Anonymous group.

Chapter 6 examines co-dependency's embodiment in social relationships, its creation of new "mediating institutions." The discourse organizes both patterns of social interaction (in the form of CoDA and similar groups) and identities (co-dependents/process addicts) in ways that embody co-dependency's truths. The analysis will show that people become co-dependent through a process of conversion in which they acquire a new identity that provides them with ongoing access to a community of sorts and to commonly held symbols, rituals, and experiences that have become elusive since the rise of liberation psychotherapy. Co-dependency, then, interweaves identity, belief, and social experience in ways that mirror the processes by which any social reality is created and maintained.

Chapter 7 explores what co-dependency means by recovery. As the analysis will show, the discourse's adherents strive to become liberation psychotherapy's ideal self: the self-actualized individual. Like their predecessors in self-actualization, CoDA converts follow a course of action that destabilizes their social relationships, particularly with those who are not adherents of co-dependency. Unlike their self-actualizing predecessors, however, co-dependents are not emancipated into a cultural and social limbo; by dint of the concept of process addiction, they have access to an alternative set of relationships and alternative institutions.

Chapter 8 explores what I call the "ironies of cultural change," the unintended social consequences that often result from the transformation of symbolic–moral systems. This discussion will show that liberation therapy was never intended to be a revolutionary discourse—that it was, instead, a discourse of reform—and trace the factors contributing to this disparity between liberation therapy's intentions and its consequences. This chapter also illustrates that in many ways co-dependency—reflecting its utter fealty to liberation psychotherapy—duplicates the same ironies and, in doing so, has a profound impact on converts' relationships with others.

The conclusion will explore the implications of and lessons to be learned from co-dependency and the co-dependency movement, arguing that, although an adequate level of understanding of this phenomenon is essential, such an understanding cannot be reached through a literal reading of the various co-dependency treatises; nor does the spate of criticisms that those treatises elicited provide a satisfactory understanding of the discourse's creation and public selection.

A final proviso is in order before beginning the analysis in earnest: It would be a mistake to read the foregoing and forthcoming observations about liberation psychotherapy's cultural and social impact as one more traditionalist's screed against relativism or "situation ethics" or the like. Rather, I take the core principles of liberation psychotherapy, and the cultural and social consequences of public acceptance of those principles, as logical and empirical considerations. What is important now is not to quibble over whether the changes are "good" or "bad"but to try to understand what the changes mean for U.S. culture and society. Although significant in its own right, the emergence and public selection of co-dependency provides one way of addressing this larger question, for the co-dependency movement itself is the product of people's attempts to respond to and deal with conditions of instability and uncertainty grounded in and issuing from these fundamental cultural and societal changes.

Co-dependency offers to those who need it (if one is to judge from their adoption of the discourse as their own) a way to make sense of their lives and to redress their problems. The discourse's capacity to make such an offer has been the principal basis of its public appeal. Co-dependency affirmed liberation psychotherapy's status as a new conventional wisdom about self and social world while simultaneously solving the principal problems that liberation therapy's anti-institutional orientation has presented for believers and nonbelievers alike. The discourse had such a far-reaching appeal because it offered people the prospect for communal belief and purpose that liberation psychotherapy by itself has heretofore failed to provide and that older cultural norms are no longer able to articulate or sustain, at least in any compelling or convincing way. Being co-dependent—believing in co-dependency—provides people with a stable and shared footing upon which to build enduring social relationships, which, in turn, are the foundations for a stable sense of self.

Regardless of whether one accepts or rejects, approves or disapproves of, what co-dependency defines as psychological health and ethical conduct, its emergence and selection is a poignant testimonial to the far-reaching consequences of cultural and social change and to the enduring significance of and desire for communal purpose and a genuinely social existence; for better or worse, co-dependency recognized and responded to that desire and, in doing so, provided people with one way of being part of a shared system of belief, purpose, and action.

Notes

1. The information presented in this section draws heavily upon Beth Ann Krier, "Excess Baggage: People-Pleasers Carry a Suitcase Full of Woes, but That's about All Co-Dependency's Leaders Can Agree On," *Los Angeles Times*, 14 September 1989, especially 21. Sales figures are from Wendy Kaminer, *I'm Dysfunctional, You're Dysfunctional: The Recovery Movement and Other Self-Help Fashions* (Reading, Mass.: Addison-Wesley, 1992).

2. See Krier, "Excess Baggage." It should be noted that, despite Wegscheider-Cruse's efforts, Hazelden Treatment Center in Minneapolis —perhaps the most influential addiction treatment facility in the nation—declined to offer a treatment program for co-dependency, citing the term's lack of diagnostic specificity, at least as Wegscheider-Cruse and her fellow advocates conceptualized it.

3. See Joseph Kahn, "Bradshaw Comes to Town—and, Maybe, to TV." *Boston Globe*, 18 February 1993, 57. It is not surprising that Bradshaw's emphasis upon the "inner child" resonates with Spielberg, whose movie *Hook* can be easily read as a parable about what happens when one "loses touch" with that inner child.

4. Health Communication's sister firm, U.S. Journal Inc., sponsored the First National Conference on Co-Dependency.
5. Beattie's newest titles are being published and distributed by Prentice-Hall/Parkside.
6. Quotes are from, respectively, Krier, "Excess Baggage," 21; John Bethune, "Pens and Needles," *Publisher's Weekly*, 20 July 1990, 23.
7. This term must be used carefully, and it generally has not been. Kaminer, in her critique of co-dependency's ideology (*I'm Dysfunctional, You're Dysfunctional*), repeatedly refers to the "recovery movement" in ways that artificially and incorrectly lump new twelve-step groups, such as Co-Dependents Anonymous, together with established groups like Alcoholics Anonymous. CoDA and AA hold diametrically opposed views about the appropriate relationship between the individual and society, as I will explain in more detail in chapter 1.
8. The countries in which CoDA meetings are currently held include Australia (six groups meeting weekly), Canada (thirty-six), the United Kingdom (thirteen), Sweden and the Netherlands (two each), and Guam, India, Japan, Mexico, and Saudi Arabia (one each). These figures, of course, should not simply be taken at face value. The organizers of any large-scale "movement" will be likely to over- rather than underestimate its membership and growth. Data from the addiction field are especially notorious in this regard. The actual daily rate is closer to two new groups per day. For example, in September 1989, there were 1,500 weekly meetings. Ten months later, there were 2,088—an increase of 588, or 58.8 a month, or approximately two per day; still, a significant rate of growth. As noted, this is not restricted to the formation of CoDA groups. (All data taken from CoDA's member newsletter, "Connections." Growth rates derived from a comparison of the number of meetings listed in this newsletter in September 1989 and November 1990.)
9. Margaret Jones, "The Rage for Recovery." *Publishers Weekly*, 23 November, 1990, 16. Take, as one example of the cultural cachet of the concept, the comments of Steven Stark, a political analyst for the *Boston Globe*. In his regular weekly column for 19 June 1992 (p. 15), Stark offered recommendations to resuscitate Bill Clinton's then-foundering presidential campaign. Stark suggested that Clinton could "Run a 'Prince of Tides' Campaign," noting that "from his handling of the Flowers and draft episodes, to his failure to inhale, to his inability to recall much of his childhood, Clinton has come across as somewhat dysfunctional. While voters may have considerable sympathy for the problems he had growing up in an abusive environment, they won't elect him to the presidency without more of an explanation. Thus, unless Clinton can recast his life story and person from that of tragic victim to heroic survivor, he can't win." Stark concluded that "if Clinton can convince voters that—like Nick Nolte's character in 'Prince of Tides'—he is in recovery, not denial, he has a chance to show growth and place himself in the middle of the therapeutic ethic so prominent in popular culture. If not, he'll remain written off as unacceptable." Although Stark's usage of "recovery" is characteristic only of the newest of the twelve-step subculture's groups, it is striking to find childhood experience and the therapeutic norm of full personal disclosure being offered as a serious campaign strategy. Clinton's "bio-pic" during the Democratic National Convention and to some extent the emphasis upon Bush's personal history during the Republican National Convention suggest that Stark's recommendations (or someone else's similar recommendations) fell on receptive ears.

10. Anne Wilson Schaef, *Co-Dependence: Misunderstood—Mistreated.* (New York: Harper and Row, 1986), 6.

11. Smalley is cited in Schaef, ibid., but Schaef offers no specific citation of Smalley's works and notes only that Smalley "conducts numerous workshops on co-dependence in the Minneapolis area and has written several pamphlets on the subject" (p. 14). One is left with the general impression that Schaef's reference to Smalley derives from, perhaps, their personal acquaintance. There are a couple of things that bear mention in this regard. First, the core of the co-dependency movement, as I have noted, is still little more than a handful of therapists—each of whom draws liberally upon the others' ideas. Schaef, Wegscheider-Cruse, Beattie, Subby, Bradshaw, and Whitfield cite one another frequently. Each of these authors also recurrently refers to other counselors' opinions; presumably, these are coworkers (either past or present) or acquaintances from the many workshops and seminars that are common to the addiction industry (as with any industry). Second, and somewhat more tangentially, the uninitiated may be mystified as to why Minneapolis figures so prominently in co-dependency's emergence. The Hazelden Treatment Center, which, as I have already mentioned, is one of the original and most highly regarded of the addiction treatment facilities in the nation, is headquartered there. Hazelden, apparently, acts as something of a magnet for those interested in addiction. Similarly, the original treatment center for "sex and love addiction" operates out of Golden Valley, Minnesota.

12. Quoted in Schaef, ibid., 14-15, and in Charles Whitfield, *Healing the Child Within* (Baltimore: Charles Whitfield, The Resource Group, 1986), 23. All references to Whitfield in this study are taken from this vanity press publication, which was subsequently picked up and issued in revised form by Health Communications, Inc. The vanity press edition was given to me by a psychiatric social worker with whom I had discussed co-dependency; he had purchased the book at a Whitfield lecture.

13. Robert Subby, *Lost in the Shuffle: The Co-Dependent Reality* (Deerfield Beach, Fla.: Health Communications, 1987), 26-27.

14. Whitfield, *Healing the Child Within*, 23.

15. Quoted in Krier, "Excess Baggage," 1.

16. See Anne Wilson Schaef, *When Society Becomes an Addict* (New York: Harper and Row, 1987).

17. Whitfield, *Healing the Child Within*, 24.

18. John Bradshaw, *Bradshaw On: The Family* (Deerfield Beach, Fla.: Health Communications, 1988), 172.

19. Schaef, *Co-Dependence*, 14.

20. Schaef, *When Society Becomes an Addict*, 15. Citing Larsen's statistics in an earlier work (see her *Co-Dependence*, 18), Schaef finds the idea that the true prevalence of a disorder can exceed the possible number of potential victims "interesting and impressive!"

21. Social theorists as diverse as Michel Foucault, Raymond Williams, Robert Wuthnow, and Wolf Lepenies have all shown that what Wuthnow calls "cultural products"—a term subsuming the various beliefs, truths, ideologies, myths, and symbols characteristic of any culture—are the end result of complex social processes in and through which those products are selected from among an array of alternative possibilities. Foucault addresses the issue of selection in a variety of works, but perhaps most explicitly in the appendix of *The Archaeology of Knowledge* (New York: Pantheon, 1972). Raymond Williams's emphasis upon the im-

portance of selection is concisely articulated in *The Long Revolution* (New York: Columbia University Press, 1961), particularly the chapter "Analysis of Cultures." Wuthnow stresses selection in *Meaning and Moral Order: Explorations in Cultural Analysis* (Berkelely: University of California Press, 1987), and still more explicitly examines the processes of selection involved in the development of pivotal Western ideas in his *Communities of Discourse: Ideology and Social Structure in the Reformation, the Enlightenment, and European Socialism* (Cambridge, Mass.: Harvard University Press, 1989). Lepenies, in the same vein, explains the rise of the discipline of sociology as the outcome of selective processes; see his *Between Literature and Science: The Rise of Sociology,* trans. R. J. Hollingdale (Cambridge: Cambridge University Press, 1988).

22. Unless one subscribes to the nonsensical view that what people say they believe is irrelevant to understanding why they behave as they do, it seems worth trying to understand what courses of action are most likely from those who hold particular beliefs; not least because these courses of action have tangible social consequences. Nonetheless, a variety of intellectual camps either directly or indirectly define away the significance of humans as meaning-creating creatures. The current enthusiasm for genetics as the key to behavior is only the most visible example. But determinism is hardly restricted to the biological realm; the social sciences are also prone to the same impulses. Behavioral psychology tends to reject the idea that people act on the basis of symbolic meanings. Although they emphasize learning, they rely upon a markedly attenuated conception of that process, extrapolating principles of human behavior from the capacities and activities of rats and pigeons. Moreover, even Freudian and neo-Freudian psychologies—with their putatively greater attention to the symbolic aspect of human existence—espouse a decidedly deterministic point of view. Since Freud, the idea that people act on the basis of "unconscious" motivations has been a centerpiece of all "insight" psychologies. So, too, the practitioners of a structurally deterministic sociology tend to treat social structures as sentient beings rather than as the more or less tangible outcomes of human activity. For a recent example of such sociological determinism, see Theda Skocpol, *States and Social Revolutions* (Cambridge: Cambridge University Press, 1979); Skocpol's argument is forcefully criticized in Michael Taylor, "Structure, Culture, and Action in the Explanation of Social Change," *Politics and Society* 17, no. 2 (1989): 115–62. To my mind, perhaps the most compelling evidence against such hard-line determinism is also the simplest: Those making such arguments not only effectively outline the irrelevance of everyone's beliefs but their own (always an occasion for healthy skepticism), but they have no way of explaining their own intellectual activities; everyone else's behavior but their own is determined.

23. Philip Rieff, *The Triumph of the Therapeutic: Uses of Faith after Freud*, 2d ed. (Chicago: University of Chicago Press, 1987).

1

Co-Dependency, Discourse, and Cultural Change

Clifford Geertz once observed that "[o]ne of the most significant facts about [human beings] may finally be that we all begin with the natural equipment to live a thousand kinds of life but end in the end having lived only one."[1] Why do we end up having lived only one kind of life? Geertz's answer is that culture, understood as an inherited system of symbolic forms that operates as "a set of control mechanisms—plans, recipes, rules, instructions—for the governing of behavior,"[2] channels individual conduct, and sculpts our innate physiological capacities into specific, repetitive forms.

The analysis of the co-dependency phenomenon presented in this book is informed by much the same understanding of culture. Of particular importance to the analysis is the connection between symbolic and relational systems. As Geertz's references to "control mechanisms" and the "governing of behavior" indicate, the symbolic systems comprising culture—ranging from whole cosmologies through discrete systems of meaning such as theories, religions, "isms," and ideologies— necessarily take social form in "relational systems," social structures, recurrent patterns of social action and interaction. At the most abstract level, these two systems, the symbolic and the relational, cultural and social structures, fit together and affect one another in specifiable ways to form a social and cultural whole—a reality.[3]

Co-dependency, as a form of folk-psychological discourse, is one of these discrete, secondary symbolic systems, derived from a more encompassing symbolism and taking on social structural form in the people identifying themselves as co-dependents in self-help groups like Co-Dependents Anonymous and in a veritable "co-dependency movement"—all organized around and embodying the discourse's constitutive themes. But it is not enough to say that co-dependency is a cultural structure, a discourse that expresses a distinctive symbolic logic; nor, as pointed out in the introduction, is it enough to say that this discourse was selected by a significant minority of the population and that it affects the behaviors of those who selected it. Such observations are true enough, but they are only the starting point for a more comprehensive, theoretically informed understanding of the phenomenon of co-dependency. This chapter is devoted to providing this more comprehensive framework, as a necessary preamble to the analysis that follows it.

Discourse, Articulation, and Cultural Change

A clear understanding of the phenomenon of co-dependency requires a consideration of general types of discourse and of the roles the different types play in social and cultural change. Especially throughout the modern age, discourses such as co-dependency have played a pivotal role both in maintaining and in changing the nature of a given social reality; they are the vehicles in and through which the satisfactions and the discontents of an age are expressed, extolling the merits or deriding the demerits of a status quo.

Which role they play, which themes these discourses express, is a matter of their articulation with the most abstract symbolic and relational systems of the larger reality in which they are created and selected. Antonio Gramsci's term "articulation" refers to the fit between, a "jointing together" of belief and practice, of symbolic and relational systems, into a plausible, more or less coherent, and palatable whole.[4]

Gramsci's particular intellectual concern, long a centerpiece of neo-Marxist thought, was how to account for the relative stability of capitalist societies. Among neo-Marxists, this stability represents a problem that must be understood and overcome, for, according to the original logic of historical materialism, the antagonisms and progressively worsening inequities of capitalism would engender the working class's awareness of themselves as a class for themselves and as the engine of historical change, an awareness that would eventually lead to a revolution against capitalism; in turn, the revolution would engender a just society. A central question for neo-Marxist theorists was (and is) why this scenario had not come to pass.

For Gramsci, the answer to this question lay in culture (the "super-structure"), which, in conventional Marxist thought—or at least in one of the most common caricatures of Marxist thought—had been concep-tualized as "epiphenomenal," as "determined by" more fundamental economic and material conditions.[5] Gramsci, contrary to this line of reasoning, argued that cultural factors—specifically, ideology, but not used in the customarily pejorative or reductionist sense of that word—played a central role in *reproducing* the status quo by securing the rul-ing class's position of "moral leadership" and the working class's consent to that leadership. In essence, Gramsci focused on what can be called "discourses of reproduction," symbolic–moral systems, expressed in discursive form and aimed at maintaining a larger—in this case, capital-ist—reality. These discourses, for Gramsci, were the products of what he called "organic intellectuals"—symbolic specialists whose function in society is translating abstract philosophical systems into practical commonsense knowledge about everyday life. Acting as mediators be-tween more "traditional intellectuals" and the "masses," organic intel-lectuals simplify the abstractions, rendering the symbolic and relational systems of capitalism as, in essence, natural facts and thus presenting the whole of the reality itself as simply to be taken for granted. Organic intellectuals, then, secure the working class's consent to the moral au-thority of the "ruling class." This juxtaposition of leadership and con-sent, which Gramsci called "hegemony," stabilized and legitimized the system of social relations under capitalism. Hegemony, as a form of articulation, fosters the *reproduction* of a social and cultural status quo.[6]

But articulation of the sort that Gramsci describes is only one form that the relationship between discourses and larger social realities may take. As Robert Wuthnow, who has also focused on the articulation be-tween cultural and social structures, puts it, an adequate analysis of dis-course and cultural change "must not only ask about the [social] conditions that shape [a discourse]...but also inquire into the reasons why these conditions did not shape it more."[7] As Wuthnow's observa-tion rightly suggests, discourses do not just formulate and express pub-lic consensus and satisfaction, fostering stability and hegemony; they also express discontent and engender cultural and social change.

In short, discourses are the "carriers" of both stability and change. Any analysis of the processes of change, then, must consider the dy-namics in and through which new discourses, new symbolic systems, are produced and publicly disseminated; the circumstances and conditions that contribute to their public selection; and their "institutionalization," their transmutation into relational systems—either by reorganizing established social relationships and institutions or by engendering new institutions, new patterns of social action and interaction.

As the foregoing comments suggest, cultural change should also be broadly understood as a dialectical process, in which these discourses of discontent play a particularly significant part. It is in and through discourse that the inadequacies of a given reality receive systematic and coherent exposition, and—depending in part on how the discourse frames and portrays these inadequacies—it is also in and through discourse that the necessary changes in belief, conduct, or both are mapped out. In broad strokes, the cycle of cultural change is one of order–disorder–new order, and discourses of discontent provide the symbolic bridge between the different orderings of cultural and social structures.

If a discourse is to have any tangible effect, it must be adopted by some significant segment of the general population. Discourses are produced by symbolic specialists: intellectuals, elites, and, in the present era, the army of experts and professionals; that is, those with the requisite training, knowledge, education (which, of course, is not quite the same thing as knowledge), literacy, and skills to be assigned or to take upon themselves the responsibilities for producing and maintaining or amending and changing a society's symbolic and relational order. But any of these outcomes, especially societal and cultural change, is contingent upon successfully persuading people to act. The social and cultural consequences of discourses of discontent, then, depend upon their *selection* by a public.

The public selection of a discourse is a function of several factors. Most obviously, the discourse must be able to reach its audience: Its creators must have access to the resources and institutional mechanisms through which their ideas can be publicly disseminated and thus become available for selection. But production and dissemination do not guarantee that a discourse will fall on receptive ears or attract a following; its public selection is principally a matter of a confluence between the historical *context* in which the discourse becomes available and the *content* of the discourse.

The probability that a new discourse will be selected sharply increases in periods marked by disruptions in established patterns of social action and interaction—periods in which already established symbolic systems, for whatever reasons, no longer fit well with or make adequate sense of lived experience. It has been extensively documented that new discourses (cultural systems, ideologies, and the like) emerge, indeed proliferate, when social relations are unstable and when the sources, nature, and redress of that instability cannot be explained by existing symbolic resources.[8] Clifford Geertz, for example, observes that ideologies—invariably a form of discourse—merge "precisely at the point at which a [social] system begins to free itself from the immediate governance of received tradition," when symbolic guides for behavior, thought, and feeling, are weak or absent. Such conditions, Geertz contends, engender "a loss of orientation," and it is this loss "that most directly gives rise to ideological activity." Ideologies, then, become crucial sources of social meanings and attitudes when neither a society's general cultural orientations nor its pragmatic ones work any longer.[9]

Discourses of Reform

In addition to the significance of the larger historical, cultural, and societal context, a new discourse's probability of public selection is directly related to its symbolic content—to how well it appears to capture the conditions in the larger reality and, on a closely related note, to how well its themes lend themselves to immediate practical action in dealing with the problems the public is experiencing.

The forms of practical action that a discourse *does* elicit can and do vary. There are two general types of discourses of discontent, and these can be analytically distinguished in terms of their thematic–symbolic content—the symbols they invoke and how those symbols are arranged to convey a larger message—as well as in terms of the courses of action they seek to or do produce. Using these criteria, it is possible to distinguish very generally between *discourses of reform* and *discourses of revolution.*

There are two analytically distinct but overlapping judgments underlying discourses of reform: (1) Fundamental cultural principles are basically sound, but (2) existing social structures do not measure up to those ideals. These reformist impulses, and the dialectical nature of the social processes they engender, are clearly reflected in the recurrent cycle of revivalism in U.S. history. In each new instance of revivalism, political, economic, and technological developments contributed to fairly wide-spread disruptions in established social structures and relationships; in each instance, this instability fostered a fervor for reform, embodied in a wide variety of discourses that expressed, at the most abstract level, "deliberate, conscious, organized effort[s] to construct a more satisfying culture";[10] in each instance, these efforts were undertaken by a small group of concerned activists who called public attention to what they saw as a set of social and moral problems, and sought to isolate causes, provide convincing evidence of the overarching malaise, and offer solutions to those problems. The solutions, in each case, entailed bringing people and errant institutions back in line with what the activists saw as the appropriate and legitimate symbolic–moral system; it entailed, in a word, reform.

To provide one brief, but illustrative, example, consider Mary P. Ryan's analysis of the Second Great Awakening, the wave of religious revivalism that swept across the United States in the early 1800s.[11] Ryan locates the intense and sudden outburst of religious enthusiasm in western New York state in the early 1800s amid the tumult accompanying such broad-based social changes as industrialization and urbanization. In keeping with the general correlation between reform and malaise to which we have just referred, Ryan observes that these structural changes engendered a period of pronounced instability in social relationships and argues that the revivals, and the accompanying wealth of voluntary associations dedicated to social reform, were a response to this social disorganization. The revivals and reform organizations were the crucible in which cultural adaptations to the new realities were formed and in which those new realities were themselves forced to accommodate the established symbolic–moral system. Gender and family roles were reconceptualized in ways that enabled people to adapt to the separation of home and workplace and the disruption in family relations that came with the rise of an industrial economy. The nuclear family—the "cradle of the middle class"—emerged out of the new symbolic status that reformers assigned to children and women. Because fathers began to work outside the home, and because the rise of large urban centers transformed the public sphere into a threatening world of strangers, many people were concerned about how the proper moral training could be instilled in children. Over time, reformers and activists successfully accommodated the demands of the age and the fears born of them by constructing religious justifications for a new division of labor in the family. According to the new symbolism that was developed, children were not, as had previously been the view, depraved creatures in need of forceful paternal control. Moreover, although some church authorities sought out and pointed to biblical prescriptions against, and thus opposed, women playing a large role in the moral tutelage of children, a compromise position was eventually carved out. As Ryan describes this compromise, it was agreed that "as long as they acted through persuasion, rather than authority, women [could exercise] extensive power, particularly over children, and even over patriarchs."[12] By thus adapting the established symbolic order to the new relational realities, it became possible to make sense of those new realities and to bring social relations into line with religious and moral ideals.

Discourses of reform, then, are in agreement with the established cultural ideals of the historical period in which they emerge. At the symbolic level, they reveal a high degree of articulation with those ideals, and at the relational level, they seek to bring social practices and structures into line with them. Frequently, the reform itself entails a process of accommodation, of constructing a basis for rapprochement between the symbolic and the relational. As Ryan's work indicates, for example, reformers in the Second Great Awakening had to find a middle ground between the monumental changes that industrialization and urbanization represented and the established religious ideals to which the new relational systems were poorly matched. The reformers adapted religious ideals to the new realities, and the new realities, in turn, were partially adapted to those older but now modified ideals. Robert Heilbroner has also observed this process of cultural and religious adaptations to capitalism: "In every pre-capitalist society," Heilbroner points out, "we find acquisitive activity disliked or despised.... Nowhere was this distaste more pronounced than within Christianity, where the taking of ordinary interest [on loaned money] was declared to be an excommunicable offense." With the rise of capitalism, it was necessary to "forg[e] a new attitude toward the central activity of the capitalist socioeconomic system—the search for profit."[13]

Discourses of Revolution: The Triumph of the Therapeutic

No such accommodating spirit infuses discourses of revolution. These discourses are characterized by a repudiation of both the symbolic and the relational systems of an existing reality. Like their reform-oriented counterparts, revolutionary discourses also call attention to what their creators see as the inadequacies and injustices of existing social institutions and relations, but their assessments of the source of those problems lay the blame squarely on fundamental flaws in established and central cultural principles. Discourses of revolution seek no less than the destruction of an old reality and the creation of a new one.

As many observers have maintained, we need look no further than events in our own era, and particularly the events of the last thirty years, for an example of the workings of a revolutionary discourse, and it is in the context of and in relation to these events that co-dependency's emergence and public selection must be understood. This revolution, however, entails nothing so fearsome or dramatic as what the term usually connotes: The changes that *have* occurred in the United States in recent decades have not included, say, the rise of a totalitarian state, massive redistributions of land or wealth, or the enforced transition to a collectivist or socialist economy. Rather, this has been an "expressive," more or less "silent" revolution centering on fundamental changes in public attitudes regarding the appropriate relationship between the self and society[14]—changes, that is, in the realm of psychology and, most especially, in the role that psychology plays in everyday life. By those accounts, we have witnessed "the triumph of the therapeutic," the "shrinking of America," the rise of "psychological man," the emergence of the "impulsive self," the birth of the "psychological society," the development of a "culture of narcissism," and a thoroughgoing "therapeutic attitude" dominated by an emphasis upon "expressive individualism"—all or any of which has led to the "fall of public man," and a pervasive "modern malaise."[15]

In general terms, the view that Americans and U.S. society reveal an increasingly psychologistic orientation is well supported and is reflected in a variety of trends, not the least of which is the increasing frequency with which people turn to the guidance of psychotherapeutic professionals—rather than, say, family or clergy—in times of trouble. Over the last three decades, the number of Americans consulting mental health professionals has, by conservative estimates, more than tripled, from 4 to 14 percent of the population. Even by these cautious estimates, a substantial minority of Americans—approximately 37 million people—regularly consult psychological wisdom in order to make sense of themselves and of a changing social world. Moreover, this increase in formal help seeking only captures a portion of the larger trend; the recent explosion of therapeutic self-help groups, which chapter 2 will discuss in more detail, is also part of the overall picture.

In the same vein, it is reasonable to expect that a culture organized around therapeutic symbols and a therapeutic ethic should generate accompanying occupational and professional opportunities and careers. This expectation is borne out by dramatic increases in the number of therapeutic practitioners. For example, in 1968 there were 12,000 clinical psychologists in the United States (no other nation at that time counted more than 400); as of 1990, that number had mushroomed to 42,000. In the fifteen years between 1975 and 1990, 10,000 new psychiatrists (from 26,000 to 36,000) were added to the fold, the number of clinical social workers grew from 25,000 to 80,000, and the ranks of marriage and family counselors swelled from 6,000 to 40,000. Moreover, the numbers of unlicensed, or "paraprofessional," counselors (including chemical-dependency counselors, such as those who created co-dependency) also grew rapidly: Virtually nonexistent ten years earlier, by the mid-1980s there were more than 130,000 such unlicensed therapists. The National Institute of Mental Health reported that between 1976 and 1984 the total number of people employed in psychiatric facilities increased from 375,000 to 441,000. Concomitantly, the number of those facilities has also grown considerably: Private psychiatric hospitals increased by 47 percent; the number of general hospitals offering separate mental health services saw a 59-percent increase, and community mental health centers showed similar patterns of expansion.[16]

Further evidence of the overall growth of this psychological orientation is reflected in comparative data revealing that in the United States there are more counselors than there are librarians, firefighters, or mail carriers; there are nearly two psychotherapists for each dentist or pharmacist. Of the nearly 100,000 psychiatrists worldwide, over one-third are American; of the 4,000 members of the International Psychoanalytic Association, one-half practice in the United States; far more than half of all the clinical psychologists in the world are Americans.[17]

Naturally, the profusion of practitioners is also reflected in education statistics. For example, between 1971 and 1987, the number of doctorates conferred in all the social sciences (including economics, sociology, anthropology, and political science) declined by 20 percent (from

3,659 to 2,916), while doctorates in psychology (which are now tallied separately from the other social sciences) increased nearly twofold (from 1,782 to 3,123). In 1987, then, 207 more doctorates were awarded in psychology than in all the remaining social sciences combined.[18]

Although these data undeniably point to significant social and cultural trends, simple references to an increasingly psychological or therapeutic worldview are not in and of themselves especially informative. Historically, most psychologies have buttressed rather than supplanted established societal arrangements and cultural codes. As Peter L. Berger and Thomas Luckmann explain this immanent conservatism, psychologies provide "the interpretative schemes for disposing of problematic cases...[thereby] serving to legitimate the identity-maintenance and identity-repair procedures established in the society, [and] providing the theoretical linkage between identity and world."[19] In the United States up to and throughout the 1950s, the predominant psychological discourses performed the fundamentally reproductive function to which Berger and Luckmann refer; the principal therapeutic impetus was adaptational, aiming to secure the individual's adjustment to the established reality and to instill what can fairly be called "an ethic of self-denial," in which the central principle was that society outweighed the individual in judgments about the morality of behavior and the normality of the self. Although the conformity that is now associated with life in the United States in the decade of "peace and prosperity" has perhaps been somewhat overemphasized in retrospect, it was more or less accepted that psychological well-being and, in the argot of that era, "maturity" were functions of fitting in and adapting oneself to conventional social norms.[20]

Given the historically conservative role that psychological discourse has played, it is clear that the cultural and societal significance of the increasingly therapeutic worldview to which so much evidence points does not issue from a psychological orientation, as such. Rather, that significance stems from the growing public acceptance of what I will call "liberation psychotherapy." By this term I do not mean a single mode of therapeutic theory and practice, such as Gestalt Therapy or Transactional Analysis. Rather, liberation psychotherapy refers to a set of assumptions and presuppositions—about human nature, culture, and society and about the right way to structure the relationship between the individual and society—that may be and are shared by any number of therapeutic theories and techniques. Chief among these core assumptions and presuppositions is that conventional culture and society make individuals sick by thwarting the development of the "real self" in the interests of social conformity. To get well, in this view, the self must get out from beneath the repressive thumb of culture and society; hence, "liberation" psychotherapy.

Liberation psychotherapy's status as a revolutionary discourse stems from this rather simple premise, for in the seemingly innocuous conviction that the individual's subjection to communal purpose is the cause of psychological sickness lies a rejection of previously established cultural principles regarding the appropriate relationship between self and society. This rejection comprises an ethical shift. An ethic is a moral and conceptual map, a guideline for deciding an appropriate course of action and for explaining—both to oneself and to others—why *this* course of action, rather than another, is appropriate. Liberation psychotherapy's symbolism is informed by and espouses what I will henceforth call the "ethic of self-actualization," which assigns ultimate moral priority to the self, over and against society. Those who subscribe to this ethic will and must behave in accordance with inner directives, expressing their autonomy from, rather than their subordination to, conventional social expectations. For self-actualized individuals, then, any action governed by social convention rather than individual preference—staying in an intimate relationship or abiding by the demands imposed by educational institutions or an inherited religious faith—is tantamount to self-violation. To be well, to be ethical, requires leaving the marriage, finding a new faith, and so on. To simply conform to social expectation is to be, in varying degrees, psychologically sick.

A closer look at the data on the psychologization of U.S. culture and society reveals this more fundamental ethical shift.[21] These data show that since liberation psychotherapy's emergence in the 1960s and among the generational cohort most affected by and most likely to have embraced it—namely, the baby boom generation[22]—the self, rather than society, has become by far the more important partner in the relationship between the two. The self's overarching moral significance, expressed by the claim that every person has a right to autonomy from social and cultural proprieties, is liberation psychotherapy's central organizing principle. The influence of this principle is reflected in a growing emphasis upon the importance of self-direction and self-expression and an accompanying reluctance to submit to collective social expectations. For example, Ronald Inglehart, a political scientist who has been clocking these trends for nearly two decades, has observed that "[t]hroughout advanced industrial society...for the past several decades, adherence to traditional cultural norms has been in retreat." Summarizing his own findings, Inglehart concludes that the magnitude of the changes involved constitutes a "silent revolution," a monumental "culture shift."[23]

Echoing Inglehart's findings, *The Inner American*—an extensive longitudinal study conducted over the twenty-year period from 1957 to 1976 and published in 1981—revealed "a shift from a *socially* integrated paradigm for structuring well-being, to a more *personal* or *individuated* paradigm for structuring well-being" (emphasis in original). Resonating with liberation psychotherapy's emphasis upon the self's autonomy from external controls, the results of this research found "the 1957 population taking much more comfort in culture and the 1976 population gathering much more strength in its own personal adaptations to the world."[24]

Further reflecting liberation psychotherapy's belief in and emphasis upon the moral ultimacy of the self, *The Inner American* pointed to three common changes in how people think about and organize the self-to-society relationship: (1) a general diminution of adherence to role standards as the basis for defining psychological adjustment, manifested in, among other things, a clear decrease in the positive regard that Americans have for parenthood and an increasing tendency for people to "feel restricted by role assignments that enforce patterns of life or are too rigidly defined"; (2) an increased focus on self-expressiveness and self-direction, at least partially reflected by sharp increases in dissatisfaction with work and the accompanying urge toward workplace "democracy," as well as by generally negative views toward norms and practices that restrict self-expression; (3) a clear shift away from a social–organizational integration of self and a concomitant shift toward personal authenticity.[25]

These findings were most recently reaffirmed by Cheryl Russell, a social demographer who has specialized in studying the impact of the baby boom and of the values characteristic of many members of that generation upon U.S. culture and society. In her book *The Master Trend* (which she subtitled *How the Baby Boom Generation Is Remaking America*), Russell argues that baby boomers constitute the first full generation of what she calls "free agents"—people for whom "the interests of the individual take precedence over the needs of the family, the rights of an organization, or the power of the state. This perspective," she goes on, "is more emotional than intellectual, more psychological than political."[26] In essence, Russell's free agents are liberation psychotherapy's self-actualized individuals—they are the selves of a still-emerging therapeutic age, selves whose existence is made possible by and testifies to a shift in U.S. culture from the ethic of self-denial to the ethic of self-actualization.

In the Wake of the "Revolution"

The significance of all these data and the trends they document is manifold, but two very general points, having to do with symbolic and relational systems and the fit between them, are especially important for understanding liberation psychotherapy's impact and its relationship to the public selection of co-dependency.

First of all, the widespread public embrace of liberation psychotherapy as a symbolic system entails a profound transformation in the function that psychologies have historically performed. Rather than legitimating the symbolic–moral order of an existing reality, liberation therapy represents an alternative symbolic–moral order, a different vision of reality itself. This transformation is reflected in and issues from the core premises of that discourse—particularly the conviction, as we have seen, that the conventional reality makes people "sick" by imposing moral and normative demands upon the self.

This conviction informs Carl Rogers's lament that "the Protestant Christian tradition…has permeated our culture with the concept that man is basically sinful, and only by something approaching a miracle can this sinful nature be negated." Asserting that "the basic nature of the human being, when functioning freely, is constructive and trustworthy," Rogers offers a counterview of life as a "process" in which a person is encouraged to express and explore all emotions: "I like to think of [this process] as a 'pure culture,'" in which "the individual…is coming to *be* what he *is*" (emphasis in original). Given the evident assumptions underlying these remarks, Rogers concludes that the key to psychotherapeutic health is the liberation of the self from cultural influences and effects.[27]

As does any discourse of revolution, the view that culture and society are the cause of psychological sickness constitutes a fundamental repudiation of established cultural principles and the social relations that embody those principles. At the same time, however, as the data showing the public acceptance of the ethic of self-actualization indicate, liberation psychotherapy has become, for many, an alternative symbolic–moral system, a new model of and for reality.

The second significant aspect to liberation therapy's rise to a position of cultural authority also issues from its core premises as a symbolic system. By defining collective control of the self as the cause of psychological sickness, liberation therapy espouses a fundamentally anti-institutional—and, really, an anticultural—worldview. This, moreover, is a generic, all-encompassing anticulturalism and anti-institutionalism: Rather than simply assailing the symbolic–moral system of *midcentury U.S. culture,* such writers as Abraham Maslow and Carl Rogers effectively defined *culture per se* as something the self must overcome to be well: *Any* imposition of collective will—which is the principal mechanism by which any culture sustains itself—ostensibly constitutes the repressiveness which is said to give birth to psychological sickness. Liberation therapy's anti-institutionalism derives from this anticulturalism, for institutions are ultimately the aggregated patterns of behavior that obtain in the collective imposition of symbolic–moral demands. Without the capacity to speak to individuals with what Karl Barth called "binding address," a culture cannot structure individual behavior.[28] Indeed, as Rieff maintains, "[a] culture survives principally...by the power of its institutions to bind and loose [people] in the conduct of their affairs with reasons which sink so deep into the self that they become commonly and implicitly understood."[29]

Because of this anticultural, anti-institutional stance, liberation therapy has proven an inordinately difficult discourse to institutionalize, particularly at the level of such informal social relationships as friendship, courtship, family, community, and the like. This difficulty, moreover, has been evident since the earliest stages of liberation therapy's ascendancy. The communal movement of the late 1960s and early 1970s—the first attempts to translate liberation psychotherapy's model of reality into tangible form—illustrates this point quite clearly. Rosabeth Moss Kanter, in what is among the most comprehensive and thoughtful of many analyses on this topic, observes that the ethic of self-actualization, expressed colloquially as "'[d]oing your own thing,' [was] a pervasive ethic in many...communes." When guided by that ethic, she continues,

> the individual constructs his own world out of the myriad choices confronting him.... [Therefore,] the chances that many others will construct theirs in exactly the same way is much more limited than in the less diverse environment of the last century. Without a strong set of beliefs to indicate to the person why he should suspend the option, he generally continues to exercise them in the new communes.[30]

The communes, Kanter concluded, by and large did not work and did not last as alternative social orders because the ethic of self-actualization "places the person's own growth above concern for social reform, political and economic change, or the welfare of the community. The person is free to leave when no longer satisfied; his involvement with the group is limited."[31]

Now, a generation later, the evidence indicates that this worldview is even more widely accepted and is the foundation for how millions of people think about and conduct their relationships with their families, friends, churches, schools, neighborhoods, and so on. The anticultural, anti-institutional core to liberation psychotherapy's vision of a new reality is a persistent subtext to social science analyses of the status of contemporary U.S. life. Consider, as one case in point, the recent volume *America at Century's End*, a comprehensive collection of research papers examining the condition of U.S. culture and society as we approach the millennium. In his summary remarks to that volume, the sociologist and political scientist Alan Wolfe, although not speaking of the rise of liberation therapy as such, nonetheless offers observations that resound with the consequences of that development. Wolfe observes, for example, that one of the threads linking the otherwise disparate analyses in the book is that for many, old rules and ways of arranging family life, marriage, religion, education, and so on, do not work.[32] In light of "the absence of models that define what is expected of them—both older models that no longer seem valid as well as ones so new they have not yet been formed," Wolfe says, "Americans will increasingly have to define for themselves the rules by which they will structure their lives."[33] He concludes that, when one examines the available evidence, "[i]t is as if the United States is caught between two moral codes, one of which no longer applies and the other of which has not yet been developed."[34]

These themes inform analyses of virtually every institutional domain in U.S. social life. Studies on the family, for example, reveal precisely Wolfe's combination of rejected or irrelevant models of action from the past and yet-to-be assembled alternatives. For example, Judith Stacey speaks of the present era as "a tumultuous and contested period of family history, *a period following that of the modern family order but preceding what, we cannot foretell....* [C]ontemporary family arrangements in the United States are diverse, fluid, and unresolved" (emphasis added).[35] Kathleen Gerson, discussing a wide variety of "family strategies" by which contemporary U.S. families respond to current conditions, echoes Stacey's general observations, noting that *"[t]he foreseeable future is unlikely to provide a return [to old family patterns]...[b]ut clear-cut and fully satisfying resolutions to the dilemmas and conflicts of unequal and uneven change have yet to emerge"* (emphasis added).[36]

The themes Wolfe raises to broadly characterize these and many similar research findings resonate with liberation psychotherapy's impact. To say that the old moral code "no longer applies" is one way to talk about the repudiation of the central principles of pre-1960s' culture. So, too, liberation therapy's influence is implied in the accompanying observation that a new moral code "has not yet been developed." But, when liberation therapy's widespread public acceptance is taken into consideration, it is also clear that Wolfe's conclusions bear reformulation: It is less that a new moral code has not yet been developed than that the symbolic–moral code that *has* been developed is structured around anticultural and anti-institutional premises. This is why, as Wolfe says, people must "structure their lives" on an improvisational basis rather than relying upon and abiding by established normative and institutional guidelines.

Co-Dependency as a Discourse of Reform

This larger set of historically specific conditions serves as the *context* in which co-dependency's creation and, most important, its public selection make sense. Among no segment of the population have these changes and conditions been more concentrated than in the baby boom generation, those nearly 75 million Americans born between 1946 and 1964; this is particularly true for the white, middle-class men and women most likely to have embraced the liberation psycho-therapy ethos or to have come of age alongside those who did. To be sure, for some proportion of this population, therapeutic emancipa-tion has provided freedoms and opportunities they might otherwise have never known. For many others, however, the conditions that lib-eration psychotherapy has brought to bear—the demise of old beliefs and practices and the absence of viable social alternatives to those that have been rejected—have translated into a seemingly endless string of disillusionments and disappointments: failed relationships, friend-ships, marriages; an overarching and pervasive ambiguity about how to decide among all but limitless courses of action; the demise of the established social and cultural foundations from which most people, historically, have arrived at some stable sense of themselves, of their world, and of their place in that world. It is principally among mem-bers of this generation that liberation psychotherapy's cultural and social impact has been more negative than positive, more confound-ing than liberating, more isolating than uplifting. It is less than sur-prising that, of the 547 members of Co-Dependents Anonymous groups (on both the East and West Coasts and in the Midwest) that I encoun-tered in the course of my research, virtually all of them were white baby boomers.[37]

Co-dependency's appeal lies in its status as a *discourse of reform*—a status that the remainder of this book will explicate at some length. Re-call, though, that discourses of reform are the products of judgments that, on the one hand, fundamental cultural principles are basically sound, moral, and just but that, on the other hand, existing systems of social relations do not measure up to those larger ideals. One source of the discourse's appeal is simply that the fundamental cultural principles that co-dependency views as moral and just are those of liberation psycho-therapy—a symbolic system with which white baby-boomers are espe-cially likely to be familiar, simply because they came of age at the same time, and under the same conditions, that liberation psychotherapy's influence was on the rise.[38] Co-dependency found a receptive audience, though, not simply because of its articulation with, and hence reitera-tion of, liberation psychotherapy's core premises. More appealing is that the discourse offers a reformed version of liberation therapy, a ver-sion that makes it possible—and indeed, as we will see, necessary—to forge a healthy identity in and through stable social relationships.

As we have seen, liberation psychotherapy's anticultural and anti-institutional principles do not lend themselves to the self's immersion in or submission to the communal purposes from which social institutions are formed and maintained. The brunt of liberation therapy's anti-institutionalism has been borne by those largely informal institutions—such as friendship, courtship, intimate relations, family, community—that stand between and mediate the relationship between the individual and the abstract and exceedingly powerful structures of state and economy; it is these mediating institutions with which individuals are in daily and nearly constant contact. Because liberation therapy directs its invective almost exclusively toward these institutions, remaining largely mute about political and economic institutions, self-actualizing individuals have devoted the bulk of their search for autonomy from group constraint to declarations and demonstrations of independence from family, community, and so on.

These observations are not offered in elegy or lamentation. Rather, the significance of these processes lies in the close, indeed, the dialectical, relationship between these institutions and individual identity. These are the institutions in and through which identities are formed and sustained; at the same time, those identities are the vehicles in and through which the institutions are themselves formed and maintained. Peter Berger, making essentially this same point, has pointed out that "identity is socially bestowed, socially sustained, and socially transformed."[39] Because they are, in this sense, mutually constitutive, their fortunes are closely intertwined: The destabilization of one implies the destabilization of the other as well.

This has been liberation therapy's chief dilemma since its ascendancy: How does one create social—especially mediating—institutions that do not obstruct the individual's search for autonomy from collective constraint? This is at the same time a question of how to create identities that are amenable to but not bound by communal purpose. The failure to resolve this dilemma is the key to understanding the difficulties of institutionalizing liberation therapy.

It is this dilemma to which co-dependency's reformist impulses are directed. The discourse provides its adherents with a way of thinking and talking about their lives and identities; it offers them a life narrative that is, in its broad themes, entirely in keeping with the central principles of liberation psychotherapy:[40] Co-dependents' lives, the narrative explains, are troubled—in any of an all but infinite number of ways—because they are psychologically sick; they are sick because of the repressions they experienced at the hands of culture and society; they must therefore negate those cultural and societal influences in order to recover from their sickness and alleviate their troubles.

In this general outline, though, co-dependency offers nothing different from liberation therapy itself. These, after all, are the very same premises that fueled the instabilities and relational problems to which co-dependency offers a response. But the discourse offers them a reformed version of liberation psychotherapy: As we will see, co-dependency's adherents are not merely pychologically sick, they are "addicts"; as addicts, the discourse informs them, they not only can but must seek redress in self-help groups designed to deal with addiction. These groups, in effect, represent the first informal, mediating institutions of what is still, in co-dependency, a liberation therapy reality. The groups provide the ongoing social recognition and support through which a more or less coherent sense of self and identity can be maintained. In providing these opportunities, in bringing social relations into line with liberation therapy's core principles, co-dependency aligns itself with its historical predecessors—it is simply the latest in a long line of discourses of reform.

* * * * *

I would introduce two final and closely-related caveats before beginning the analysis of co-dependency in earnest. First of all, because co-dependency theorists are ardent believers in liberation psychotherapy, their assessment of the problems they confronted simultaneously includes *and* excludes particular themes. Subsequent chapters will examine what is included, at some length, but what is excluded is no less important and should not pass unnoticed. What is of particular significance in this regard is the exclusion of everything that has transpired in the wake of liberation therapy's quite profound impact on U.S. culture and society. There are, I think, simple enough reasons for this exclusion. Liberation psychotherapy ultimately has but one explanatory mechanism for any and all psychological and social problems: societal and cultural repression of the self. Because of its perfect articulation with liberation psychotherapy, then, co-dependency predictably continues to dip from that thematic well for its own explanations; in doing so, the discourse excludes the cultural and social changes that have followed from widespread public acceptance of liberation psychotherapy. What is thus missing from co-dependency, of course, is any consideration of the ways in which liberation therapy's *impact* may be related to people's contemporary problems.

The second caveat flows from the first. I am not suggesting that co-dependency theorists were or are explicitly conscious of the problems involved in institutionalizing or legitimating liberation psychotherapy. I do maintain that co-dependency has helped in accomplishing both of these outcomes, but I would argue that the outcomes were serendipitous rather than consciously or carefully planned. It is much more likely that co-dependency theorists were simply working with the conceptual elements that they had at their disposal, trying to make sense of their mounting caseloads. Because of their intellectual commitments, to both liberation psychotherapy and conventional wisdom about addiction, they happened upon a conceptual alchemy that led to the creation of a discourse well-suited to interpreting and dealing with the problems of the therapeutic culture: a discourse of reform. It is to an analysis of that discourse that the remainder of this book is addressed.

Notes

1. Clifford Geertz, "The Impact of the Concept of Culture on the Concept of Man," in *The Interpretation of Cultures* (New York: Basic Books, 1973), 45.
2. Ibid., 44.
3. For this distinction between cultural and relational structures, see Sharon Hays, "Structure and Agency and the Sticky Problem of Culture," *Sociological Theory* 12, no. 1 (1994): 57–72. For a similar but somewhat more problematic analysis, see Anne Kane, "Cultural Analysis in Historical Sociology: The Analytic and Concrete Forms of the Autonomy of Culture," *Sociological Theory* 9, no. 1 (1991): 53–69.
4. Antonio Gramsci, *Selections from the Prison Notebooks,* ed. and trans. Quentin Hoare and Geoffrey Nowell-Smith (London: Lawrence and Wishart, 1971).
5. Marx is often taken as an advocate of the view that "culture" is determined by economic social structures. Although Marx, in *The German Ideology,* does observe that it is possible to "explain all the different theoretical products and forms of consciousness, religion, philosophy, ethics, etc., etc., and [to] trace their origins and growth from [their] basis [in economic imperatives]"—a fairly clear instance of deterministic thought—he also goes on to discuss the importance of examining "the reciprocal action of these various sides on one another." If culture and economic structures are locked in such "reciprocal" fashion, then theirs is not a linear relationship; culture is plainly no more epiphenomenal than is social structure (Karl Marx, *The German Ideology,* in *Karl Marx: Selected Writings,* ed. David McLellan [Oxford: Oxford University Press, 1978], 172). By the same token, it is also common to see Max Weber as a proponent of the opposite form of

determinism, focusing on the ideals and ideas paving the way for capitalism—the symbolic grounding that made that set of social arrangements both possible and palatable. Weber, though, concludes *The Protestant Ethic* with the nondeterministic admonition that "it is, of course, not my aim to substitute for a one-sided materialistic [i.e., Marx's and Engels's view] an equally one-sided spiritualistic causal interpretation of culture and of history. Each is equally possible, but each, if it does not serve as the preparation, but as the conclusion of an investigation, accomplishes equally little in the interest of historical truth" (Max Weber, *The Protestant Ethic and the Spirit of Capitalism*, trans. Talcott Parsons [New York: Charles Scribner's Sons, 1958], 183).

6. Emile Durkheim, of course, maintained much the same interest throughout his scholarly life, focusing, for example, in *The Elementary Forms of the Religious Life*, on the ways in which the religions of totemic societies engendered symbolic systems that simultaneously represented society itself and imbued it with a sacred significance that provided a sense of common purpose and identification. Unlike Gramsci, however, for Durkheim the primary question to be answered about modern industrial societies was less *how* than *if* they would hold together. Durkheim's concern—itself a variation on the notion of articulation, though he did not put it this way—issued from the extremely high division of labor characteristic of industrial societies. Durkheim feared that the citizenship of modernity, fragmented as it was into specialized tasks, would face a paucity of shared symbolic meanings and common causes and thus an impoverishment of the ritual activities that he believed held cultures and societies together across time (see Emile Durkheim, *The Elementary Forms of the Religious Life* [New York: Free Press, 1965] and *The Division of Labor in Society* [New York: Free Press, 1965]). Later generations of social theorists influenced by Durkheim—so called neo-Durkheimians—uncovered what they saw as alternative forms of symbolic and ritual activity, arguing that Durkheim's fears may have been overstated. Among the alternatives for representing and expressing solidarity that the neo-Durkheimians pointed to are various affairs of state and national ceremonies, as reflected in, for example, William Lloyd Warner's analysis of Memorial Day, Edward Shils's and Michael Young's study of the significance of the coronation in English society, and Robert N. Bellah's work on "civil religion" (William Lloyd Warner, "An American Sacred Ceremony," in *American Life: Dream and Reality* [Chicago: University of Chicago Press, 1962], 1-26; Edward Shils and Michael Young, "The Meaning of the Coronation," *Sociological Review* 1 [1953]: 63-81; Robert Bellah, "Civil Religion in America," in *Beyond Belief: Essays on Religion in a Post-Traditional World* [New York: Harper and Row, 1970]). Both the neo-Marxist and neo-Durkheimian versions of a reproductionist, or integrationist, view have been roundly criticized. Against Gramsci, Abercrombie et al. maintain that the stability of advanced industrial capitalist societies is a matter of "pragmatic" rather than "normative" acceptance of the relational structures in which they are enmeshed. It is not, these authors argue, that everyone consents to the ideologies that purportedly legitimate the existing systems as just, but that the "imperatives of everyday life" engender no less compelling "imperatives of cooperation" (Nicholas Abercrombie, Stephen Hill, and Bryan S. Turner, *The Dominant Ideology Thesis* [London: George, Allen and Unwin, 1980]; chapter 6 provides a cogent summary of the main points of their analysis; see also Weber's discussion of "formally free labor" in *The Protestant Ethic*). It should be mentioned, as well, that from at least one standpoint both neo-Marxists and their critics, whatever

their intentions, present a somewhat anemic conception of culture. As Marshall Sahlins has persuasively argued, the economic systems of large-scale industrial societies are themselves organized around and embody a symbolic system and, moreover, have become the principal producers of symbolism. To treat the "imperatives of everyday life," however tacitly, as somehow more fundamental and tangible than the "fuzzy" and putatively ephemeral realm of culture and symbol is to ignore the fact that everyday life and its imperatives are already the social and relational embodiment of an underlying symbolic logic (see Marshall Sahlins, *Culture and Practical Reason* [Chicago: University of Chicago Press, 1976]; for a related argument, see Jeffrey C. Alexander, "The Promise of a Cultural Sociology: Technological Discourse and the Sacred and Profane Information Machine," in *Theory of Culture,* ed. Richard Munch and Neil J. Smelser [Berkeley: University of California Press, 1992], 292–323). Finally, Steven Lukes has taken issue with the neo-Durkheimian view, singling out the just cited works of Warner, Shils and Young, and Bellah. Notably, he objects to this view on the same grounds as do critics of the neo-Marxist approach: namely, that they assume that "consensus" underlies social integration. Lukes also goes beyond assailing the underlying assumptions of theories of reproduction, arguing that symbol and ritual can be and are used to exacerbate conflict and work against social integration, at the same time contributing to the solidarity of oppositional groups. Thus, Durkheimian theory can show the ways in which symbolic and ritual action "can serve to integrate and strengthen subordinate social groups" as effectively as it can illuminate the processes engendering social and cultural stability (Steven Lukes, "Political Ritual and Social Integration," *Sociology* 9 [1975]: 298, 299–300). For a recent extension and application of Lukes's points in regard to oppositional activities, see Eric W. Rothenbuhler, "The Liminal Fight: Mass Strikes as Ritual and Interpretation," in *Durkheimian Sociology: Cultural Studies,* ed. Jeffrey C. Alexander (New York: Cambridge University Press, 1988), 66–89.

7. Robert Wuthnow, *Communities of Discourse: Ideology and Social Structure in the Reformation, the Enlightenment, and European Socialism* (Cambridge, Mass.: Harvard University Press, 1989), 5. My discussion of the need to attend to the processes and the context of cultural change, as well as the content of discourses, is beholden to the framework for cultural analysis that Wuthnow lays out in this work.

8. The relationship between social and cultural instability and periods of ideological ferment has produced a huge literature; one much too large to cite fully here. The following, then, are representative examples: Anne Swidler, "Culture in Action: Symbols and Strategies," *American Sociological Review* 51 (1986): 273–86; Robert Wuthnow, *Meaning and Moral Order: Explorations in Cultural Analysis* (Berkeley: University of California Press, 1987); Wuthnow, *Communities of Discourse.* Victor Turner's work on "liminality"—a singularly thoughtful body of writing— is also informed by this theme. See his *Dramas and Social Metaphors: Symbolic Action in Human Society* (Ithaca, N.Y.: Cornell University Press, 1974), in which the following essays are especially helpful: "Social Dramas and Ritual Metaphors," 23–50; "Metaphors of Anti-Structure in Religious Culture," 272–99; "Passages, Margins, and Poverty: Religious Symbols of Communitas," 231–71. See also his *The Ritual Process: Structure and Anti-Structure* (Ithaca, N.Y.: Cornell University Press, 1977; originally pubished in 1969) and *The Forest of Symbols: Aspects of Ndembu Ritual* (Ithaca, N.Y.: Cornell University Press, 1986; originally published in 1967). These works, either explicitly or implicitly, are at least partially beholden to Anthony F. C. Wallace's seminal and widely cited article

"Revitalization Movements" (*American Anthropologist* 58 [1956]: 264–81), which argued that throughout history periods of profound social disorganization have always engendered social movements, embodying and fueled by alternative symbolic systems, which restored and revitalized society. Three excellent works explicitly employ Wallace's theory: James G. Moseley, *A Cultural History of Religion in America* (Westport, Conn.: Greenwood Press, 1981), explores the impact of cultural innovations in periods of social instability. Moselely, using Wallace's notion of revitalization movements, traces the cultural cross-fertilization by which Americans girded themselves for revolution and describes how they organized themselves afterward. Thoughout U.S. history, Moseley argues, religious and political thought have intermixed in ways that stabilized and revitalized the nation. Frances Fitzgerald, *Cities on a Hill* (New York: Simon and Schuster, 1987; originally published in 1981) applies both Turner's notion of liminality and Wallace's concept of revitalization movements to a thoughtful analysis of the enduring cultural significance of community in American life, especially as it relates to larger social instabilities. William G. McLoughlin, *Revivals, Awakening, and Reform: An Essay on Religion and Social Change in America, 1607–1977* (Chicago: University of Chicago Press, 1977), offers the unique argument that the United States has been through five distinct periods of revivalism and revitalization, including, most recently (and most relevantly to the present argument), the still-unfolding legacy of the 1960s. There are also numerous historical studies that plainly reveal the link between instability and the creation of new symbolic-moral systems and discourses of reform, although they do not employ the same conceptual vocabulary as I am using here. Among the best of these are Mary P. Ryan, *Cradle of the Middle Class: The Family in Oneida County, New York, 1790–1865* (Cambridge: Cambridge University Press, 1981); Paul E. Johnson, *A Shopkeeper's Millennium: Society and Revivals in Rochester, New York, 1815–1837* (New York: Hill and Wang, 1978); Cedric Cowing, *The Great Awakening and the American Revolution: Colonial Thought in the 18th Century* (Chicago: Rand McNally and Co., 1971), which focuses upon these dynamics exclusively in relation to the Revolutionary War era; Whitney Cross, *The Burned-Over District: The Social and Intellectual History of Enthusiastic Religion in Western New York, 1800–1850* (New York: Harper and Row, 1965; originally published Ithaca, N.Y.: Cornell University Press, 1950), which is perhaps the most comprehensive analysis of the social, economic, ideological, and cultural factors associated with the Second Great Awakening and plainly reveals the same social and cultural processes. Rosabeth Moss Kanter, *Commitment and Community: Communes in Sociological Perspective* (Cambridge, Mass.: Harvard University Press, 1972), revealing the dialectical nature of cultural change, maintains that there have been three waves of utopian community building in the United States, with each wave corresponding and contributing to periods of societal and cultural upheaval. Finally, each of the following works echoes the overarching theme of the close connection between cultural and societal tumult—in this case, again, the 1960s—and the proliferation of new cultural products and alternative social forms: Hugh Gardner, *The Children of Prosperity: Thirteen Modern American Communes* (New York: St. Martin's Press, 1978); Judson Jerome, *Families of Eden: Communes and the New Anarchism* (New York: Seabury Press, 1974); Benjamin Zablocki, *The Joyful Community* (Baltimore: Penguin Books, 1971).

9. Geertz, "Ideology as a Cultural System," in *The Interpretation of Cultures*, 219.

10. Moseley, *A Cultural History of Religion in America*, 146–47.

11. See Ryan, *Cradle of the Middle Class*. For an analysis offering similar conclusions but focused on the Rochester revivals and disruptions in authority relations in the new industrial workplace as well as the larger community, see Johnson, *A Shopkeeper's Millennium*.

12. Ryan, *Cradle of the Middle Class*, 74. Occurring, as it did, some 170 years ago, the transformation of children's cultural status underscores the value of placing contemporary events in broader historical perspective. As we will see, co-dependency's creators, perhaps especially John Bradshaw, write as if the view of children as little beasts held sway in U.S. culture through the 1940s and 1950s.

13. Robert Heilbroner, *The Nature and Logic of Capitalism* (New York: W.W. Norton, 1985), 109, and chapter 5, more generally.

14. The notion of an "expressive revolution" is taken from Bernice Martin's eloquent *A Sociology of Contemporary Cultural Change* (New York: St. Martin's Press, 1981); that of a "silent revolution," from Ronald Inglehart, *The Silent Revolution: Changing Political Styles among Western Publics* (Princeton: Princeton University Press, 1977). See also Inglehart's more recent work, *Culture Shift in Advanced Industrial Societies* (Princeton: Princeton University Press, 1990).

15. See, respectively, Philip Rieff, *The Triumph of the Therapeutic: Uses of Faith after Freud*, 2d ed. (Chicago: University of Chicago Press, 1987); Robert Boyers, *Psychological Man* (New York: Harper and Row, 1975); Ralph H. Turner, "The Real Self: From Institution to Impulse," *American Journal of Sociology* 81 (1976): 989–1016; Philip Gross, *The Psychological Society* (New York: Random House, 1978); Christopher Lasch, *The Culture of Narcissism: American Life in an Age of Diminishing Expectations* (New York: W.W. Norton, 1979); Robert Bellah et al., *Habits of the Heart: Individualism and Commitment in American Life* (New York: Harper and Row, 1985); Richard Sennett, *The Fall of Public Man: On the Social Psychology of Capitalism* (New York: Random House, 1978); James Davison Hunter, "The Modern Malaise," in *Making Sense of Modern Times*, ed. James Davison Hunter and Stephen C. Ainlay (London: Routledge and Kegan Paul, 1986), 76–100.

16. See Joseph Veroff, Elizabeth Douvan, and Richard A. Kulka, *The Inner American: A Self-Portrait from 1957 to 1976* (New York: Basic Books, 1981); Bernie Zilbergeld, *The Shrinking of America* (Boston: Little, Brown, 1983), 30ff.; Stuart A. Kirk and Herb Kutchins, *The Selling of DSM: The Rhetoric of Science in Psychiatry* (New York: Aldine de Gruyter, 1992), 8–9. The growth of the addiction-treatment industry, discussed in chapter 2, is also a manifestation of this trend.

17. Zilbergeld, *The Shrinking of America*, 31.

18. U.S. Bureau of the Census, *Statistical Abstracts of the United States* (Washington: Government Printing Office, 1990), 162; Charles Anderson, Deborah J. Carter, and Andrew G. Malizio, *Fact Book on Higher Education* (New York: MacMillan, 1990). Additionally, in 1988, American universities awarded 3,058 Ph.D.'s in psychology. Among doctorates awarded in a variety of other scientific disciplines, only the physical and biological sciences awarded more. Although in absolute terms the number of doctorates awarded in psychology decreased from 1987 to 1988, the overall trend is toward an ever widening disparity in the number of these Ph.D.'s and those awarded in economics, political science, sociology, anthropology, and history. For the former, the trend has clearly been one of dramatic increases; for the latter, it has been one of substantial decreases.

19. Peter L. Berger and Thomas Luckmann, *The Social Construction of Reality: A Treatise in the Sociology of Knowledge* (Garden City, N.Y.: Doubleday, 1966), 176.

20. On the definitions and cultural importance of "maturity" in the 1950s, see Barbara Ehrenreich, *The Hearts of Men: American Dreams and the Flight from Commitment* (Garden City, N.Y.: Doubleday/Anchor, 1983), 17. See also Cheryl Russell, *The Master Trend: How the Baby Boom Generation Is Remaking America* (New York: Plenum, 1993), 13-14. In terms of the caricature-like renditions of the 1950s, one needs only to recall that the Beat movement was the cultural and intellectual precursor to the 1960s' counterculture. As Russell points out, conformism notwithstanding, the baby boomers' parents also valued self-reliance highly and raised their children accordingly. These are not the values one would expect to find underlying a repressive cultural and societal order.

21. See Berger and Luckmann, *The Social Construction of Reality*, 104-16.

22. Cheryl Russell aptly documents this generational aspect to the cultural changes of recent years; see Russell, *The Master Trend*.

23. Inglehart, *Culture Shift*, 205; *The Silent Revolution*.

24. Veroff et al., *The Inner American*, 529, 532.

25. Ibid., 530.

26. Russell, *The Master Trend*, 27-28. Although her description of free agency plainly reflects liberation psychotherapy's view of what constitutes the right relationship between self and society, Russell pays little attention to the therapeutic aspects, per se, of free agency, and so her argument is not as conceptually focused as it might be. Russell attributes the trend toward free agency to individualism, a view that vastly oversimplifies both individualism itself and its current manifestations. Individualism has historically had a variety of different meanings and usages, and these can and must be distinguished from one another. Steven Lukes, for example, has explored in some detail the important differences among and between political, economic, religious, ethical, epistemological, and methodological individualism (see Steven Lukes, *Individualism* [Oxford: Basil Blackwell, 1973]). Moreover, as James O'Connor has pointed out, "[p]rior to the development of the European idea of the intrinsic and supreme value of the individual, or the 'self,'... 'individual' meant 'not divisible' from the collectivity" (see James O'Connor, *Accumulation Crisis* [New York: Basil Blackwell, 1986], 15). Russell is, in fact, referring to the impact of liberation psychotherapy upon contemporary conceptions of the self and its right relationship to society. In many ways, this impact has produced perhaps the most all-encompassing interpretation of individualism to date.

27. Carl Rogers, *On Becoming a Person: A Therapist's View of Psychotherapy* (Boston: Houghton Mifflin, 1961), 91, 111-12.

28. Karl Barth, *The Church and the Political Problem of Our Day* (London: Hodder and Stoughton, 1939), 82; quoted in P. Rieff, *The Triumph of the Therapeutic*, 19.

29. P. Rieff, *The Triumph of the Therapeutic*, 2.

30. Kanter, *Commitment and Community*, 172-73. See also Fitzgerald, *Cities on a Hill;* Gardner, *The Children of Prosperity;* Jerome, *Families of Eden;* Zablocki, *The Joyful Community*.

31. Kanter, *Commitment and Community*, 166-67. See her chapter 7, generally, for a discussion of some of the problems communes of the 1960s and 1970s faced in organizing themselves as groups. Frances Fitzgerald, in her analysis of latter-day lifestyle enclaves, has recently echoed Kanter's conclusions. The governing presumption underlying the counterculture's critique of conventional U.S. life in the 1960s, Fitzgerald notes, was that "all institutions of society were empty and had to go." Guided by those convictions, she continues, "[t]he counter-culture was

not an alternate culture so much as an anticulture where all structures and conventions were dissolved" (Fitzgerald, *Cities on a Hill,* 408.)

32. Alan Wolfe, "Out of the Frying Pan, into…What?" in *America at Century's End,* ed. Alan Wolfe (Berkeley: University of California Press, 1991).

33. Wolfe, "Out of the Frying Pan," 468.

34. Wolfe, "Introduction," in *America at Century's End,* ed. Wolfe, 8.

35. Judith Stacey, "Backward toward the Postmodern Family: Reflections on Gender, Kinship, and Class in the Silicon Valley," in *America at Century's End,* ed. Wolfe, 19. See also Judith Stacey, *Brave New Families: Stories of Domestic Upheaval in Late Twentieth-Century America* (New York: Basic Books, 1990).

36. Kathleen Gerson, "Coping with Commitment: Dilemmas and Conflicts of Family Life," in *America at Century's End,* ed. Wolfe, 57.

37. Reliable demographic information about the participants in the co-dependency movement has heretofore been scarce and hard to come by. CoDA has not surveyed its membership, nor have the dozens of other new Anonymous groups loosely modeled after Alcoholics Anonymous that have emerged in the past decade. Claims about the newest groups and members, those organized around the beliefs associated with co-dependency, have relied upon anecdotal information and undocumented assertions, which have themselves been informed by the observers' theoretical presuppositions. (See, for example, my comments about Kaminer's assertions later in this note.) Although the data underpinning this study are not statistically generalizable, they do provide an empirical, rather than an anecdotal, starting point. Although I did not explicitly survey CoDA groups on demographic information, I did count the number in attendance and note their demographic makeup. Because there was so little racial and ethnic variation, I have summarized only the numbers attending each meeting and the ratio of men to women in them. These are presented in Appendix A. Gender, of course, is self-evident. My remarks about race and age, although based upon my own judgment, nonetheless seem reasonable enough. It is not difficult to tell teenagers and grandparents from those in middle-age; nor does it require unusual skill to distinguish caucasians from African-Americans, Hispanics, or Asians (a skill, I should add, that I was required to exercise on only three occasions: I encountered one black woman, one Asian-American woman, and one Arab-American man during the course of my research). Among the 547, there were no children and only a handful of teens and elderly people. In addition, although women constituted 61 percent of those attending the meetings, this ratio was not what one would expect to find given what some have seen as the gender-specificity of co-dependency's symptoms. Wendy Kaminer, in *I'm Dysfunctional, You're Dysfunctional,* has asserted that the co-dependency movement appears to be disproportionately female. In large part, however, this observation is based upon her attendance at a 1991 conference on co-dependency, sponsored by the exclusively recovery-oriented publisher, Health Communications, Inc., and held at the Wyndham Franklin Plaza Hotel in Philadelphia. At best, this is dubious evidence. The conference was, as Kaminer notes, "billed as a women's conference" (88–89). As such, the predominance of women in attendance does not constitute particularly convincing evidence about the composition of the co-dependency movement. The assumption that co-dependency is gender-specific lies in the additional assumption that excessive denial of self for others is an exclusively female province. The latter assumption may well be warranted, but, at least by my own experience, it is at best only loosely connected to the membership composition at Co-Dependents

Anonymous meetings. Moreover, as subsequent chapters will show, the emphasis upon self-abnegation ignores the fact that co-dependency's meanings are multireferential: As I have already indicated, many of the problems to which co-dependency is presented as a solution have very little to do with self-denial.

38. Ronald Inglehart discusses at some length the significant relationship between historical circumstances and the values that a generation holds (see his *Culture Shift*). As a number of analysts, including Inglehart, have noted, the baby boomers—particularly white baby boomers—were raised in affluence and thus had an extended adolescence and far greater access to leisure time and education, which led to their holding far higher expectations of life than did their parents, whose characters were forged against the backdrop of world wars and the Great Depression (see, for example, Gardner, *The Children of Prosperity;* Wade Clark Roof, *A Generation of Seekers: The Spiritual Journeys of the Baby Boom Generation* [New York: HarperCollins, 1993]).

39. Peter L. Berger, *Invitation to Sociology: A Humanistic Perspective* (Garden City, N.Y.: Doubleday, 1963), 98.

40. On the narrative essence of identity, see Alasdair MacIntyre, *After Virtue,* 2d ed. (Notre Dame, Ind.: University of Notre Dame Press, 1984). See also Jerome Bruner, "Life as Narrative," *Social Research* 54 (1987): 11–32; Charles Taylor, *Sources of the Self: The Making of Modern Identity* (Cambridge, Mass.: Harvard University Press, 1990). These views bear no small family resemblance to George Herbert Mead's social psychology; see, for example, his *Mind, Self, and Society,* ed. Charles W. Morris (Chicago: University of Chicago Press, 1934) and *On Social Psychology,* ed. Anselm Strauss (Chicago: University of Chicago Press, 1977).

2

A Genealogy of Co-Dependency:
Truth Rules and the Twelve-Step Subculture

Co-dependency's emergence onto the U.S. cultural and social land-scape was the culmination of *selection* by two groups. The discourse literally became a social phenomenon through its selection by a public, without which there would be no phenomenal sales of co-dependency treatises to report, nor would there have been—as we will see later in this chapter—an explosion in the number and types of self-help groups modeled, in style if not substance, after Alcoholics Anonymous.

This chapter will be concerned more with the selection of the themes, images, concepts, and symbols that went into co-dependency's cre-ation as a discourse, making it available for public use. The produc-tion and creation of co-dependency was the labor of a specific set of symbolic specialists: Searching for a clinical vocabulary suited to the array of problems they encountered as alcohol and drug-addiction counselors, Melody Beattie and the other advocates of co-dependency selected key concepts from the realms of family therapy and family systems theory, the twelve-step philosophy of Alcoholics Anonymous, and the psychotherapies of people such as Abraham Maslow, Carl Rogers, and Virginia Satir. Those who identify themselves as co-de-pendent, then, have adopted ideas that had already been selected and organized in the particular and distinctive ways that produced co-de-pendency as a specific mode of discourse.

Examining a discourse's origins is an integral part of any cultural analysis, an exercise designed to yield not only an understanding of the discourse itself but also—and more important, in the end—an un-derstanding of what exactly is being selected, of what courses of ac-tion the discourse's adherents are encouraged to pursue, and, ultimately,

47

of why people selected it. The origins of co-dependency are particularly instructive in all of these ways, for analysis reveals that the discourse has been but poorly understood. Co-dependency emerged out of what I will call the twelve-step subculture[1]—and also fueled substantial growth in the numbers of people and groups *in* that subculture—and has therefore been portrayed in evolutionary terms: that is, as a natural outcome of the progressive accumulation of knowledge about the workings of addiction.

As this chapter will show, however, this evolutionary view ignores the "therapeutic revolution"—it ignores the cultural and societal context in which co-dependency was produced and selected. The discourse relies heavily on the assumptions and principles of liberation psychotherapy and, in doing so, introduces an altogether different symbolic logic into the twelve-step subculture. This infusion of a foreign point of view, as we will see, led to an uneasy fit between co-dependency and the older twelve-step groups—those that were founded prior to the rise of the therapeutic culture and that therefore reflect and are organized around a more conservative, socially and culturally reproductive symbolism.

Genealogy and the Emergence of Co-Dependency

The French social philosopher Michel Foucault offered the outline of a useful method—what he called a "genealogy"—for examining the origins of a new discourse.[2] This chapter will apply a modified version of Foucault's genealogical approach towards co-dependency's emergence. The key premise governing a genealogical analysis is that new belief systems, theories, ideologies, and the like do not emerge—or at least do not often emerge—as the result of continuities in or the progressive accumulation of knowledge but, rather, from discontinuities in established knowledge, from breaks with their own intellectual and theoretical traditions. New discourses often emerge and become established in the larger world through an amalgam of "accidents, chance, passion, petty malices, surprises,...and [bids for] power" rather than through a smooth or logical developmental process.[3] As I have already noted, however, co-dependency's origins have been portrayed and understood in evolutionary terms, as a culmination of progressive insights about alcoholism and addiction. Anne Wilson Schaef's rough sketch of the chro-

nology and logical processes by which co-dependency emerged epitomizes this point of view:

> As I understand the development of the concept of co-dependence within the CD
> [chemical dependency] field, it has been employed in relation to the treatment of
> the alcoholic.... As Virginia Satir developed her concepts of family therapy, Vernon
> Johnson, Sharon Wegscheider-Cruse, and others began to look at alcoholism as a
> family disease, and the entire field opened itself to the awareness that the alcoholic
> was not the only person affected by the disease.... [T]he next phase in the devel-
> opment of this concept was recognizing that...the co-dependent was also in a
> great deal of pain and needed help. Concurrently with this phase was the realiza-
> tion, statistically, that children of alcoholic families tended to become alcoholics
> and/or develop serious problems adjusting to life.[4]

Although this evolutionary model of co-dependency's emergence is
inadequate conceptually, the chronology of events it offers is accurate. In
this view, the discovery of co-dependency is simply the latest installment
in the long history of the disease model of alcoholism, originally ex-
pounded by Benjamin Rush in 1785. Rush (one of the signers of the Dec-
laration of Independence), considered the father of U.S. psychiatry, was
puzzled that some people could drink alcohol both freely and relatively
often without experiencing adverse effects while others repeatedly drank
themselves into physical, psychological, and social difficulties. For Rush,
it was only sensible to assume that problem drinkers could not control
themselves and that this loss of control signified an underlying malady—
a disease or addiction—that prevented moderation.

One hundred and fifty years and several reincarnations later, Rush's
model was rechampioned by "the alcoholism movement,"[5] an unofficial consortium of advocates dedicated to effecting public acceptance
of the idea that serious alcohol problems are the product of disease rather
than of moral intransigence, as had always before been thought. Throughout the 1930s and 1940s, the disease model was the focus of research
and protracted advocacy by the Yale (now Rutgers) Center for Alcohol
Studies and the National Council on Alcoholism. Coupled with the apparent successes of the then-new self-help group Alcoholics Anonymous (founded in 1935), which also took the disease model as the
foundation for its twelve-step philosophy, these efforts eventually, in
1956, persuaded the American Medical Association to recognize alcoholism as a bona fide disease. This recognition was a major step toward
legitimating the disease model, a precursor to the eventual passage of
the 1970 Comprehensive Alcohol Abuse and Alcoholism Prevention

and Rehabilitation Act (revised in 1976). With that legislation, alcoholism was socially, publicly, and legally designated as a disease and, in keeping with the intention of the act, has since received medical treatment rather than criminal sanction.[6]

Two provisions in the Comprehensive Alcohol Abuse Act effectively institutionalized this new orientation toward alcohol problems. The first called for the creation of the National Institute on Alcohol Abuse and Alcoholism (NIAAA), which was formed in 1971 and coordinates, funds, and disseminates a vast body of research, all of it informed by the disease model. A second provision called upon the insurance industry to provide coverage for alcohol treatment in regular health care packages. By the late 1970s, many insurers had begun to comply. Health care providers, themselves only recently redefined as self-consciously corporate entities,[7] were quick to capitalize upon the murmurings of a fledgling market. Between 1979 and 1989, the total number of privately owned addiction-treatment centers more than doubled, rising from 2,935 to 6,036 facilities. The U.S. Department of Health and Human Services' 1990 study of treatment facility censuses reported that nearly one and a half million persons had received some form of addiction treatment during 1987; nearly double the figures from only two years earlier.[8]

In this evolutionary model of co-dependency's emergence, the rise of the treatment industry is a logical next chapter in a straightforward story of progressive increases in knowledge about the workings of addiction. This, as I will discuss in more detail later in this chapter, reflects a serious misreading of events, not least because the treatment industry itself fostered major changes in the nature of the disease model. For the present, it is enough to say that the industry quickly cultivated close ties with existing twelve-step groups (AA, Al-Anon, Ala-Teen), drawing upon their memberships for a steady supply of paraprofessional counselors to staff treatment facilities, referring their patients to twelve-step groups and meetings, and garnering a substantial number of referrals from those groups in the bargain.[9] "Treatment" is commonly an abbreviated variation upon and introduction to the disease model and the twelve-step "program," and the accompanying links between the professional and self-help approaches, as the figures reported above imply, drew substantial numbers of new adherents to the twelve-step philosophy.

The twelve-steps provide a simple formula for living and promise that if believers follow the steps faithfully, they will achieve dramatic improvements in their lives. That promise, the simplicity of the steps, and the far-wider public exposure to the AA philosophy that the treatment industry provided have contributed to the twelve-steps' applications to an ever-growing number of life troubles—including spouse abuse, a penchant for spending more money than one earns, or any of the problems represented in the following list of national support groups and anonymous organizations:[10]

Alcoholics Anonymous
Batterers Anonymous
Co-Dependents Anonymous
Debtors Anonymous
Depressives Anonymous
Divorce Anonymous
Drugs Anonymous
Emotional Health Anonymous
Emotions Anonymous
Emphysema Anonymous
Families Anonymous
Fundamentalists Anonymous
Gamblers Anonymous
Grandparents Anonymous
Homosexuals Anonymous
Impotents Anonymous
Incest Survivors Anonymous
Marriage Anonymous
Molesters Anonymous
Messies Anonymous
Narcotics Anonymous
Neurotics Anonymous
Overeaters Anonymous
Parents Anonymous
Potsmokers Anonymous
Prison Families Anonymous
Sex Addicts Anonymous
Sex and Love Addicts Anonymous
Workaholics Anonymous

In addition to these groups, there are such variations as[11]

Cocaine Anonymous
Men for Sobriety
Pills Anonymous
Shoplifters Anonymous

Smokers Anonymous
Spenders Anonymous
Survivors of Incest Anonymous (primarily male victims)
Twelve Steps for Christian Living Group
Twelve Steps for Spiritual Growth
Women for Sobriety
Women with Multiple Addictions

In a general sense, these broader applications of the twelve-steps required no more than a change in terminology. AA's first step asks members to admit a "powerlessness over alcohol," but "alcohol" can be and has been easily replaced by virtually any problem over which people feel they have no control. As the lists of AA imitators suggests, contemporary Americans apparently consider themselves powerless over much of life, and more people, more problems, and more groups are being added all the time.

In addition to those directly afflicted with an addiction or "addiction-like" problems, it is a common conviction in this burgeoning twelve-step subculture that addicts have a "primary" disease and that their mates, friends, and children suffer a set of "secondary" problems caused by living with or being close to someone who has the disease. This belief has been a catalyst for rapid expansion in the number of secondary groups in the subculture: More organizations for addicts means more organizations for those close to them. For virtually every Anonymous group there is also a secondary support group for nonaddicted friends and family. AA's well-known counterpart, for example, is Al-Anon, whose members were originally said to suffer from "co-alcoholism"; just so, "Co-S.A." for the mates of "sex addicts" or "Gam-Anon" for the intimates of compulsive gamblers. Co-*dependency*, as the term was originally used, denoted the loved ones of "chemical dependents," a term born of the addiction treatment industry.

As I have noted, from an evolutionary perspective, all of these developments were the logical outgrowth of progressive increases in knowledge about addictions and their treatment: As we have learned more, this reasoning runs, we have discovered a nationwide "epidemic" of addictions. The many new members and groups in the subculture, in turn, are understood as logical descendants of AA and Al-Anon. But this portrait of the phenomenon is woefully inadequate. The version of co-dependency that spawned such widespread public interest and enthusiasm in fact represents a radical reversal in the traditional twelve-step view of the relationship between self and society—a reversal that echoes liberation therapy's worldview and indicates the influence of that worldview. That this reversal is repeatedly overlooked is evident in the common tendency to refer to co-dependency as "psychological." At a very high level of abstraction, it is certainly true that Freudian psychoanalysis, Skinnerian behaviorism, the humanistic psychotherapy of Carl Rogers, and the AA model of addiction are all "psychological," but it is not at all clear what such an attribution really reveals. These are very different ways of thinking, and a failure to distinguish among them results in precisely the sort of misunderstandings that have led even co-dependency's most thorough observers to lump AA and CoDA together as if they are largely indistinguishable elements within a broader "recovery movement."[12] The differences between AA and many of the newest twelve-step groups, such as CoDA, are profound, and the exponential increase in the numbers and types of twelve-step groups cannot be interpreted as the logical continuation of the legacy of AA. Guided by a completely different understanding of recovery from that of AA, the newer groups are better seen as a co-dependency movement. In short, another history is needed—one both more detailed and more attuned to the important differences among and between the pre- and post-co-dependency groups, in terms of what they consider to be legitimate statements and valid truths about reality.

Truth Rules, Discursive Formation, and the Twelve-Step Subculture

All clinical psychologies have a common subject matter—the self in (a usually troubled) relation to society—but each makes different assumptions about the individual and the social world; each seeks to achieve different purposes; each makes a different life story possible and, as such, requires and helps to create a different individual. "Psychology," then, is in fact many psychologies; each constrained by its own truth rules.[13]

All ideologies, theories, worldviews, and the like are governed by tacit rules as to what will and will not count as true statements. The combination of rules and statements produces a characteristic mode of discourse, or what Michel Foucault called a "discursive formation."[14] The rules governing therapeutic modalities are derived from practitioners' assumptions about the parties whose conflict psychotherapy is designed to mediate: distressed individuals and the social and cultural context in which they live. Thus, depending upon the therapist's assumptions about human nature and culture, a person's adaptation to, compromise with, or liberation from the demands of culture can all be, and have been, construed as therapeutic. Freud, for example, argued that cultures are intrinsically repressive by dint of their efforts to channel human behavior into similar, "civilized" patterns. But, he maintained, even if overly stringent, these efforts were necessary because humans are by nature aggressive beings. The convergence of these assumptions led Freud to conclude that the individual's reasoned compromise with cultural demands was the appropriate course of action and the only possibility of psychological well-being. For Freud, to reject culture altogether was to invite chaos but to adapt to it uncritically was to be psychologically ill.[15]

Adaptationally oriented psychologies, conversely, assume that humans are by nature aggressive and potentially dangerous creatures and that culture is the source of human morality. These implicit rules also generate a distinctive point of view and way of talking. For example, only an adaptationally oriented psychologist would observe that "[o]ne of the outstanding effects of the discipline found in the average home and school" is that the "very deep-lying, bestial, primitive, psychic life in us [is] buried under a mass of training."

Case studies such as that of Peter, an eighteen-year-old boy who "classed himself as a homosexual," also illustrate the workings of adaptational truths. One reads that, under the guidance of his psychologist, Peter "worked out a plan for contacts with the opposite sex" and that within the year he "was far enough along to get married. Whether he was completely cured is not the question."[16] As Peter apparently learned, the rules for adaptational truth hold that, along with other external demands upon the self, culture's gender assignments must be obeyed. When they are not, they must be reasserted; patients must adapt to existing cultural mandates, and their psychological health is gauged by the extent to which they do so.

Adaptational psychologies are, in essence, discourses of reproduction: They see no problems with the larger reality and operate to maintain that reality. AA is beholden to an adaptational psychology. Reflecting its reproductive orientation, AA takes a violation of existing cultural standards as the basis for diagnosis and defines the cure as learning to accept and live according to those standards. These tacit truth rules engender intrinsically restitutive themes. For example, the first of the twelve-steps, as noted earlier, observes that "We admitted we were powerless over alcohol, that our lives had become unmanageable." This reflects the organization's implicit but nonetheless thoroughgoing cultural conservatism. The alcoholic is "powerless" to behave in accordance with existing normative standards, and this powerlessness is manifested in a pattern of "unmanageable" conduct.

AA's eighth and ninth steps also illustrate the adaptational nature of its program of recovery from alcoholism. These steps are logical companions: The eighth requires alcoholics to make a list of all persons they have harmed, and the ninth stipulates that amends must be made to the people on that list. Lying, cheating, stealing, and other transgressions are invariably considered in terms of their effect upon others, from immediate family through society as a whole. "When we take such personality traits as these into shop, office, and the society of our fellows, they can do damage almost as extensive as that we have caused at home."[17]

Those about to take AA's ninth step are given one admonition, also informed by adaptational concerns for obligations to others and framed in terms of the existing moral order:

> There can only be one consideration which should qualify our desire for a complete disclosure of the damage we have done. That will arise in the occasional situation where to make a full revelation would seriously harm the one to whom we are making amends. Or—quite as important—other people. We cannot, for example, unload a detailed account of extramarital adventuring upon the shoulders of our unsuspecting wife or husband.... [The general rule, then, is] [l]et's try to avoid harming third parties, whoever they may be.[18]

As the foregoing quote suggests, AA members are also expected to direct their attention to the damage done *by* the addiction to themselves and to others rather than to seek a cause for the addiction in damage done *to* themselves. In AA, claims that one drinks, for example, because of a bad marriage or a troubled childhood are characterized as symptoms rather than explanations of the disease; the search for a social etiology to addiction is interpreted as a manifestation of "denial," or "stinkin' thinkin'":

> [T]he majority of AA members have suffered severely from self-justification during their drinking days. For most of us, self-justification was the maker of excuses;

excuses, of course, for drinking, and for all kinds of crazy and damaging conduct. We had made the invention of alibis a fine art. We had to drink because times were hard or times were good. We had to drink because at home we were smothered with love or got none at all. We had to drink because at work we were great successes or dismal failures. We had to drink because our nation had won a war or lost a peace.... We thought "conditions" drove us to drink, and when we tried to correct these conditions and found that we couldn't to our entire satisfaction, our drinking went out of hand and we became alcoholics. *It never occurred to us that we needed to change ourselves to meet conditions, whatever they were.* (Emphasis added)[19]

The italicized passage aptly summarizes AA's view of the right relationship between alcoholics and society. The organization neither seeks cultural reform nor calls for compromise between its members and their social worlds. The therapeutic goal is adaptation to existing social and cultural standards. The logical consequence of this orientation is, then, reproduction of the status quo.

Historically, the "secondary" twelve-step groups have been guided by the same truth rules. Throughout the 1940s, many of the wives of early AA members accompanied their husbands to meetings, and, although they were not allowed to attend the meetings per se, they oversaw coffee making and cleanup chores, planned group outings, and the like.[20] These informal gatherings eventually developed into AA Family Groups and AA Auxiliaries. They adopted and adapted the twelve steps in an effort to recover along with their mates.

In 1951, Anne "B." and Lois Wilson (AA cofounder Bill "W."'s wife), created an umbrella organization that subsumed these various Family Groups. Al-Anon, the name on which the members finally settled, would henceforth coordinate and disseminate information about meeting times and locations, provide public information, and select what has since come to be called "conference-approved literature" (CAL) for use by the membership.

Al-Anon's growth kept pace with AA's. By the late 1950s, the organization had occupied first one, then two floors of space in an office building on East Twenty-Third Street in Manhattan. Much of their success was fueled by favorable media coverage—newspaper features, a positive piece in *The Saturday Evening Post*, an episode on the popular Loretta Young television show.[21] In 1962, an Ann Landers column on Al-Anon generated 4,000 inquiries from readers. Shortly after that, Landers ran an Illinois woman's letter singing Al-Anon's praises, and the organization received 10,000 letters in response; a later reprint of the same letter brought another 11,000 inquiries. The public interest translated into organizational growth and prosperity. By 1978, Al-Anon had created its own World Service Office at One Park Avenue in Manhattan; in 1985, they relocated to 1372 Broadway.

By the late 1980s, there were 28,000 Al-Anon groups worldwide; 15,000 in the United States. Half of the membership, which is and for several years has been 88 percent female, have at least some college education; most work outside the home, and over 25 percent hold managerial or executive positions. This composition, according to members, differs from thirty years ago, when the majority were housewives, many of whom either worked part-time or did not work outside the home and very few of whom were divorced. The membership has also changed in other ways. Early members tended to be almost exclusively the mates of recovering (AA) alcoholics. Current members now reflect "the only criterion for membership...[which is] that an important person in your life be an alcoholic," recovering or not, including "husbands, parents, children, brothers and sisters, 'live-ins' [lovers], employers [or]...employees."[22]

These changing demographics both reflect and are reflected in ideological changes. The goal of keeping the marriage and family together at virtually any cost has been supplanted by the conviction that loving an alcoholic does not have to entail the destruction of the nonalcoholic's life as well. As one member said, "Hey, I can love him or her forever, but I don't have to stay with this alcoholic." But although Al-Anon's "focus on oneself, rather than on the alcoholic"[23] and the stress placed upon the interpersonal (rather than internal, disease-based) etiology of the members' psychological troubles constitute a slightly different perspective from AA's, members' attentions have by and large focused upon the damage done *by* the addiction *to* the family members. As such, Al-Anon's ways of thinking and talking about the self remained more or less congruous with the original rules for addictive truth.[24]

Treatment, Family Systems Theory, and Adult Children of Alcoholics

"Children of alcoholics" were the subject of an Al-Anon presentation during AA's twentieth anniversary conference in 1955. Ala Teen was formed in 1957, and the first meeting was held in Pasadena, California, that same year. As both of these events indicate, the twelve-step subculture has long been concerned about the impact of addiction upon family members. However, the treatment industry, which emerged as a powerful force in the late 1970s, slightly modified and dramatically intensified this long-standing concern with families. The modifications helped to spawn the Adult Children of Alcoholics movement; the intensification was evident in a new claim that if one person in the family was addicted, everyone in the family was also sick and in need of treatment.

In part, the intensified interest in the family can be seen as a marketing strategy. The introduction of insurance revenues for addiction treatment presented providers with strong incentives for finding and creating more and more problem populations. To fully tap into the wellspring of third-party reimbursement, the treatment industry actively "discovered" new forms of addiction and crafted new rationales for "intervention," creating new treatment populations and programs. The patients' family members were a natural target of this new entrepreneurialism.[25] The discoveries leading to and legitimating these intensified efforts were made by recovering alcoholics and addicts (such as John Bradshaw and Melody Beattie) and the family members of alcoholics and addicts (such as Sharon Wegscheider-Cruse), who—because of the treatment industry's aforementioned fondness for hiring people who had "been there"—had found a way to transform their pasts into career tracks, becoming, as they have been called, "professional ex-'s."[26] In the course of their training as substance-abuse counselors, these professional ex-'s were exposed to and heavily influenced by so-called family systems psychotherapies—a theoretical framework born of schizophrenia studies in the 1950s that has been expanded upon ever since.[27]

It is no more useful to speak of family systems theory as a unified discourse than it is to speak of co-dependency as "psychological," but there are certain core concepts shared by most family systems therapists. These concepts are derived primarily from the influential Palo Alto Group and their efforts to combine tenets of general systems theory with studies of "dysfunctional communication patterns" into a single theory of family psychopathology.[28] In essence, the theory asserts that the family's interactions are the cumulative product of a shared history and that those interactions are explicable in terms of "circular causality" and governed by a set of implicit "family rules."

In the early 1980s, a group of treatment industry activists who were heavily influenced by this systemic view began to apply it specifically and clinically to families with alcohol and drug problems.[29] It has since become commonplace to speak of addiction as a "family disease." As the phrase implies, the guiding assumption underlying this view is that one member's addiction indicates that the entire family is sick, or, as John Bradshaw puts it, "[t]he theory of family systems accepts the family itself as the patient with the presenting member being viewed as a sign of family psychopathology."[30]

In essence, this is sociological "role theory" applied to the "addicted family."[31] Because family roles are interwoven, the presumption is that no one gets sick alone. The addict constitutes a "threat" to the other family members, all of whom adapt behaviorally in response. These "accommodations," as Wegscheider-Cruse calls them, become patterned into roles, each of which is, in effect, a symptom of an alcoholic family system. The names assigned to each general pattern of adaptation imply the nature of the roles. Black, for example, identifies "The Responsible One," "The Adjuster," "The Placater," and "Acting-Out Child." Renamed and expanded, the list of roles now includes "the enabler" (most often the spouse, who covers up for the addict), "the family scapegoat," "the family hero," "the lost child," and "the mascot."[32]

Adult Children of Alcoholics (ACoA), founded in 1977, is the social embodiment of these treatment industry creations. The ACoA "syndrome," as it is called, is predicated upon the argument that the alcoholic family roles learned in childhood continue into adult experience, manifesting themselves in an inability to forge lasting or close relationships. A capacity for intimacy is presumably precluded because of the lingering influence of the alcoholic "family rules" learned as children, rules an ACoA slogan concisely summarizes as "don't talk, don't trust, don't feel."

When ACoA first became popular, it was unclear where it belonged in the twelve-step subculture. In part, this was an organizational quandary, exacerbated by ACoA's extremely rapid growth: In 1981 there were fourteen ACoA meetings registered with Al-Anon's World Service Organization; as of April 1990 there were over 1,500 meetings in the United States, and over 200 registered in ten foreign countries. Faced with this rapid infusion of newcomers, Al-Anon asked, "how can we welcome them all into the Al-Anon family?"[33]

But Al-Anon's concerns went beyond the organizational logistics of "welcoming them all." The same editorial that expressed that concern went on to note that "[m]any adult children of alcoholics feel they're all different from the spouses, parents, and others in our fellowship," and asked, "But haven't adult children always been a part of Al-Anon?"[34] A 1984 policy statement, drafted by an Al-Anon World Service Conference and addressed to Al-Anon Adult Children of Alcoholics groups, also indicates that Al-Anon's concerns went beyond infrastructural problems. It was puzzling out ACoA's relationship to established twelve-step philosophy:

> Although there have always been adult children in our fellowship, recently Al-Anon has been recognized as a resource for those whose lives had been affected, perhaps years ago, by the alcoholism of a parent. Many of these members felt that they benefitted most when they shared at meetings with other adult children of alcoholics. To attract those with similar experiences, they called their Al-Anon groups "Adult Children of Alcoholics," "Children of Alcoholics," and "Sons and Daughters of Alcoholics." The formation of these groups seems to be a response to a need expressed within the fellowship.

Al-Anon goes on to note that, in light of ACoA's rapid growth, "confusion has arisen concerning Al-Anon's policy on registering these groups." In order to resolve the confusion, the organization reiterated its registration policy:

> Like other groups with a category of membership in the title (parents, men, women, etc.) the World Service Office does register them. By doing so we acknowledge their place in the Al-Anon family *provided they keep their doors open to anyone whose life is or has been affected by someone else's drinking and with the understanding that they will abide by Al-Anon's Twelve Traditions.* (Emphasis in the original)

The last passage is instructive. In it, Al-Anon defines and literally emphasizes the terms upon which ACoA's official induction into the twelve-step subculture was contingent. This emphasis suggests that Al-Anon's concerns transcend a strain upon organizational resources. The reference to the "Twelve Traditions"[35] points ACoA members toward the key principles by which twelve-step groups and identities are organized. This is also the point to Al-Anon's insistence that "only CAL [conference approved literature] be used at Al-Anon [Adult Children] meetings. This practice maintains the Al-Anon focus, reinforces our unity, and avoids any implication of affiliation."[36] If ACoA groups observed these requirements, the conference would incorporate their "stories" in forthcoming CAL titles in return.

Al-Anon's concern with and insistence upon unity and fidelity to the principles of the twelve-step subculture issued from its philosophical differences with ACoA. In turn, these philosophical differences are grounded in the larger cultural changes that took place in the years between the founding of Al-Anon and the founding of AcoA. Although Al-Anon appears not to recognize it, or at least does not publicly acknowledge as much, ACoA introduced a rival discourse and different rules for truth into the subculture; ACoA is reliant upon the truths of liberation psychotherapy. By predicating ACoA's twelve-step legitimacy upon an adherence to traditional addiction truths, Al-Anon sought to minimize the potentially deleterious impact of these new truths.

There are at least two important ways in which the "adult children" movement introduced liberation therapy truth rules into the twelve-step subculture.

First, the adult children programs' emphasis upon personal history contrasts with AA's and Al-Anon's more pragmatic techniques. The disease model requires no great "insights" and points no fingers. It merely calls for a tactical recognition of one's illness and the damage it has done, followed by a methodical agenda for the righting of wrongs and building life anew. According to original twelve-step truths, dwelling in the past, running it repeatedly through one's hands, is a symptom rather than a cause of the disease. Liberation psychotherapy, conversely, requires attention to childhood: The cultural and societal repressions meted out in the course of primary socialization are the source of the psychological problems of adulthood.

Second, but directly connected with the historical emphasis, ACoA fosters a qualitative reversal of the mood in which recovery is conceived and exercised. AA and Al-Anon members take a very selective journey through their pasts, a journey in which the significant landmarks commemorate wrongs done by the members (in the throes of their addictions or relationships with addicts) rather than the wrongs done to the members. ACoA, following the logic of liberation psychotherapy, reverses this trajectory, focusing upon wrongs done to the members and attributing blame. This different approach fosters what some have seen as a penchant for a counterproductive hostility and anger. Pat, who has made a career in the subculture, observes that, especially in non-Al-Anon ACoA groups,[37] it is common for meetings

to degenerate into emotional upheavals, ritual purgings.... It's a bunch of new people, nobody with longevity. They blame, they point fingers, they comment on each other—"My Christmas was worse than your Christmas."...In ACoA, it's a we-them situation: "You did this to me, and it's your fault," and the payoff is, "I can feel self-righteous self-pity." It's the narcissism of pain. The issue is really how to integrate the trauma into your life—how you make peace with it, come to terms with it.[38]

A colleague of Pat's, a board member of the National Association of Children of Alcoholics (NACoA), seconded her misgivings, saying, "If we [NACoA, ACoA] don't watch out, the next movement will be the Children of Adult Children of Alcoholics."

ACoA's emphasis upon personal biography and the insights into the present that are presumably to be gained from attending to one's past are Freudian legacies, but so are AA's and Al-Anon's efforts to, as Pat says, "integrate the trauma," to "make peace with it," and to "come to terms with it." The apparently vengeful mood of at least some adult children signals the presence of another symbolic order, another set of truth rules, a different discursive formation; it signals the presence, and the influence, of liberation psychotherapy.

The Sources of Discontinuity

Rather than the product of a smooth evolution of thinking and knowledge, the emergence of "adult child" discourse in fact constituted a radical break with the twelve-step subculture's original truth rules. This break issues from the larger cultural influence of liberation psychotherapy.

There *were* other factors contributing to this break; chief among these is the treatment industry. Given that its rise signaled the legitimation of the disease model and, as a result, the successful destigmatization of alcohol problems, it is ironic that the treatment industry at least partially helped to facilitate profound changes in the disease model. In large part, it did this by subjecting "recovery" to the exigencies of commerce. Whatever else it may be, at its most fundamental level the provision of treatment is a fee-for-service commodity, whose profitability is entirely contingent upon observing the time limits that insurance providers place upon reimbursement. These limits demand quick results—certainly not one of the long suits of traditional addiction discourse. In AA, there is no "right" period of time in which to get well; recovery is still viewed as a lifetime commitment that must proceed at each individual's pace. Treatment cannot and does not operate that way: Families want their parents, children, or spouses back in the fold; hospitals want patient turnover rates that will maximize revenue; insurers want to minimize claims expenses; the courts want responsible citizens, lighter dockets, less-crowded jails; employers want their workers back on the job. Yet all want results. In an effort to satisfy these somewhat contradictory demands for both celerity and tangible improvements in the patients' behaviors, as well as its own concerns with profitability, the treatment industry encouraged and crafted a marriage of convenience between the twelve-step philosophy and the most practical tenets from family systems and other psychotherapies. In the process, traditional addictive discourse was necessarily streamlined and abbreviated; its truth rules diluted.[39]

Still, although the treatment industry fostered this intermarriage of conflicting therapeutic truth systems and thus a discontinuity with established addiction discourse, the present faultline in the twelve-step subculture runs wider and deeper than this connection can fully explain. The original purpose of treatment was social control; it was devised as an alternative to more severe sanctions—jail time, divorce, job loss, school expulsion. As such, it was oriented by adaptational goals and toward reproducing the status quo: toward creating better citizens, more reliable spouses, productive workers. The industry had no mandate for cultural reform. Co-dependency, in sharp contrast, questions and criticizes some of the very institutions in whose stead and service the treatment industry was originally designed to act.

Co-dependency's critical stance toward what it portrays as conventional society and culture reflects the rise of liberation psychotherapy. Bradshaw, Beattie, and their colleagues list such influences as Abraham Maslow, Virginia Satir, and Carl Rogers—all representatives of liberation psychotherapy's symbolic order, an order in which childhood experiences become determinative forces in one's life, and, far more important, culture is seen as the cause of psychological sickness rather than the standard for normality.

The truth rules of liberation psychotherapy engender a discourse with revolutionary, rather than reproductive, aims. Its assumptions that human nature is innately gentle and loving and, more important, that culture is unduly repressive but not particularly necessary or valuable are precisely the opposite of the assumptions undergirding the adaptational psychologies from which AA was derived. True statements in liberation therapy discourse must reflect the assumptions that humans are innately benevolent creatures, that the "true self" is sequestered behind a wall of defenses born of repressive cultural authority, and (or), that this true self is most easily apprehended in and through the realm of emotional experience and expression. Thus, as we saw in chapter 1, Carl Rogers asserts that "the basic nature of the human being, when functioning freely, is constructive and trustworthy" and that the principal source of human suffering is the sociocultural order that requires and creates the "defensively-organized" person.

Given these assumptions, for Rogers, the key to psychotherapeutic health must be to liberate the individual from cultural and societal influences and effects, rather than to reproduce those influences and effects: "When we are able to free the individual from defensiveness, so that he is open to the wide range of his own needs...his reactions may be trusted to be positive, forward-moving, constructive."[40]

ACoA discourse plainly imported the liberation psychotherapy view of culture into the twelve-step subculture. Co-dependency takes this influence a step further, abiding by and emphatically espousing all of liberation therapy's truth rules. Bradshaw, for example, maintains that, "all of us are born with a deep and profound sense of worth. We are precious, rare, unique and innocent." Just so, Subby views children as "creative, tenacious, and persevering spirits," and cautions his readers that "it would be a grave mistake to think that...the fragile spirit of a child...is resilient to the hideous abuses, tensions, and emotional trauma of a troubled family." Schaef, too, takes issue with culture's impact upon human nature, observing that "[w]e all know how frank children can be, yet much of their training teaches them how to be 'nice,' 'polite,' and 'tactful.'"[41]

Perhaps nowhere in co-dependency discourse is the presence and impact of these new truth rules more apparent than in a thoroughly revised reading of the relationship between addicts and their families. Filtered through liberation psychotherapy's baseline assumptions, co-dependency defines the "alcoholic family" as a subtype of the "dysfunctional family." Wegscheider-Cruse was a leader in this reconceptualization. For her, all of the alcoholic family roles (the enabler, the mascot, the scapegoat, the lost child, the hero) "are symptoms of the disease of co-dependency, in which the primary compulsion is to act in a manner which accommodates the dependent." But, reflecting liberation psychotherapy's influence, she maintains that it is not only the family members of "dependents" who must accommodate others in this way. Indeed, "[r]igid families...who carry an overload of traditional dogma about the roles of family members, also provide a prime breeding ground for co-dependency."[42] In co-dependency, addicted and more generically dysfunctional families share, among other qualities, this "rigidity" in belief and conduct. Expanding on this theme, Bradshaw asserts that "[e]very dysfunctional family...has certain structural similarities," including a "dominant dysfunction [that] causes a threat to which all members respond. The adaptation to the threat causes the system to close up in a frozen and rigid pattern...[that] is maintained by each member playing one or more rigid roles." As a result of this frozen pattern, "[a]ll members have lost their own reality. Each is out of touch with his own feelings, needs and wants. Each is a false self who has given up his individual uniqueness for the sake of loyalty to the system."[43]

Although "loyalty to the system" may not be the right phrase for what Bradshaw portrays as an act of unconscious obedience and systemic domination, what is most important to see, here, is the claim that a family's dysfunctionality issues from any "threat" that results in group control over the individual members and a reduction in the range of their choices. This threat, Bradshaw says, takes many forms, including

> Dad's drinking or work addiction; Mom's hysterical control of everyone's feelings; Dad or Mom's physical or verbal violence; a family member's actual sickness or hypochondriasis; Dad or Mom's early death; the divorce; Dad or Mom's moral/ religious righteousness; Dad or Mom's sexual abuse. Anyone, who becomes controlling in the family to the point of being experienced as a threat by the other members, initiates the dysfunction.[44]

Co-dependency shares ACoA's angry mood and emphasis upon past experience, but because it assigns a generic causal capacity to group subordination of the individual, co-dependency asserts that "addicted families" are no different from and are really only a subtype of the "dysfunctional family." These changes in truth are reflected in the increasingly generic application of the "adult child" appellation. As John Friel and Linda Friel, both addiction and co-dependency treatment specialists, maintain, one may now be an adult child by virtue of any ostensibly repressive, oppressive, or traumatic socialization experience:

> As countless professionals in our field [chemical-dependency treatment] are at last beginning to recognize, it's not just the alcoholic or cocaine addict in the family who has a problem. Even if there is no chemical dependency in the family, the entire family can operate just like an alcoholic family if the rules that govern the system are the same. In other words, it is not just Adult Children of Alcoholics

(ACoAs) who can profit from a twelve-step group. It is Adult Children of Dysfunctional Families (Adult Children) who can profit, too.[45]

The adjective that the Friels, and all of co-dependency's advocates, use to characterize families points to precisely what the evolutionary view of co-dependency overlooks and what a genealogical analysis—and an attention to discontinuities in logic—reveals. Functionality, like efficiency, beauty, or truth, is a matter of perspective. To say that a family, or any social institution, is not functioning as it should implies a standard against which its performance is gauged. What is it that the institution is expected to do? What function is it supposed to perform? In 1935, when AA was founded, families were expected to raise their children to fit into the established social and cultural world. A high premium was placed upon conformity, on playing by existing rules, on performing one's social roles as expected, and on an orientation toward social approval. So, too, in 1951, when Al-Anon was founded, or in 1957, when Ala-Teen began, the individual's psychological well-being was assessed by compliance with and adjustment to, as the previously quoted instruction from AA put it, existing "conditions...whatever they were." In the relationship between self and society, the latter was accorded ultimate authority and priority.

By the 1960s and 1970s, when the treatment industry arose and the adult children movement began, that standard had been reversed. Reflecting the cultural impact of liberation psychotherapy, psychological health had come to be assessed primarily in terms of a person's ability to negate the moral demands of a culture and society that had been adjudged poorly qualified to issue such demands; its militarism, sexism, racism, materialism, and rewarding of unthinking conformity left the status quo embattled and fighting from a position of moral weakness.

Given these larger cultural changes, it is less than surprising that when recovering-addicts-turned-treatment-industry-professionals consulted prevailing therapeutic wisdom in order to complement their own treatment regimens, they found—and found convincing—a predominance of clinical approaches grounded in a profoundly critical view of conventional culture and society. Families, as the frontline institutions in the dissemination of cultural standards, were among the principal targets of these approaches. Instructing children in an ethic of self-denial and—to use Wegscheider-Cruse's term—"accommodation" to the status quo, fostering a subordination to social authority and encouraging them to meet the normative demands from which social roles take shape, were by this time routinely blamed for psychological illness. Families that abided by these expectations were now "dysfunctional," mainly because the functions they were expected to meet had changed. From the new vantage point, it seemed apparent that the pivotal issue for the individual's psychological health was to prevent anything that undercuts or interferes with the self's unfettered development. Thus, again, the dysfunctional family is "just like" the alcoholic family because, in both, group dynamics eclipse the self and restrict its choices.

For all of these reasons, it is more than just an incidental oversight to speak of co-dependency as "psychological," or, as some have asserted, "religious."[46] Such characterizations contribute little, if anything, toward understanding what claims co-dependency makes and, by extension, what commitments believers are expected to make. In the same vein, it is clear that the newest members of the twelve-step subculture have very little in common with those "brown shoe alcoholics" (as they sometimes refer to themselves) whose twelve-step roots run back fifteen, twenty-five, or even fifty years. Long-standing members carry altogether different biographical passports and are guided by fundamentally different conceptions of their relationship to society. Not only do co-dependents not necessarily have an addiction to alcohol or other drugs, but such addicting substances need not figure in their lives at all. Rather, the necessary entry ticket is now a subjection to the repressions of a collective and external authority—liberation psychotherapy's basic causal mechanism. That such an explanation was heretofore taken as a *symptom* of alcoholism underscores just how fundamentally the adult children movement and co-dependency have altered the twelve-step subculture's rules for what counts as true—and for what counts as psychological sickness or health.

Notes

1. "Subculture," perhaps especially since the late 1960s, has come to be a loaded term. As it is used here, it is not intended to signify subversive or counterrevolutionary connotations. Rather, it is intended to signify a group or groups united by beliefs and practices not shared by the majority of the population. David Matza has employed the term in a similar fashion in his discussion of the "delinquent subculture" (see David Matza, *Delinquency and Drift* [New York: John Wiley and Sons, 1964]). The present usage shares Matza's contention that it is misleading to

68   A Disease of One's Own

view a subculture as being organized around the rejection of the dominant culture; rather, the dominant culture and subcultures often share similar values. Attention to their similarities and to the ties between them is more fruitful than a focus upon presumed oppositions. It is this perspective that informs Matza's deliberate use of the term "subculture of delinquency" rather than "delinquent subculture"—the distinction is intended to highlight correspondences rather than rifts between culture and its subcultures. Often, he argues, subcultural norms and values are directly traceable to and inadvertently encouraged by the dominant culture, a view with obvious relevance in this context.

2. Foucault's "genealogical" method is inseparable from what he called the "archaeological" method, both of which inform the discussion of truth rules in this chapter. The latter is devoted to exploring the rules that distinguish discourses from one another; the former traces the history of those rules and the discontinuities that engender new discourses. I have found the following works by and about Foucault especially useful: Michel Foucault, "Truth and Power," in *Power/Knowledge: Selected Interviews and Other Writings, 1972–1977*, ed. Colin Gordon (New York: Pantheon, 1980), 109–33; *The History of Sexuality*, vol. 1 (New York: Vintage Books, 1980), an excellent example of both the genealogical and archaeological approaches; *The Foucault Reader*, ed. Paul Rabinow (New York: Pantheon, 1984), to my mind, the best and most diverse source. Four articles in that volume were of particular relevance and value for this study: "On the Genealogy of Ethics: An Overview of Work in Progress," 340–72; "We Other Victorians," 292–300; "The Repressive Hypothesis," 301–29; and "Neitzsche, Genealogy, History," 76–100. In addition, it should be noted that Foucault has a reputation for being less than explicit—for some, obtuse—about his methods and terminology. The best of numerous Foucault exegeses, in my view, is Hubert L. Dreyfus and Paul Rabinow, *Michel Foucault: Beyond Structuralism and Hermeneutics* (Chicago: University of Chicago Press, 1982). See also David Couzens Hoy, ed., *Foucault: A Critical Reader* (Oxford: Basil Blackwell, 1986).

3. Arnold I. Davidson, "Archaeology, Genealogy, Ethics," in Hoy, ed., *Foucault: A Critical Reader,* 224.

4. Schaef, *Co-Dependence,* 4–6.

5. On the alcoholism movement, see Robin Room, "Treatment-Seeking Populations and Larger Realities," in *Alcoholism Treatment in Transition*, ed. Griffith Edwards and Marcus Grant (London: Croom-Helm, 1980), 205–24; Kaye Middleton Fillmore and Dennis Kelso, "Coercion into Alcoholism Treatment: Meanings for the Disease Concept of Alcoholism" (Berkeley, Calif.: Alcohol Research Group, monograph B299, 1986); Joseph W. Schneider, "Deviant Drinking as Disease: Alcoholism as a Social Accomplishment," *Social Problems* 25 (1978): 361–72; Constance M. Weisner and Robin Room, "Financing and Ideology in Alcohol Treatment." *Social Problems* 32 (1984): 167–84.

6. Gallup polls conducted periodically over the past forty-five years unmistakably illustrate that the alcoholism movement has succeeded in effecting public acceptance of the disease model. In the years 1946 to 1951, only 20 percent of those polled agreed with the disease model view; by 1955–1960, 60 percent agreed. Finally, as of 1982, 80 percent of respondents agreed that alcoholism is a disease (cited in Stanton M. Peele, *The Meaning of Addiction: Compulsive Experience and Its Interpretation* [Lexington, Mass.: D.C. Heath, 1985], 28).

7. The Nixon administration's Health Maintenance Organization Act of 1970 explicitly defined hospital and other health care providers as essentially no different

than any other corporate enterprise. The rationale behind this legislation, which sought to subject the health care industry to "the discipline of the market," reflected that point of view; see Paul Starr, *The Social Transformation of American Medicine* (New York: Basic Books, 1982) for an overview. For an analysis of the relationship between defining hospitals in this way and the rise of "alternative delivery systems," especially for alcohol treatment, see John Steadman Rice, "'A Power Greater Than Ourselves': The Commodification of Alcoholism" (master's thesis, University of Nebraska at Omaha, 1989). For a related discussion, on the artificiality of the health care "market" and its failure to "behave" as a market, see W. Boyd Littrell, "Competition, Bureaucracy, and Hospital Care: Costs in a Midwestern City," in *Bureaucracy as a Social Problem*, ed. W. Boyd Littrell, Gideon Sjoberg, and Louis A. Zurcher (Greenwich, Conn.: JAI Press, 1983), 251–69.

 8. See National Institute on Drug Abuse and National Institute on Alcohol Abuse and Alcoholism, "Highlights from the 1989 National Drug and Alcoholism Treatment Unit Survey" (thirteen-page early report from the *National Drug and Alcoholism Treatment Unit Survey*; Washington: Government Printing Office, 1990); and U.S. Department of Health and Human Services, *Seventh Special Report to the U.S. Congress on Alcohol and Health from the Secretary of Health and Human Services* (Washington: U.S. Department of Health and Human Services, 1990), especially chapter 7. Drawing upon 1985 data, Norman K. Denzin reported that as many as 800,000 persons annually receive some form of treatment for alcohol problems (see his *The Recovering Alcoholic* [Beverly Hills, Calif.: Sage, 1987], 17).

 9. For discussions of these interrelationships, see Rice, "'A Power Greater Than Ourselves,'" and J. David Brown, "The Professional Ex-: An Alternative for Exiting the Deviant Career," *Sociological Quarterly* 32 (1991): 219–30.

10. The list was supplied by the National Self-Help Clearinghouse, Washington, D.C., in response to a request for a comprehensive nationwide listing of twelve-step and/or Anonymous groups.

11. This list is adapted from a list of self-help groups in the Minneapolis/St. Paul area. The entire list may be found in the *Utne Reader,* Nov./Dec. 1988, 62, in a piece that was itself a reprint from the August 1988 issue of *The Phoenix.*

12. Wendy Kaminer has frequently used the term "recovery movement" as if there are no differences among and between the various groups in the twelve-step subculture. As this chapter demonstrates, however, AA and its imitators hold almost completely contradictory points of view; see Kaminer, *I'm Dysfunctional, You're Dysfunctional.*

13. Sigmund Freud's split with his most promising students (C. G. Jung, Alfred Adler, Otto Rank, Wilhelm Reich) is perhaps the quintessential example of the differences among "psychologies." In *The History of the Psychoanalytic Movement,* trans. A. A. Brill (New York: Johnson Reprint Corporation, 1970; originally published in 1917), Freud explicitly broke with his students and explained why it was necessary to do so: They were not practicing psychoanalysis but psychotherapy — promising "cures" of various stripes that, for Freud, were no more than different ways to be sick. In the terminology of the present study, they were guided by different rules for making true statements.

14. Michel Foucault, *The Archaeology of Knowledge* (New York: Pantheon, 1972), 99ff.

15. The clearest exposition of these views may be found in Sigmund Freud, *Civilization and Its Discontents* (New York: Norton, 1961). See also Philip Rieff, *Freud: The Mind of the Moralist,* 3d ed. (Chicago: University of Chicago Press 1979; originally published in 1959), and *The Triumph of the Therapeutic.*

16. The examples of adaptational discourse are from, respectively, Edmund S. Conklin, *Principles of Abnormal Psychology*, rev. ed. (New York: Henry Holt, 1946), 4, 14; and Vernon B. Twitchell, "A Psychologist Looks at Psychotherapy," *The American Mercury*, August 1950, 172–73. As I discovered in the course of archival research, Conklin's and Twitchell's views are endlessly reiterated in psychology textbooks published prior to the 1960s. I selected their remarks because they provided especially clear examples of the adaptational orientation that was dominant at the time.

17. Alcoholics Anonymous, *Twelve Steps and Twelve Traditions* (New York: Alcoholics Anonymous World Services, 1985), 81. In the newer additions to the twelve-step subculture, the steps have been somewhat altered (Appendix B shows, for example, CoDA's twelve steps).

18. Ibid., 86.

19. Ibid., 47.

20. In AA's early years it was widely believed that only men became alcoholics; thus the supporting role of the wives during this time. This, of course, has changed radically.

21. Nan Robertson, *Getting Better: Inside Alcoholics Anonymous* (New York: Morrow, 1988), 162. The Loretta Young episode about Al-Anon was called "The Understanding Heart."

22. Robertson, *Getting Better*, 164.

23. Quoted in ibid., 164, 160, respectively. The demographic materials presented in this section are also derived from Robertson.

24. This, however, has begun to change. Both AA and Al-Anon have been affected by the influx of mainstream psychotherapeutic views.

25. Fillmore and Kelso, "Coercion into Alcoholism Treatment"; Patricia Morgan, "The Political Economy of Drugs and Alcohol," *Journal of Drug Issues* 13 (Winter): 1–7; Weisner and Room, "Financing and Ideology in Alcohol Treatment"; and Rice, "'A Power Greater Than Ourselves,'" all examine the rise of the treatment industry from a political–economic perspective.

26. Brown, "The Professional Ex-."

27. See, for example, C. F. Midelfort, *The Family in Psychotherapy* (New York: McGraw-Hill, 1957); Murray Bowen, *Family Therapy in Clinical Practice* (New York: Jason Aronson, 1978); Nathan Ackerman, *The Psychodynamics of Family Life* (New York: Basic Books, 1958), and *Treating the Troubled Family* (New York: Basic Books, 1966); Salvadore Minuchin, *Families and Family Therapy* (Cambridge, Mass.: Harvard University Press, 1974), and *Family Kaleidoscope: Images of Violence and Healing* (Cambridge, Mass.: Harvard University Press, 1984); R. D. Laing and A. Esterson, *Sanity, Madness, and the Family*, 2d ed. (New York: Basic Books, 1971).

28. Ludwig von Bertalanffy's systems theorizing was an important influence on Palo Alto family systems theorists; see, for example, Bertalanffy, "An Outline of General Systems Theory," *British Journal of the Philosophy of Science* 1 (1950): 134–65. Family systems psychotherapy is one strain of structural–functional theory. Although this influence is seldom noticed or acknowledged, some feminist theorists have argued that all family systems therapies are indebted to R. F. Bales and Talcott Parsons, *Family, Socialization, and Interaction Process* (New York: Free Press, 1951). Deborah Anna Luepnitz, for example, observes that "all [of the]...basic categories for conceptualizing families...derive from Parsons's work," including "the idea that the family [has] a 'structure'...that it performs 'functions' that involve 'contracting' and 'role negotiation' and that it must 'adapt'

to society" (Deborah Anna Luepnitz, *The Family Interpreted: Feminist Theory in Clinical Practice*. [New York: Basic Books, 1988], 64–65); see also Virginia Goldner, "Feminism and Family Therapy," *Family Process* 24 (1985): 31–47. Although Luepnitz's position is, as she admits, inferred rather than demonstrable (see 65*n*), her point is not without merit. The logic of explanation in both the sociological and family therapy versions of systems theory is strikingly similar, if inverted. Sociological studies in this camp see the system as functional and argue that seemingly dysfunctional phenomena, such as inequality, are in fact important for the smooth functioning of the system (Kingsley Davis and W. E. Moore, "Some Principles of Stratification," *American Sociological Review* 10 [1945]: 242–49; but see also Herbert Gans, "The Positive Functions of Poverty," *American Journal of Sociology* 78 [1972]: 275–89). Family systems therapy, conversely, views the system as dysfunctional and maintains that seemingly functional behaviors actually perpetuate the systemic dysfunction. Leading authors and significant works from the Palo Alto Group include Gregory Bateson, D. Jackson, J. Haley, and J. Weakland, "Toward a Theory of Schizophrenia," *Behavioral Science* 1 (1956): 251–64; Jay Haley, "Marriage Therapy," *Archives of General Psychiatry* 8 (1963): 213–34, and *Strategies of Psychotherapy* (New York: Grune and Stratton, 1963); Don D. Jackson, "Family Rules: The Marital *Quid pro Quo*," *Archives of General Psychiatry* 12 (1965): 589–94, and "The Myth of Normality," *Medical Opinion and Review* 3, no. 5 (1967): 28–33; Virginia Satir, *Conjoint Family Therapy* (Palo Alto, Calif.: Science and Behavior Books, 1967). The focus upon dysfunctional communication patterns may be found in P. Watzlawick, *An Anthology of Human Communication: Text and Tape* (Palo Alto, Calif.: Science and Behavior Books, 1964), and *The Language of Change: Elements of Therapeutic Communication* (New York: Basic Books, 1978); P. Watzlawick, J. H. Beavin, and Don Jackson, *Pragmatics of Human Communication* (New York: W. W. Norton, 1967).

29. See especially Claudia Black, *It Will Never Happen to Me* (Denver, Colo.: M. A. C., 1981); Janet G. Woititz, *Marriage on the Rocks* (Deerfield Beach, Fla.: Health Communications, 1979), and *Adult Children of Alcoholics* (Deerfield Beach, Fla.: Health Communications, 1983); Sharon Wegscheider, *Another Chance: Hope and Help for the Alcoholic Family* (Palo Alto, Calif.: Science and Behavior Books, 1981); Sharon Wegscheider-Cruse, "Co-Dependency: The Therapeutic Void," in *Co-Dependency: An Emerging Issue*, edited (no editors cited) (Deerfield Beach, Fla.: Health Communications, 1984), 1–4, and *Choicemaking: For Co-dependents, Adult Children, and Spirituality Seekers* (Deerfield Beach, Fla.: Health Communications, 1985).

30. Bradshaw, *Bradshaw On: The Family*, 27.

31. Norman K. Denzin provides a cogent discussion of the relationship between role theory and the concept of the alcoholic family roles in his recent book *Hollywood Shot by Shot: Alcoholism and the American Cinema* (Chicago: Aldine de Gruyter, 1991), see especially chapter 7.

32. See Black, *It Will Never Happen to Me*, chapters 2 and 4; Wegscheider-Cruse, *Choicemaking*, 129.

33. "It's All in the Family" (editorial), *Inside Al-Anon: Special Issue for and about Children of Alcoholics* Oct./Nov. 1986: 1; reprinted in 1989. Membership data are taken from an ACoA brochure, dated April 1990, entitled "What Is IWSO?" [International World Service Organization]. It is indicative of ACoA's growth, as well, that the 1,500 meetings in 1990 represent a 50-percent increase over the 1,000 meetings listed in January 1988.

34. "It's All in the Family," 1.
35. See Appendix B for a copy of CoDA's Twelve Traditions.
36. All material relating to the 1984 IWSO are taken from "It's All in the Family."
37. Despite Al-Anon's efforts, there are still unaffiliated ACoA groups, although most have been absorbed into the twelve-step subculture.
38. All comments attributed to Pat, a clinical psychologist who works with alcoholic families, are taken from Robertson, *Getting Better*, 181–82.
39. See Rice, "'A Power Greater Than Ourselves,'" for a discussion of the impact of referral sources and profit orientations upon the structure of addiction treatment in one hospital-based facility.
40. Rogers, *On Becoming a Person*, respectively, 91, 194, 91, 111–12, 113, and 194.
41. Bradshaw, *Bradshaw On: The Family*, 46; Subby, *Lost in the Shuffle*, 63, 62; Schaef, *Co-Dependence*, 69.
42. Wegscheider-Cruse, *Choicemaking*, 129, 7, respectively.
43. Adapted from a list of the dysfunctional family's characteristics; Bradshaw, *Bradshaw On: The Family*, 179–80.
44. Ibid., 164. The punctuation in the last sentence is Bradshaw's.
45. John Friel and Linda Friel, *Adult Children: The Secrets of Dysfunctional Families* (Deerfield Beach, Fla.: Health Communications, 1988), 5.
46. Wendy Kaminer has been the principal exponent of what she sees as co-dependency's "religious" nature. See her *I'm Dysfunctional, You're Dysfunctional*.

3

The Anatomy of Co-Dependency

This chapter and the next will focus on the articulation between liberation psychotherapy and co-dependency *as symbolic systems,* examining their fit *at the level of meaning.* Over the course of these two chapters, we will see that in many respects the fit between the two systems is all but perfect; co-dependency largely reproduces liberation psychotherapy's core tenets. But there are differences, and the differences are important, not least because they reveal co-dependency's reformist impulses, its attempts to conceptualize and deal with problems born of liberation psychotherapy's instability as a social form, especially at the level of intimate relationships, primary groups, and identities. This reformist impulse will be the focus of chapter 4; this chapter is devoted to an examination of co-dependency's core premises and causal logic.

As chapter 2 showed, evocative terms and phrases such as the "triumph of the therapeutic" and the "psychological society," although heuristically helpful, fail to adequately differentiate among the varieties of psychotherapeutic discourse, theory, and practice, and as such they provide only partial purchase on the nature and significance of the cultural changes to which they and so many other theoretical treatises and empirical studies refer. The cultural changes of recent decades reflect the increasing—though as I have emphasized, not universal—public acceptance of psychologies I have subsumed under the heading of liberation psychotherapy: that is, those that share and espouse the same convictions about self, about society and culture, and about the appropriate relationship among them.

The "triumph of the therapeutic," as we have seen, represents a profound transformation in the historical function of psychology in relation to its societal and cultural context—a transformation from means to end, from a body of theoretical knowledge and discourse *legitimat-*

ing a larger cultural vision to *being* that larger vision itself. As Peter L. Berger and Thomas Luckmann have pointed out, historically, "psychology always presupposes cosmology."[1] In short, psychologies—and here I have in mind any and all theories and practices that explain, classify, and seek to rectify puzzling behavior—do more than minister to troubled selves: More important, they also maintain the viability and plausibility of the larger symbolic and relational systems in which they operate and that provide the baseline from which psychological diagnoses, classifications, and practices can make any sense at all. The eminent psychiatrist Jerome D. Frank, commenting on the culturally and socially contingent nature of psychological categories and theories, has pointed out that

> [s]ymptoms that in the Middle Ages were viewed as evidence of demoniacal possession to be treated by exorcism are now regarded as signs of mental illness to be treated by a psychiatrist. In World War II Russian soldiers were never classified as having psychoneuroses, because, as far as one can see, the Russian army did not recognize this condition. Presumably soldiers with complaints that Americans would term psychoneurotic were regarded either as malingerers subject to disciplinary action or as medically ill and therefore treated by regular physicians.[2]

There are two points to be emphasized here: First of all, unlike its intellectual predecessors, liberation psychotherapy did not legitimate but, instead, forcefully critiqued and ultimately supplanted the cosmology from which it was born. Among its exponents and devotees, this particular brand of psychology became an alternative model of culture; no longer a psychology per se, it became instead the cosmology that new forms of psychology would presuppose and seek to legitimate. Second, it is my contention that the discourse of co-dependency is best understood as a manifestation of the new types of psychology that the therapeutic culture requires.

To speak, with Berger and Luckmann, of "problematic cases" for which psychologies provide "interpretative schemes" is to speak of what Mary Douglas refers to as cultural "anomalies," the all but inevitable instances of phenomena that slip through the cracks of any symbolic system. The significance of anomalies centers on the issue of a symbolic system's legitimacy. Anomalies elude the existing structures of meaningfulness; they defy explanation by way of a culture's available interpretive concepts, theories, and discourses. Too many inexplicable phenomena threaten the plausibility of the cultural system itself, raising fundamental questions that promise to undo that system; questions such as "what good is a cultural system if it cannot account for all—or nearly all—of the events in the world? How can we be certain that what the cultural-symbolic system tells us is right? And, if it is not right, then why should we continue to believe—or, at minimum, to behave as if we do?"

Anomalies, Douglas maintains, cannot be ignored, except at peril to the cultural system itself; they must be accounted for, or dealt with in some way.[3] Psychologies are mechanisms for dealing with cultural anomalies at both the symbolic and the relational levels. At the symbolic level, the diagnostic act itself situates problematic instances within the limits and logic of the larger symbolic system, making the problems explicable in relation to and in terms of that larger system. Thus, through the creation of diagnosable categories, a behavior or event may be deviant, pathological, or aberrant, but it is within the explanatory power of the existing meaning system and can be categorized accordingly. At the relational level, psychologies perform, or enable, a social control function. Once named and classified—by cause and nature—problem behaviors become amenable to intervention; therapeutic techniques can be devised and brought to bear, bringing miscreants into line with convention and custom and thereby restoring things to their appropriate and expected order.

Acting in these capacities, psychologies articulate with existing symbolic and relational systems in ways that *reproduce* those systems, legitimating both the sensibility and validity of established meanings and the social relationships that embody them. As I noted at the outset of this chapter, co-dependency's articulation with liberation psychotherapy is of a *reformist* character: The discourse is organized around and reflects the conviction that the key principles of liberation psychotherapy are fundamentally sound, moral, and just, but they are not borne out as effectively or as fairly as they should be in the systems of social relations. It is to an accounting of these relational problems that co-dependency discourse offers both explanation and redress: The nature of the explanation reveals the discourse's articulation with liberation psychotherapy at the level of meaning; the character of the proposed means of redress reveals the reformist impulse. This chapter is concerned with the first of these functions: with the nature of the explanation of people's problems that co-dependency offers.

The Symbolic and Narrative Structure of Co-Dependency:
The Making and Meaning of the Co-Dependent

At the symbolic level, co-dependency discourse articulates perfectly with liberation psychotherapy; it mirrors and is structured by liberation psychotherapy's cardinal principles, taking as unquestionably true the assumptions that human nature is innately benevolent and constructive, that culture and society are overly repressive, and that those repressions are the source of virtually all psychological and, by extension, social problems. Drawing extensively and all but exclusively from these elements, co-dependency portrays a distinctive vision of an ideal social world. This vision amounts to a psychotherapeutic version of utilitarianism, in which it is assumed that each person's pursuit of emotional and experiential self-interest will engender a just and harmonious social order. The ethic of self-actualization, then, is the foundation for an alternative cultural and social reality, and it is against that reality that co-dependency situates the problems it seeks to explain.

The linchpin to this utilitarian worldview is the most fundamental of liberation psychotherapy's principles: the presumption of the innate benevolence of human beings. In co-dependency, the child—which is also variously identified by such synonyms as the true self, the higher self, the inner child, and the divine child—symbolizes this view of human nature. Whichever term is used, the meaning is constant; the child always refers to what Charles Whitfield, one of the symbol's principal architects, describes as "the part of us that is ultimately alive, energetic, creative and fulfilled. This is our Real Self—who we truly are" (capitals in original).[4]

The child image surely contributed to co-dependency's popular appeal, for in contemporary U.S. life, children and childhood have become heavily loaded symbols, icons of an Edenic time in life, a brief haven of innocence and authenticity. Viviana Zelizer's *Pricing the Priceless Child* convincingly and capably documents the progressive attachment of these meanings to childhood, showing that as children's economic value has declined over the past seventy-five years, their emotional value has increased commensurately; their growing economic uselessness, to put it bluntly, has been balanced by and transmuted into emotional pricelessness. The net result of this change in children's cultural status, Zelizer observes, has been a "sacralization" of childhood experience and a proliferation of symbols reflecting that change in status.[5] In light of this larger cultural trend and, particularly, its isomorphism with liberation psychotherapy's view of human nature, it is predictable that co-dependency should have employed the child as a symbol of an idealized self; equally predictable is that the symbol should hold a special resonance for co-dependency's adherents.

As the symbol of an ideal self, the child contains multiple references and connotations, all of which are plainly informed by liberation psychotherapy's view of human nature as well. Whitfield, again, invokes the child image interchangeably with what he calls the "true self," a usage that plainly underscores the assumptions about human nature that structure co-dependency discourse. For Whitfield, before society and culture begin to impose their requirements upon the individual, the self is "spontaneous, expansive, loving, giving, and communicating.... [It] feels... [a]nd it expresses those feelings.... [It] is expressive, assertive, and creative. It can be childlike in the highest, most mature, and evolved sense of the word.... It is healthily self-indulgent, taking pleasure in receiving and being nurtured."[6]

The child is the metaphorical rock upon which co-dependency's symbolic structure is built. Using that image as a foundation, the discourse conceptually divides the social world into a set of binary oppositions, contrary units of meaning that, despite their opposite connotations, rely upon their opposition to convey their respective meanings. This symbolism reflects and performs an essentially anthropological operation, situating human social experience within a framework of meaningfulness, charting the boundaries between normality and deviance, and ultimately mapping out a template for social action. Just as such symbolic oppositions as the sacred and the profane, the raw and the cooked, and the pure and the polluted are mutually constitutive symbols defining an overarching cosmology, in co-dependency, beliefs and practices, social relationships and institutions are either functional or dysfunctional, depending upon their treatment of and impact upon the child.[7]

The significance of this child image is nowhere more apparent than in the symbolic opposition that co-dependency draws between individuation and socialization as the representative child-rearing practices of two opposed cultural and social systems: The discourse pits the liberation therapy culture against the culture that, for purposes of convenience and clarity, I will call "mainstream culture" throughout the remainder of this book. The relationship between liberation therapy culture and mainstream culture is like that between such symbolic oppositions as sacred and profane: Mainstream culture is paired with, opposed to, and thereby helps to define the liberation therapy culture. Guided by opposed imperatives, these contradictory symbolic systems also produce opposite selves. Mainstream culture, by way of socialization, manufactures false selves, co-dependents; liberation therapy culture, fostering individuation and an ethic of self-actualization, engenders the true self, the self-actualized individual.

These differences derive from the opposed view of human nature that informs the two symbolic systems. Contrary to liberation therapy's benign view, mainstream culture sees human nature as instinctively aggressive, even potentially predatory. Because it holds to this view, its treatment of the child is oriented by and designed to instill an ethic of self-denial, in which the self learns to accept its subordination to externally- imposed demands for appropriate conduct. Mainstream culture socializes children; its institutions—especially its families, churches, and schools—impose a set of values and norms upon the self, the child. Because these institutions promulgate the message of self-denial, they are dysfunctional. Reflecting the same logic, functional institutions are guided by the ethic of self-actualization, aiming to secure the self's individuation, a full autonomy from others and from social control.

Individuation, as the symbolic opposite of socialization, is the guarantor of psychological health. As John Bradshaw explains, the key to psychological well-being is not belonging but differentiation: "The process of differentiation of self is essential to us all. The difference between individuation and belonging is one's place on a continuum. We are all somewhere on the continuum and all in need of becoming more differentiated. Our individuality is equivalent to our identity."[8]

As a psychological discourse, co-dependency's principal concern is with the mental and emotional well-being of self and with the factors contributing to or undermining that well-being. Because the "cosmology" that co-dependency "presupposes" is liberation therapy, the model of psychological well-being is the self-actualized individual, whose counterpart and opposite number is the co-dependent.

"Co-dependent," in short, is a diagnosis. Every diagnosis contains an implicit narrative—a story that explains, in this case, the making of the co-dependent; the transformation, over time and as the result of specific factors, of the child into the co-dependent.[9] Reflecting its powerful articulation with liberation therapy, the story of the making of the co-dependent is essentially one of repression. In co-dependency, repression is reframed in terms of two inter-related equivalences: socialization is repression and, more important, repression is "contamination," "abandonment," and "abuse."

The origins of the co-dependent's sickness lie in the child's exposure during socialization to the "rules" of mainstream culture; its tutelage in the ethic of self-denial. Reflecting this emphasis upon the causal significance of self-denying rules, Robert Subby characterizes the disease of co-dependency as *"the product of delayed or interrupted identity brought about by the practice of dysfunctional rules"* (emphasis in the original).[10] All co-dependency treatises maintain that these dysfunctional rules are woven into the very fabric of mainstream culture, a conviction that is readily apparent in John Bradshaw's contention that *"[t]he [dysfunctional] family itself is [only] a symptom of society at large"* (emphasis added).[11]

For Bradshaw, mainstream culture foments a "poisonous pedagogy," a set of rules that "glorify obedience, orderliness, logic, rationality, power and male supremacy... [and] are flagrantly anti-life." Underscoring the notion that the entire social and cultural order has been poisoned, Bradshaw goes on to argue that "[m]any of our religious institutions offer authoritarian support for these [rules]. Our schools reinforce them. Our legal system reinforces them.... [They] *are carried by family systems, by our schools, our churches, and our government. They are a core belief of the modern 'consensus reality'"* (emphasis in the original).[12] According to Bradshaw, the poisonous pedagogy's rules encompass a wide range of commonly accepted albeit tacit beliefs, including:

1. A feeling of duty produces love.
2. Hatred can be done away with by forbidding it.
3. Parents deserve respect because they are parents....
4. Children are undeserving of respect simply because they are children.
5. Obedience makes a child strong.
6. A high degree of self-esteem is harmful.
7. A low degree of self-esteem makes a person altruistic.
8. Tenderness (doting) is harmful.
9. Responding to a child's needs is wrong.
10. Severity and coldness toward a child gives him [*sic*] a good preparation for life.

11. A pretense of gratitude is better than honest ingratitude.
12. The way you behave is more important than the way you really are.
13. Neither parents nor God would survive being offended.
14. The body is something dirty and disgusting.
15. Strong feelings are harmful.
16. Parents are creatures free of drives and guilt.
17. Parents are always right.[13]

Though only one is the topic of discussion, Bradshaw's list really describes two diametrically opposed, realities—one that socializes children and one that fosters their individuation. Socialization—the process by which cultures impress their core beliefs upon the self—is the driving force in the creation of psychologically sick selves, passing on poisonous beliefs by way of unnecessary and cruel practices.

Although running like a red thread throughout the entire co-dependency corpus, this line of reasoning is especially evident in Bradshaw's works, which repeatedly maintain that, because of its reliance upon socialization and external control of the individual, mainstream culture "abandons and abuses" the child. Seeing socialization as abandonment and abuse, Bradshaw acknowledges, requires "stretch[ing] the old meanings of our words." For example, to see things in this way demands that we learn to "expand the meaning of the word abandonment to include various forms of *emotional abandonment*: stroke deprivation, narcissistic deprivation,... the neglect of developmental dependency needs and family system enmeshment... [and] all forms of abuse." Since socialization per se is really abandonment and abuse, the catalogue of abusive practices cannot help but be a lengthy one. Indeed, Bradshaw goes on to explain that dysfunctional families also abandon and abuse children by "not modeling their own emotions for their children,... not being there to affirm their children's expression of emotion,... not providing for the children's developmental dependency needs,... [and by] not giving them their time, attention and direction."[14]

It is clear that Bradshaw is doing more than, as he says, "expand[ing] the meanings" of abandonment and abuse. Rather, he supplies those practices with entirely new meanings—meanings grounded in the core principles of liberation psychotherapy: Anything that does not foster individuation, anything that places the individual in a subordinate relationship to society, is abandonment and abuse.

The concepts of abandonment and abuse are a variant on what Mary Douglas has called symbols of pollution and purity, which are perhaps the most fundamental, culturally universal, form of binary opposition.[15] When systematically paired with opposed symbols of purity, pollution images engender an entire system of meaning and an accompanying model of social organization. Symbols of pollution, Douglas argues, denote defilement, and "[d]efilement is never an isolated event. It cannot occur except in view of a systematic ordering of ideas.... The only way in which pollution ideas make sense is in reference to a total structure of thought."[16] When set in opposition to individuation, then, the concepts of abandonment and abuse delineate moral and symbolic boundaries and a total structure of thought. They outline two symbolic worlds with a single set of symbols, assigning to only one a moral status and utilizing the other to punctuate that moral status.

In co-dependency, socialization is not cultural instruction but systematic violation, routinized defilement. This theme was most readily apparent in Bradshaw's 1990 PBS miniseries *Homecoming*. In his introductory remarks, Bradshaw announced that the program would explore the causes and consequences of being "wounded" and "contaminated" as a child. Asking the question, "Did your child get wounded?" Bradshaw directed the audience's attention to an enormous placard beside him on the soundstage. The placard listed a set of symptomatic traits the audience should look for in themselves to help them "see if you got your childhood needs met." Bradshaw, employing one of his favorite rhetorical devices, presented the symptoms born of these unmet needs in the form of an acronym, with each letter in the word "contaminate" serving as the first letter of a symptom of a wounded inner child, a polluted true self:[17]

Co-dependence
Offender Behavior
Narcissistic Disorder
Trust Issues
Acting Out/Acting In
Magical Beliefs
Intimacy Dysfunction
Non-Disciplined Behavior
Addictive/Compulsive
Thought Distortions
Emptiness

Bradshaw's image of contamination draws sharp moral boundaries between the liberation therapy culture and mainstream culture; the latter, by its practices, pollutes an otherwise pure self with what Bradshaw calls "toxic shame." Toxic shame, he explains, is an existential condition, a "being wound" routinely incurred by the children of mainstream culture. This being wound translates into an intensely negative self-image: The wounded person, he says, tends to think "I *am* a mistake," rather than "I have made a mistake."[18] Shame, then, is a sense of oneself as intrinsically flawed. Melody Beattie, seconding this view, says that "[s]hame is...the belief that whether what we did is okay or not, who we are isn't. Guilt is resolvable.... Shame isn't resolvable.... Hold a light to shame and call it what it is: a nasty feeling dumped on us to impose rules—usually someone else's rules."[19] In co-dependency, again, socialization—the imposition of "someone else's rules"—impedes self-actualization. Socialization, then, is by definition the practice of a dysfunctional society. Mainstream culture, by routinely telling children that, as Beattie says, "who they are is not okay," mass-produces co-dependents.

The discourse's various descriptions of the central personality traits, the symptoms, of the co-dependent provide a checklist of the consequences of raising children according to the ethic of self-denial. All of co-dependency's advocates offer similar lists of symptoms, and all agree that the central characteristic co-dependents share is an excessive orientation to something or someone outside of themselves. Consider Schaef's discussion of the co-dependent's qualities. According to Schaef, because mainstream culture requires self-abnegation and placing others first, "the perfect co-dependent...gets her identity completely from outside herself; she has no self-esteem or self-worth...[and] she is isolated from her feelings." This penchant for what Schaef calls "external referencing...[is] the most central characteristic of the...disease of co-dependence." Through this "cultural co-dependence training," Schaef goes on,

> we learn that the reference point for thinking, feeling, seeing, and knowing is external to the self, and this training produces people without boundaries.... In order to have and experience boundaries, a person must start with an internal referent (knowing what one feels and thinks from the inside) and then relate with the world from that perspective.[20]

Echoing Schaef's views, Sharon Wegscheider-Cruse maintains that a "reliance on others, a need for external validation, rather than the kind of validation that comes from within, from a secure sense of self"[21] is the foundation from which all of the other symptoms and manifestations of the disease of co-dependency derive. Reflecting this central premise, Schaef maintains that, since they have no choice but to seek some sense of who they are elsewhere, co-dependents are especially prone to a generalized "relationship addiction," using relationships "to get a fix" and seeking out so-called cling–clung relationships, in which each partner believes that "neither...can survive without the other."[22]

By Schaef's lights, external referenting also explains why the co-dependent "spends much of his time doing what is called impression management; trying to make others see him as he wants to be seen and believing that he can control their impressions."[23] Impression management is born of the effort to measure up to external standards, as mainstream culture demands. Because the ethic of self-denial teaches them to attach a pathological degree of importance to social proprieties, "co-dependents are always trying to be 'good' persons, and they actually believe they can control others' perceptions" of them. For Schaef, as for all of her colleagues, cultural expectations foster personal dishonesty. "For all sorts of reasons," Schaef explains,

> co-dependents are involved in a process of dishonesty. To be out of touch with your feelings and unable to articulate what you feel and think is dishonest. To distrust your perceptions and therefore be unable to communicate them is dishonest. Impression management is dishonest.... Gullibility...in fact, may be a form of personal and interpersonal dishonesty.[24]

Schaef's seemingly peculiar view of dishonesty also reveals her fealty to liberation psychotherapy. Because co-dependents are insufficiently individuated, she reasons, they do not know themselves well enough to be honestly "in touch" with what they feel or think. Therefore, they cannot help but be dishonest.

The overarching significance of individuation is also and more plainly apparent in the advocates' repeated references to co-dependents as "people without boundaries." Boundaries, in co-dependency, represent the imaginary normative markers of the individuated self's social "space"; they define the limits of the permissible, representing standards beyond which the individual will not go and beyond which others may not come without express permission. Because co-dependents, as Schaef puts it, "have no selves," they cannot and do not have such boundaries: "Co-dependents literally do not know where they end and others begin."[25] Having neither cognizance of appropriate limits to their own conduct nor a recognition of such limits in others, co-dependents exhibit an intractable self-centeredness, which is seen in their tendency to compulsively "rescue," "fix," and "caretake." Schaef defines caretaking as "making yourself indispensable." Expanding upon that theme, she explains that "[w]hen we do things for others that they *need* to do for themselves, we are making ourselves indispensable and are not helping them" (emphasis in the original). This too, Schaef maintains, is a form of self-centeredness, because caretaking is "very intrusive.... [Co-dependents] cannot respect others enough to allow them to work out their own problems.... [They] are meddlers; they believe they can and should be able to fix anything." Agreeing with Schaef, Melody Beattie contends that the co-dependent's meddling "doesn't help; it causes problems. When we take care of other people and do things that we don't want to do, we ignore personal needs, wants, and feelings...[and] we don't assume responsibility for our higher responsibility—ourselves."[26]

Co-dependents, then, are the symbolic opposites of self-actualized individuals. Whereas the latter make themselves and their own personal development the first priority in their lives—they are their own "higher responsibility," as Beattie says—co-dependents, as Schaef said, "have no selves," and they "get their identity completely from outside themselves."

* * * * *

Though using a different terminology, co-dependency's symbolic structure mirrors liberation therapy in every significant detail. The co-dependent's "sickness" comes down to a lack of individuation and a less than fully autonomous self; so too, the causes of that sickness—when such rhetorical flourishes as abandonment, abuse, and contamination are distilled to their essential logic—are variations on the basic premise of repression. There is a life story contained in the juxtaposition of these themes, a narrative that explains the transformation of the child into the co-dependent.

Tales of Abandonment: Symbolic Order and
Causal Narrative in Co-Dependents Anonymous

The simplicity and the familiarity of its meanings and the evocativeness of its dominant images combined to make co-dependency both easily understandable and powerfully persuasive. But what is important is not that co-dependency has persuasive powers but that it *did* persuade—a fact made evident by the proliferation of new twelve-step groups, like CoDA, beholden to co-dependency's truths. These groups and their members are the social embodiments of co-dependency. At CoDA meetings, it was repeatedly clear that it was co-dependency discourse that provides the occasion and the purpose for the weekly convocations.

Moreover, it was also clear that the members freely availed themselves of co-dependency's generality—a generality that is born of the discourse's binary symbolic structure and that translates into far-reaching public accessibility and applicability. Because of that binary structure and the generalities of meaning that it affords co-dependency became available to a broad cross-section of people: Guided by the discourse's causal narrative, an extremely wide range of past experiences can readily be taken as instances of abandonment and abuse; by the same token, guided by the symptoms and manifestations of the disease, a no-less-wide array of life problems, ranging from drug addiction to failed or unsatisfying relationships, can be viewed as indicators of one's sickness.

In their testimonials, CoDA members exhibited a mastery of co-dependency's symbolic order and its narrative of contamination, readily using those devices to classify and characterize themselves and their life experiences, both past and present. This mastery was also reflected in the interpretive license with which they brought the discourse to bear upon their life stories. The members took advantage of co-dependency's plasticity in two general ways: by tailoring the discourse to the particulars of their own lives and by tailoring their life stories so that they fit within the structure of the discourse.

This pattern of interpretive license was reflected in the members' conceptual improvisations upon the main themes in the discourse. For example, although they did not always use the terms "abandonment" and "abuse," they recurrently invoked those concepts through synonymous terms such as the "inner child," which serves as a symbol of the abandoned and abused true self that they must seek out in order to "reparent" and "heal." At a CoDA meeting explicitly organized around the theme of the inner child, Gina, a woman in her early thirties, had asked to address the group because she was celebrating her one-year "birthday" in CoDA. Gina said that this was a night of reflection and gratitude for her, because "my life is so much different now than then that it's just unbelievable." She went on to discuss what she saw as her co-dependent patterns prior to selecting co-dependency and joining CoDA:

> When I first came to CoDA, the extent of my relationships was the two minute, two days, two months type. What I did was, I'd go out to a bar and I'd pick up a guy or I'd let myself be picked up and then we'd have a "relationship" [using her fingers as quotation marks]. But that was never really a question, really, because I had no self-esteem and I had no boundaries, so I had to latch onto the guy...however long that lasted. And I was hurting, but that was really the only way that I knew to get out of the pain I was in. It didn't work either, but I didn't know anything else, couldn't think of anything else to do. And my self-esteem was so low that if a guy was attracted to me, well, hey—let's go.

Gina went on to conclude that her lack of self-esteem, her emotional pain, and the pattern of behavior into which she was locked—because she "couldn't think of anything else to do"—were products of childhood abandonment. Demonstrating her fluency with the discourse and her grasp of its nuances, Gina conveyed her abandonment metaphorically:

> I was born thirty-one years ago to an emotionally unavailable father and a hypercritical mother...[our family was] either totally detached or totally in turmoil. As a little girl, I wasn't particularly attractive and I was small, so I got picked on a lot. It wasn't that there was a lot of substance abuse in my family, because there wasn't. There was just an incredibly rigid set of standards and an incredibly critical set of parents who drummed it into me that there was really nothing that I could do that was okay...and so I grew up with a lot of shame and confusion.

In CoDA, "rigid standards," "criticism," and the "emotionally unavailable father" are all member-coined synonyms for abandonment; all ways of employing co-dependency's causal narrative to explain their problems and understand their lives. Echoing the causal capacity that co-dependency assigns to abandonment, Gina has learned that the rigid standards imposed upon her in childhood led to her pattern of short-term relationships with men as an adult. Growing up with the sense that "nothing...I could do...was okay," itself another synonym for abandonment, culminated with a futile search for something or someone outside of herself to reduce her negative self-conception.

In essence, Gina's story reveals a common, and sophisticated, grasp of the logic of abandonment, a logic that at its core contends that abandonment or abuse is anything that interferes with the child's right to develop naturally, according to its own prerogatives. Through such concepts as "emotional unavailability," the members consistently revealed an easy facility, a ready ability to extrapolate from that logic in order to find ways to apply the discourse to their own experiences. Invoking a more literal form of parental unavailability, more than one member traced the onset of their own co-dependency to a parent's death. For example, at the same meeting at which Gina discussed her inner child, Sheila commented that "I never had a childhood, because my father died young, so I had to become my mom's best friend, mother, sister, husband *and* daughter in a big hurry"; in the process, her true self was "abandoned," subordinated to the external demands of role performances occasioned by the loss of her father. At another meeting, Randy's story of abandonment was also of this more literal type:

> I wasn't raised in an alcoholic home. I was the oldest of three and my mom died giving birth to my little sister. My memories of my childhood, or at least the first two-and-a-half or three years of it, were great. My grandmother told me I was a happy child. But a lot of that changed when my mom died. My dad's sister came out to help raise us. My dad, I remember, just wasn't around much. He was working full-time and going to school part-time. He didn't drink, but what he did use was women. So, he was gone every night, to dances and whatever, with his girl-friends. He was also a bitter and pretty vicious... well, he wasn't vicious, he was a rageaholic. But, to be fair, I mean, here's this guy—twenty-seven years old, three kids in diapers—and his wife is dead. I'm sure he didn't have a clue *what* the fuck to do, but he *was* pretty hard on us. And, I guess, on me, especially.

Although it may seem peculiar and perhaps even unfair to characterize early death as parental abandonment and family dysfunctionality, Randy and Sheila's comments are faithful to co-dependency's broad conceptions of functionality and dysfunctionality and the causal narrative that flows from those constructs. Indeed, the discourse has taught them, and they have learned, that family dysfunctionality may be induced not only by addictions, violence, or sexual abuse but also, as John Bradshaw explains, by divorce, attempts to control others, and "actual sickness or hypo-chondriasis." Indeed, Bradshaw says that any "primary stressor," even "early death... [can be] experienced as a threat by the other members" of the family, and this sense of threat "initiates the dysfunction" from which the disease of co-dependency is inevitably born.[27]

Co-dependency's generality, then, readily facilitates its adherents' efforts and abilities to find a place for themselves within the discourse. Reflecting this wide interpretive latitude, rigid and critical parents or their untimely deaths are only two versions of abandonment that CoDA members can and do invoke. Steve, "like a lot of people, apparently," also "had an emotionally unavailable dad—just kind of passive and uninvolved." In addition to his father's affective distance, Steve said

> My mom was a pill addict, and I can remember walking around her passed out on the floor when I was getting ready for school. And she'd still be lying there in that same spot when I came home from school. Anyway, when I was fifteen, my mom killed herself and I was there to see the whole thing. She took a whole bunch of pills and drank a lot of liquor...and somehow managed to take off in the car. She died [later] in the emergency room.

It is certainly not necessary or even desirable to somehow "rank" the severity of people's troubles, but having a parent die young or witnessing one's mother's suicide are qualitatively different experiences from the far more common CoDA images of abandonment, such as a difficult divorce or, as in the following example, Gina's memory of not being allowed to express anger as a child:

> I've never been able to show my anger. Because that was just totally forbidden in my family. At least for the kids it was; not for my parents, of course, but if *we* got angry or talked back, or said what we wanted, if it contradicted our parents, well look out. And so now I'm just finding out that I've got a lot of anger. [But] I'm coming to understand that it's okay to have feelings, that they're not wrong, they just *are*, and I have a right to them, to have them, to express them. I'm a survivor of abuse and abandonment, and now I know that it's not enough to just survive—I want to live.

Co-dependency's generality is such that members tend to treat the evident differences between the events of Steve's and Gina's lives as differences of degree rather than kind. Moreover, they also tend to treat the differences of degree themselves as of relatively minor significance, so that Gina's experience of not being allowed to express her feelings as a child is no less a form of abandonment than is Steve's tragic experience. Both are instances of abandonment, because both—albeit in very different ways—are externally imposed obstructions to the child's natural course of development.

Tammi's story also illustrates the liberal interpretations of abandonment that co-dependency makes available to its adherents. She described herself as "a flaming co-dependent," largely because "I have this thing where I really can't stand to be alone." Although unsure what the basis for her fears of loneliness might be, Tammi said she was

> sure it taps into my fear of abandonment, which is really huge. But I just get terrified when I have to be alone. The abandonment that I felt as a little girl came out of my parents not being willing to let me just be who I was, and shaming me into acting like

they wanted me to act. So even though I know this fear is co-dependent as hell, I think I need to deal with that critical parent inside that's still shaming me. And if I start trying to get past the fear without dealing with that [inner critical parent], then I'd be doing the same judgmental, critical thing that got me here in the first place. You know? I need to get that inner parent to just accept that I'm scared, first, and to accept me as I am, and validate those feelings before I start trying to get past them.

Reflecting her ability to apply co-dependency's conceptual order to her own experiences, Tammi now sees that her parents' efforts to teach her to control her behavior denied who she really was and concludes that these denials have prevented her from becoming who she was meant to be. Because she was abandoned in this way once, she still suffers from a fear of being left alone; because of this lingering fear, she has been externally oriented; and because of those orientations, she is co-dependent.

The far-ranging applicability of abandonment and abuse is mirrored by equally broad applications of what constitutes the disease of co-dependency itself. Subsequent chapters will examine the many versions of the disease in more detail, so at this juncture it will suffice to say that the manifestations of the disease range across the behavioral spectrum, encompassing everything from the most withering inhibitions through the most outrageous exhibitions. In essence, members take the presence of problems in their lives as a symptom of co-dependency; by proxy, then, those problems are taken as indicators of abandonment and abuse in childhood. We have seen but a minor indication of these many faces of the disease in this chapter: Gina's string of sexual exploits is no less a sign of co-dependency than is Tammi's fear of being alone. The same plasticity of symptoms is reflected in Larry's conclusion that he has had troubled relationships with business clients in his adult life because "needing to be in control was very important to my family when I was growing up." As he rhetorically asked the other members of his group,

It was the same thing growing up, right? Because there's no mechanism in this society for a five year old to say, "Look, mom and dad, this isn't working out, so I think I'm going to try someplace else." Right? [I have the] same kind of dependence [on business clients]. So the parents assume that because they're keeping you alive that means they can treat you however they want to. I don't know. I've been thinking about this a lot, because I want to please my clients, too. And I'm not just afraid that if I don't, I won't get paid—I'm still afraid I'm going to get spanked. I mean it. That little kid inside me is still expecting to get nailed for not living up to my part of the deal in the dependent relationship. It's crazy-making; from childhood on is crazy-making.

Although Larry does not put it in these precise terms, it is clear that he understands and frames his adult fears and his identity itself according to the logic of abandonment. He conceives of his desire to please his clients as a symptom of his co-dependency, which, in turn, he acquired through the messages drummed into him by mainstream culture's rejection of his true self. As a result, he is an adult child, "still afraid that I'm going to get spanked."

* * * * *

Due to the high degree of articulation between the symbolic systems of liberation therapy and co-dependency, by selecting the discourse and using its constitutive themes and symbols to talk about their own lives the members of CoDA essentially duplicate the cultural critique that liberation psychotherapy first launched in the 1960s, tracing the cause of all their troubles to mainstream culture's various attempts to subordinate them to narrow role requirements and thus to repress their true selves. Co-dependency's adherents, in keeping with the beliefs they have selected, forcefully repudiate all that constrains individuals' actions, restricts their choices, and assigns them to prearranged slots within an established social structure, characterizing such practices as "abandonment," "abuse," and "contamination" and as the causes of a profound psychological malady. As we have seen in this chapter and will see throughout the remainder of this book, CoDA members have mastered these explanations for their life troubles and have learned to apply them accordingly.

At the same time that they duplicate liberation psychotherapy's critique of mainstream culture and society, CoDA members also locate themselves within the alternative reality—liberation psychotherapy's moral vision—that informs co-dependency's truths. Co-dependents are "deviant" in relation to that reality, and by acknowledging themselves as such they simultaneously affirm the palpability and legitimacy of that reality. In their adult lives, they have not, to reinvoke Carl Rogers's prescriptions for authentic selfhood, moved "away from facades, away from oughts, away from meeting expectations...[and] pleasing others"; nor have they moved "toward self-direction and being process."[28] In acknowledging and constructing their status as co-dependents, the members signal their concurrence with the conceptions of a healthy self contained in such prescriptions. In effect they assent both to the notions that they are not citizens of a liberation psychotherapy world, and that they want to be.

But although co-dependency's symbolic structure and its causal narrative essentially reprise liberation psychotherapy's vision of reality, the discourse also involves more than that. Indeed, if co-dependency were not different from liberation psychotherapy in some way, it is not at all clear why it should have fueled a sudden surge in the number of self-help groups comprising the twelve-step subculture. The core truths of liberation psychotherapy, after all, run counter to group identity and action, demanding people's emancipation from anything that overrides the self's uniqueness, their negation of all that interferes with self-direction. As we have seen in this chapter, that is precisely what the discourse of co-dependency does: Although the stories that CoDA members recount reveal a wide diversity of experiences, ranging from parental death and suicide through demands that anger be controlled, co-dependency's symbolic structure and causal narrative reduce that diversity to a single tale of abandonment and abuse as the cause of all adult discontents and disappointments. These adult travails, moreover, are portrayed as manifestations of disease, the shared condition of co-dependency. And the very identification of oneself as sick points to precisely those "oughts" and "expectations" from which liberation psychotherapy says the individual must be freed.

The point of these observations is not that CoDA members have "bought into" an illusory version of freedom or that co-dependency is merely an ideological ruse of some kind. Rather, the point is that co-dependency is a discourse of reform, an effort to institutionalize liberation psychotherapy and translate it into tangible social forms. The process of institutionalization is inevitably a matter of imposed controls and standardization of behavior. As a reformist discourse co-dependency both strongly articulates with the symbolic–moral system to which it subscribes and simultaneously seeks to correct the imperfect manifestations of that system in social relationships. Although ultimately beholden to liberation psychotherapy truths, those who selected co-dependency as their own truth system have taken on very different commitments from what one could expect from an unalloyed adherence to liberation psychotherapy. Co-dependency, unlike its symbolic progenitor, elicits people's commitments to submerge themselves in, to become members of, a group and to speak of themselves in ways that identify them *as* members. It is these capacities that identify co-dependency as a discourse of reform.

Notes

1. Berger and Luckmann, *The Social Construction of Reality,* 175.
2. Jerome D. Frank, *Persuasion and Healing: A Comparative Study of Psychotherapy* (New York: Schocken Books, 1961), 7-8.
3. Mary Douglas, *Purity and Danger: An Analysis of the Concepts of Pollution and Taboo.* London, New York: Ark, 1984. Anomalies can be dealt with in a number of ways: altering the larger cosmology to create a place for them; constructing an interpretation of them that corresponds with existing frameworks of meaningfulness; defining them as dangerous and effectively utilizing them as symbolic "boundary markers" beyond which lies a forbidden and perilous realm; or simply eliminating them from existence. As an example of constructing an interpretation that reduces ambiguity, Douglas cites Evans-Pritchard's account of Nuer practices for dealing with infant deformity. Deformed Nuer babies are defined as baby hippopotamuses accidentally born to humans; accordingly, they are placed where they "belong": in the river. Similarly, as an instance of the physical control of anomalies, Douglas notes that some West African tribes kill twins, because— according to their cosmology—two creatures cannot be born from a single womb (Douglas, 39).
4. Charles Whitfield, *Healing the Child Within,* 9.
5. Viviana Zelizer, *Pricing the Priceless Child: The Changing Social Value of Children* (New York: Basic Books, 1985). See also Joel Best, *Threatened Children: Rhetoric and Concern about Child-Victims* (Chicago: University of Chicago Press, 1993; originally published in 1990).
6. Whitfield, *Healing the Child Within,* 10. Whitfield coined the term "Divine Child" for this Edenic image.
7. Emile Durkheim, in *The Elementary Forms of the Religious Life* (New York: Free Press, 1965), painstakingly showed that the communicative power and meaningfulness of symbols issues from their relationship to other symbols. For Durkheim, the ability of religious systems to communicate truths to their believers rests upon a bedrock distinction between the categories of the sacred and the profane. Each of these categories derives its significance from the other: That which is profane is not sacred and vice versa. The entire world is classified according to the distinction between those two categories. See also Claude Lévi-Strauss, *The Savage Mind* (Chicago: University of Chicago Press, 1966), *Structural Anthropology* (Garden City, N.Y.: Doubleday Anchor, 1967), and *The Raw and the Cooked* (New York: Harper and Row, 1969); Mary Douglas, *Purity and Danger;* Will Wright, *Sixguns and Society: A Structural Study of the Western* (Berkeley: University of California Press, 1977).
8. Bradshaw, *Bradshaw On: The Family,* 43. To some extent, Bradshaw acknowledges that identity is formed in social interaction, but he tends to see the appropriate role of social institutions as passive, responding to and encouraging the child's self-explorations.
9. As the philosopher Arthur C. Danto has pointed out, narratives are always more than simply descriptions of events; indeed, "[n]arratives may be regarded as kinds of theories,... introducing, by grouping them together in certain ways, a kind of order and structure into events" (*Analytical Philosophy of History* [London: Cambridge University Press, 1968], 137).
10. Subby, *Lost in the Shuffle,* 55.

11. Bradshaw, *Bradshaw On: The Family*, 27.
12. Ibid., 166–67, 8, 187. "Consensus reality" is Bradshaw's term for socially constructed reality. However, although he cites Berger's and Luckmann's *The Social Construction of Reality* in *Bradshaw On: The Family*, it is unclear whether he is pitching his argument at a certain level of accessibility or whether he does not fully grasp the constructionist position. His use of "consensus" overlooks the extent to which the endurance of a sociocultural order is predicated upon "reification"—that is, upon the majority of people "forgetting" that reality *is* socially constructed, a point that Berger and Luckmann stress repeatedly. Bradshaw also argues the alternative position that the system is perpetuated through hierarchy and authoritarianism. This is a well-substantiated view but, again, one in which the relevance of consent is not clear.
13. Bradshaw, *Bradshaw On: The Family*, 8. Bradshaw has adopted the list and the notion of a poisonous pedagogy from Alice Miller, another liberation therapist. (See A. Miller, *For Your Own Good: Hidden Cruelty in Child Rearing and the Roots of Violence*, translated by Hildegarde and Hunter Hannum. New York: Farrar, Straus, Giroux, 1983, 60.)
14. Ibid., 3.
15. Douglas, *Purity and Danger.*
16. Ibid., 81.
17. Every chapter of *Bradshaw On: The Family*, for example, features a summary of the key points covered in that chapter. The summaries are all organized around acronyms, just as the symptoms are here organized around "contaminate."
18. Bradshaw, *Bradshaw On: The Family*, 2.
19. Melody Beattie, *Beyond Codependency and Getting Better All the Time* (New York: Harper/Hazelden, 1989), 108 (unlike her fellow advocates, Beattie does not hyphenate the term "codependency"); see also Whitfield, *Healing the Child Within*, 36. Bradshaw makes much the same distinction between "healthy" and toxic shame. Anthropological studies of shame, such as those working with the otherwise ill-fated distinction between "shame cultures" and "guilt cultures," more closely capture the spirit in which the term is used in co-dependency. In this literature, shame is collective control over the individual; guilt is inner control by the individual.
20. Schaef, *Co-Dependence*, 36, 45.
21. Wegscheider-Cruse, *Choicemaking*, 8.
22. Schaef, *Co-Dependence*, 44–45.
23. Ibid., 36. Notice that co-dependency also employs a "pop sociology (if there is such a genre). Erving Goffman uses the term "impression management" in his *The Presentation of Self in Everyday Life* (Garden City, N.Y.: Doubleday/Anchor, 1959), and "external referenting" harkens back to the other-directed individual of much concern in David Reisman (with Nathan Glazer and Reuel Denney), *The Lonely Crowd: A Study of the Changing American Character* (New Haven, Conn.: Yale University Press, 1950) of over forty years ago. As noted in chapter 1, "pop sociology" was also apparent in the "role theory" applied to the addicted family, the Parsonian (and Balesian) undertones of the "family system" and its "(dys)functionality." It is also evident in Bradshaw's references to "consensus reality."
24. Schaef, *Co-Dependence*, 59, 61.
25. Ibid., 45. There is, of course, some hyperbole in Schaef's remarks. If co-dependents "literally" could not distinguish themselves from others, it would likely indicate a far more serious mental disorder than what Schaef is describing.

26. Respectively, Schaef, ibid., 53, 55; Melody Beattie, *Codependent No More: How to Stop Controlling Others and Caring for Yourself* (New York: Harper/Hazelden, 1987), 83.
27. All quotes from Bradshaw, *Bradshaw On: The Family,* 164.
28. Rogers, *On Becoming a Person,* 167ff.

4

A New Theory of Addiction

Liberation psychotherapy's profound influence on contemporary U.S. life—particularly among co-dependency's primary constituency, the baby boom generation—helps to explain at least part of co-dependency's popular appeal. Co-dependency strongly articulates with liberation psychotherapy, taking much that its precursor espouses as unquestioned truth. Thus, the discourse simply tells people things they already know, conveying ideas with which they are already more than passingly acquainted. For a person to understand co-dependency requires little beyond a working familiarity with concepts that are now largely taken for granted in everyday American life, such as that childhood experience plays an important role in character development or that an overly repressive childhood may be bad for people.

But co-dependency's high degree of articulation with liberation psychotherapy is ultimately a poor explanation for the discourse's popular selection. For one thing, all of co-dependency's central ideas about causality and psychological sickness and health are already available in hundreds, indeed thousands, of liberation psychotherapy treatises, the vast majority of which antedated the arrival of co-dependency manuals on the national bookshelves: It is now conventional wisdom to see psychological sickness as a product of emotional repressions in childhood or to view psychological health as a function of individuation and autonomy from communally imposed standards. Moreover, one would expect those that hold to those ideals to be less, not more, likely to align themselves with communal purpose and action, to be more likely to distance themselves from settings and situations that impose control upon the self.

I have already noted, but it bears repeating, that the significance of this apparent disparity between the liberation psychotherapy worldview that co-dependency presupposes and the courses of action it elicits from its believers is *not* that the discourse somehow "dupes" its adherents into adopting "illusory" conceptions of self-realization. Co-dependency's adherents cannot help but know that by selecting the discourse they align themselves with a group endeavor; indeed, all of the treatises on co-dependency define this communal dimension as an integral part of the self's psychological well-being. Not only would assertions that the adherents are too easily gulled be unnecessarily puerile, they would miss the most important point, the point to which this chapter will address itself at some length: namely, that what is most significant about the disparity is that it indicates that co-dependency is appealing principally because of, not despite, the opportunities it provides people to be part of a collective experience. Moreover, this communal possibility is appealing *because* of liberation psychotherapy's profound impact, rather than— as co-dependency's founders contend—because of the public's lack of awareness of that therapeutic system.

Liberation psychotherapy is a difficult symbolic system to institutionalize. Particularly at the level of intimate and primary-group relationships and the identities that are formed in and maintained by these relationships, it does not easily lend itself to developing social alternatives to that which it rejects. It is to the problem of institutionalization and to the problems growing out of that more fundamental problem that co-dependency addresses itself. Its aim is to explain but also to redress those problems, to stabilize social relations in accordance with liberation therapy's symbolic order. Through its selective use and reinterpretation of conventional addiction discourse, co-dependency reforms liberation psychotherapy, transforming it into what it has never really been: a genuinely social doctrine. The central mechanism that makes all of this possible is what I will call a new theory of addiction—one that takes liberation psychotherapy's moral vision as the benchmark for individual conduct.

Co-Dependency and Cultural Change

In one sense, given the extensive array of problems the discourse seeks to explain, co-dependency can be read as a chronicle of the age, an unofficial index of the social consequences of a cultural and psychotherapeutic "revolution" and the period of instability following in its wake. From this vantage point, therapeutic emancipation has set into motion cultural and social processes that have created a panoply of both possibilities and problems.

It is not necessary to dwell at any length upon the possibilities, for they are more or less self-evident: Adherents of liberation psychotherapy take it as an article of faith that emancipating people from social and cultural constraints provides a greater realm of individual spontaneity and creativity, new bases for social relationships that make possible an unprecedented degree of genuine intimacy, a respect for and celebration of each person's unique qualities, and so on. Certainly, for many people, these possibilities—or near-approximations—have been realized.

However, for many others, among whom both co-dependency's creators and its constituency must be counted, the problems born of such profound cultural and social change appear to outweigh the possibilities. By their own accounts, it is clear that Bradshaw, Subby, and their colleagues, during their tenures as counselors in the addiction treatment industry over the past twenty to thirty years, have encountered a bewildering and disturbingly long litany of troubles, including not only drug and alcohol abuse and the problems—the "co-dependency"—of those who love the abusers but also a catalogue of other putatively compulsive behaviors such as incest, physical and sexual abuse, extensive sexual adventuring, gambling, eating (both over- and under-), spending, shopping, emotional volatility, and so on. The disease of co-dependency, the advocates maintain, is the primary causal agent in all of these problems, responsible not only for the excessive self-abnegation and inhibition with which co-dependency was originally associated but also for the exact opposite behaviors—for the variety of excesses to which the just-mentioned list refers.

Viewed in the context of sweeping cultural transformations, the long list of troubles that co-dependency's creators encountered and that their discourse addresses are best understood as the unfortunate manifestations of cultural and social disorganization rather than as the products of cultural repression and a resulting individual pathology. Identity itself is one of the arenas in which such cultural changes play themselves out. As Philip Rieff, for one, has pointed out, the "dissolution of a...system of common belief [is] accompanied, as it must be, by a certain disorganization of personality."[1] Shorn of its cultural and social underpinnings, identity becomes an increasingly problematic category;

a coherent organization of one's life and a stable sense of self become elusive accomplishments. When the very conception of the social is in flux, the self could hardly help but be otherwise.

To come at this point from a slightly different perspective, consider the role that liberation psychotherapy assigns to culture and its institutions. Although the view that collective constraints contribute to the individual's psychological troubles (an artifact of Freudian psychoanalytic theory and of the notion that civilization inevitably begets individual "discontents") is the linchpin of most clinical psychologies of our era, liberation psychotherapy takes this idea to its furthest extremes, largely ignoring the degree to which identity is also shaped by culture and in social institutions. As thinkers as diverse as Freud, George Herbert Mead, John Dewey, and, more recently, Peter L. Berger, Charles Taylor, and Alasdair MacIntyre have reminded us, cultures may well constrain the self, as liberation psychotherapy maintains, but they are also the foundation of the self, providing the means and materials by which the individual forms an identity and becomes a social being. Berger, concisely expressing this point of view, says flatly that "identity is socially bestowed, socially sustained, and socially transformed."[2] Likewise, for Mead, "[t]he self, as that which can be an object to itself, is essentially a social structure, and it arises in social experience." Indeed, Mead observes that "it is impossible to conceive of a self arising outside of social experience.... [O]ne has to be a member of a community to be a self."[3] MacIntyre, making much the same point, observes that "the story of my life is always embedded in the story of those communities from which I derive my identity."[4]

It is important to recognize that those who emphasize the social and cultural foundations of identity are not offering a rigid determinism; they do not argue that there is no unique self or that there is no capacity for individual freedom. Rather, these thinkers stress the dialectical—or, if you like, dialogical—nature of the self-to-society relationship: The self is both product and producer of social reality. The sociologist Eugene Rochberg-Halton, in a recent discussion of the U.S. school of philosophical pragmatism (particularly the works of Mead, Dewey, William James, and Charles S. Peirce), aptly summarizes this dialectical conception of the self. The pragmatists' conception of self, Rochberg-Halton observes, "acknowledges the uniqueness and creative potentiality of the person, and at the same time includes these qualities as social constituents of the self, rather than as asocial attributes of individualism, uncon-ditioned by the communicative act. The meaning of uniqueness, indi-viduality, and originality always resides in and for the discourse of the common good, the cultivation of the community both within and out-side the individual person, the living and the not yet born." For the prag-matists, for most sociologists and anthropologists, and, indeed, for virtually every culture in the history of the human race, the notion of a self existing outside of and thoroughly autonomous from culture and society is, at minimum, a logical absurdity. Such an extreme solipsism, Rochberg-Halton observes, "is the fiction of modern individualism.... For this separate 'I,' the 'private I,' if you will... *has no separate ex-istence of its own*" (emphasis in the original).[5]

In contrast to this dialectical conception, the self that liberation psy-chotherapy portrays and calls for is an asocial self, one whose identity is to be, and presumably can be, forged exclusively through the negation of social and cultural influences. Indeed, liberation psychotherapy effectively posits the existence of an a priori self, a true self, which cultural and soci-etal ministrations can only distort—a stance that is implied in the convic-tion that culture and society exert an exclusively pathological influence on the individual. Counseling an adversarial relationship between self and society and equating psychological well-being with emancipation from collective norms that constrain the realm of self-expression, liberation psychotherapy advocates and perpetuates "the fiction of modern individu-alism," and in so doing calls for the separation of its adherents from, to reinvoke MacIntyre's apt phrase, "those communities from which I de-rive my identity." But the separation of the individual from those commu-nities that sustain identity does not just imperil individual identity. Indeed, to the extent that many people follow this therapeutic advice—and, as I have argued in chapter 1, all of the available evidence indicates that mil-lions of people have—the communities in which identity is grounded are themselves destabilized. Under these conditions, identity itself could hardly help but be destabilized as well.

Co-dependency does not provide a cultural and societal reading such as this for the problems that it seeks to explain; nor could it, given the intellectual influences to which all of the advocates are beholden. Con-fronted by a steady stream of people clearly engaged in mighty struggles to define and maintain a coherent identity in the absence of the stable relationships necessary to that task, co-dependency's creators offered an explanation of their troubles that is vintage liberation psychotherapy. I use the adjective "vintage" quite deliberately, for co-dependency's concepts of abandonment and abuse are, to stretch the metaphor, old wine in a new bottle: They are cultural repression served up with new, and more evocative, names. Co-dependency's causal theory is also "vintage" in the sense that it ignores altogether the extensively documented changes in U.S. culture and society over the past thirty years. Indeed, the various expositions on co-dependency read as if this were still the 1940s or 1950s, as if William H. Whyte's "Organization Man" still described the "modal personality type" of our age,[6] as if conformity rather than personal uniqueness were the prevailing cultural currency, as if the psychotherapeutic tenets the discourse espouses were bold new revelations rather than an increasingly conventional wisdom by which so many of the baby boomers, and now their children, already categorize and negotiate their life experiences.

It is less than surprising, given co-dependency's strong articulation with liberation psychotherapy, that cultural repression of the self is the sole causal explanation in the discourse, for this is the only explanation for human misconduct that liberation psychotherapy has ever had at its disposal. But the significance of co-dependency's recourse to this causal logic lies less in its evident datedness than in the ways in which the discourse reinterprets and redefines the dependent variable—the nature of the psychological trouble—to which that causal logic is applied. By redefining the psychological condition that repression ostensibly causes, co-dependency provides a way of reforming liberation psychotherapy, a way of talking about and dealing with the problems engendered by that therapeutic system's public acceptance without acknowledging or recognizing that that very system was and is a principal source of those problems. Revealing its eminently reformist character, the discourse restores the social foundations to identity, giving people access to new and relatively stable relationships and communities; and it does so while simultaneously preserving the essence of and hence legitimating liberation psychotherapy's worldview.

The New Theory of Addiction

The mechanism by which co-dependency transforms liberation psychotherapy into a genuinely social doctrine is a new conceptualization of addiction, a new way of thinking about the psychological problems that are putatively caused by repression. In any psychology, the dependent variable—the condition that is caused—is always a deviation from some ideal state. In liberation psychotherapy, the self-actualized individual has always served as the yardstick against which deviance is measured. I will discuss the qualities of the self-actualized individual in more detail in subsequent chapters; at this juncture, what is essential to know is that there are two general qualities to being self-actualized and, thus, two general forms of deviance in a liberation psychotherapy world. Self-actualized individuals, first of all, have achieved full autonomy; their actions are governed exclusively by their own sense of morality rather than by an unthinking submission to conventional social norms and mores. Second, self-actualized individuals are also intrinsically benevolent people. Although they are not bound by customary rules, they remain moral agents and will therefore not harm other others in the course of pursuing their own self-actualization.

Liberation psychotherapy—especially as it has come to be popularly expressed and understood—only weakly articulates the second essential quality of the self-actualized individual. In liberation psychotherapy treatises of all stripes, the idea of the self as completely free from convention tends to be far more heavily featured than is the notion of that self's benevolence. Consider, as one example, the following comments by Carl Frederick, a devotee of EST (Erhard Seminar Training)—one of liberation psychotherapy's multiple manifestations:

> *You* are the Supreme being.
>
> Reality is a reflection of your notions. Totally. Perfectly.
>
> So you got the notion to play a little game with yourself.
>
> That is, you said to yourself, something like, "Gee, this is rather boring. Wouldn't it be more FUN TO COMMUNICATE." So you created a WORD game. That's all life is— one big word game. Don't lie to yourself about it anymore. They even wrote it down, not long after the beginning. They said: "AND THE WORD WAS GOD."
>
> Of course it was.
>
> Also notice that there isn't any right/wrong—it simply doesn't make SENSE to be unethical.
>
> You had the notion that communicating would be more fun. And you created all the rules. So you are responsible for the game as it is. All of it.
>
> And it has no significance. You're IT. Choose. It has no significance. Choose. Life is one big, "SO WHAT?" "CHOOSE."

Later in the same treatise, Frederick observes that

> human beings who LET GO and simply experience life…as I observe things, usu-
> ally end up being happy, loving, self-expressive and healthy…. Letting go of the
> notions they told you about and creating your own.
>
> That's what aliveness is all about.
>
> You see, in my view, the sole purpose of life is to acknowledge that you're the
> source, then choose to BE what you know you are. It'll all flow from there. (empha-
> sis in the original)[7]

Setting aside the evidently and eminently "sixties-ish" flavor of the prose, Frederick's remarks are very instructive. In his view, "letting go…[and] creating your own [notions]" about what courses of action to follow will engender "happy, loving, self-expressive and healthy [people]" who know that "it simply doesn't make SENSE to be unethical." To invoke ethics, as Frederick does, immediately after saying that "there isn't any right/wrong" also makes little sense, but what is clear and most important is that in his remarks he assumes, if he does not explicitly discuss, the self's innate benevolence.

All statements of liberation psychotherapy contain and are organized around this implicit assumption of benevolence. That assumption, for instance, undergirds Maslow's description of the self-actualized individual as both "an autonomous self independent of culture" and as a person who possesses a "democratic, egalitarian, and humanitarian character structure and values."[8] The same assumption informs Carl Rogers's conviction that "the basic nature of the human being, when functioning freely, is constructive and trustworthy."[9]

It is in and around the assumption of innate human benevolence that co-dependency's creators found and forged the connection between liberation psychotherapy and AA's disease model of addiction; out of this connection, the new theory of addiction was born, giving rise to the co-dependency movement. The basis for this connection between the two symbolic systems lies in the crucial phrase in Rogers's statement about human nature's benevolence: "when functioning freely." For Rogers, as for all liberation psychotherapists, it is a law of nature that, when following their own rather than culture's imperatives—"when functioning freely"—people will invariably behave in a constructive and trustworthy manner. A generation later, when the repressive grip of culture appears to have been all but broken and when people are, or appear to be, functioning freely, Anne Wilson Schaef, Robert Subby, and the rest of co-dependency's founders encountered few instances of "constructive and trustworthy" behavior; indeed, in their clinical work, they were besieged with the wide range of problems to which I have already referred—behaviors that, on the face of it, seemed to contradict the assumption of benevolence.

Although ultimately beholden to liberation psychotherapy truths, co-dependency's creators also were and are all thoroughly schooled in the disease model of addiction. As such, they were uniquely situated between two symbolic systems. As the keepers of two flames, with access to two sets of truths, the advocates were in a position to provide an answer to this turn of events, a way of explaining—and ultimately explaining away—the public impact of liberation psychotherapy by using the core principles of liberation psychotherapy itself.

The presumption of innate benevolence is both a statement of the human essence and a model of intentionality. Although AA and liberation psychotherapy hold to almost completely opposed assumptions about the self-to-society relationship, the disease model of addiction provides essentially the same model of intentionality as liberation psychotherapy. Consider the first of AA's twelve steps, which says, "we admitted we were *powerless* over alcohol, that our lives had become unmanageable." To say that the unmanageability of alcoholics' lives was the result of a powerlessness to do otherwise is to make a statement about their intentions: They did not intend to harm others and only did so because they have a disease, an addiction. Drawing upon that overlap in the causal logic between conventional addiction discourse and liberation psychotherapy but still faithful to the ethic of self-actualization, co-dependency conceptualizes the psychological condition that is caused by cultural repression of the self as an addiction. Thus, such problems as incest, the various forms of abuse, and criminality are all instances of "unmanageable" behavior resulting from people's "powerlessness" over their own actions. The liberation psychotherapist knows that incest, drug addiction, child abuse, spouse abuse, and all of the other problems co-dependency advocates encountered cannot be intentional acts because, to quote Rogers again, "the basic nature of the human being, when functioning freely, is constructive and trustworthy." Therefore, those who engage in such acts cannot be functioning freely.

This logic is reflected in the abundance of references to powerlessness and determinism in the co-dependency literature. Melody Beattie, for example, explains that "[o]ur original bond with our primary caregiver *determines* how we bond with others" (emphasis added). This original bond is forged under the rules of mainstream culture, which "position themselves in our control center. They jam things up and take over.... Once situated, they program us to do things"; the lessons from the past "control, or generate, our behaviors." Because socialization precludes the resolution of developmental challenges, "[u]nfinished business remains in the air, in us, and in our lives. We will be attracted, drawn, compelled to what is unfinished in us." Indeed, she insists, "once 'it' sets in co-dependency takes on a life of its own."[10]

Sharon Wegscheider-Cruse espouses the same ideas, arguing that "because for the co-dependent the issues and conflicts [from childhood] have not been resolved,...they tend to repeat." Co-dependents, Wegscheider-Cruse maintains, "tend to find themselves in situations and relationships similar to the ones they fled.... [T]he co-dependent... assumes fixed behavioral stances, protective defenses, repetitious, ritualistic patterns of behavior."[11]

John Bradshaw's "toxically shamed self," as discussed in chapter 3, also expresses the theme of powerlessness and the logic of addiction. According to Bradshaw, toxic shame causes individuals to freeze up, "binding" them to the roles and rules that mainstream culture imposed upon them as children. Because co-dependents are "bound" in this way, childhood experience does not simply shape but unequivocally determines identity; in fact, for Bradshaw, the adult is not an adult at all but is, rather, a "180-pound three year old"—a phrase that uniquely illustrates the meaning of the term "adult child."[12] Each time the child is "toxically shamed," Bradshaw explains, "it forms a little imprint...[a] little black hole" on their souls. These imprints, this network of "little black holes," coalesce into a set of "governing scenes...[that] the adult child keeps re-enacting." Childhood shame, Bradshaw maintains, is

imprinted on the child's brain until he [*sic*] grieves it.... The child remembers all this pain.... [I]t's all imprinted in there.... And remember, emotion is energy, so where does the energy go?...If you don't work [the emotional energy] out, you act it out or act it in. *You don't have a choice until you heal this wounded inner child.* (Emphasis added)[13]

This "shame-bound," or "shame-based" self, in turn, is characterized as the core of an addictive personality. The shame-bound individual has no choice: co-dependents act as they do because they are *bound* to do so: "[i]f you're shame-based, you're going to be an addict—no way around it."[14]

Co-dependency, then, fuses liberation psychotherapy's causal model and cultural critique with the disease model of addiction's emphasis upon powerlessness. The logic of both symbolic systems is thereby subtly but significantly changed. On the one hand, addiction is caused by cultural repression (which it never was before); on the other, all problems in living become addictions. As John Bradshaw expresses this change in logic, "All addictions are rooted in co-dependence and co-dependence is a symptom of abandonment."[15] Anne Wilson Schaef, although using slightly different terminology, propounds essentially the same premise, arguing that mainstream culture is an "addictive system" that mass produces an "addictive personality" that is slavishly and mindlessly devoted to any course of action that diverts attention from a wounded inner self.[16] Co-dependency's architects all agree that this addictive personality will drift from one addiction to another. Thus, if one is not addicted to relationships, then one is addicted to alcohol; if not alcohol, then cocaine; if not cocaine, then sex; if not sex, then gambling—and so on.

Plainly, this is a theory that requires an understanding of addiction that goes beyond the conventional, if tenuous, linkage of addiction with physiological dependence upon some mind-altering substance. Schaef, recognizing the need for a new way of thinking about addiction, makes a distinction between what she calls "ingestive addiction" and "process addiction." "An addiction to food or chemicals," Schaef explains, "is often called an ingestive addiction." Conversely,

> A process addiction is an addiction (by individuals, groups, even societies) to a way (or the process) of acquiring the addictive substance. The function of an addiction is to keep us out of touch with ourselves (our feelings, morality, awareness—our living process). An addiction, in short, is any substance or process we feel we have to lie about.[17]

Process addicts, in a nutshell, are addicted to whatever alters their moods, anything that enables them to ignore or avoid their terrible feelings about themselves—anything, as Schaef said in the just-quoted passage, that "keep[s] us out of touch with ourselves." According to Bradshaw, who espouses an identical distinction between types of addiction, because co-dependents have been abandoned and abused, "[y]ou need something outside of you to take away your terrible feelings about yourself"—feelings created by mainstream culture's socialization, and hence abandonment and abuse, of the child.[18] Whatever takes away the addicts' "terrible feelings about" themselves is their addiction.

The concept of process addiction is the logical complement to the concepts of abandonment and abuse. As we have seen, co-dependency defines any imposition of external demands upon the self—hence, in effect, the socialization process itself—as abandonment and abuse. With such an expansive logic, virtually everyone can come to see themselves as having been abandoned and abused. Mirroring that vast conceptual net, defining addiction as an attachment to mood-altering behaviors that temporarily obviate a bad self-image engenders an exhaustive catalogue of addictive behaviors. Thus, Schaef's implication that "even societies" can suffer from addictions. In the same all-inclusive spirit, according to Bradshaw, "perfectionism, striving for power and control, rage, arrogance, criticism and blame, judgmentalness [sic] and moralizing, caretaking and helping, envy, people-pleasing and being nice" are now types of addiction.[19] So, too, "[a]ny emotion can [also] be addictive"—including sadness, rage, excitement, joy, and religious righteousness. Indeed, contending that "[r]eligious addiction is a massive problem in our society," Bradshaw insists that "religious righteousness" is the "core mood alteration among religious addicts."[20]

The generality of the concept of process addiction also undergirds the "discovery" of a whole series of "activity addictions," including "[i]ntellectualizing—[which] is often a way to avoid internal states which are shame-bound...[and] a marvelous way to mood alter"—as well as such everyday activities as "working, buying, hoarding, sexing [sic], reading, gambling, exercising, watching sports, watching TV, having and taking care of pets." Bradshaw does add the proviso that "[n]o one of these activities is an addiction if it has no life-damaging consequences. But," he continues, "all of these activities can be full-fledged and life-damaging addictions. Each is a way to get so involved in an activity that one is mood-altered by doing the activity."[21]

Co-dependency's conceptualization of addiction, then, eschews any physiological dimension to addiction whatsoever. With the creation of process addiction, the addiction itself is now a rhetorical rather than a biological category. Bradshaw, clearly aware of just how radical this new conception is, offers some palliative observations:

> The genetic data would seem to refute the position that toxic shame is the core of addiction. While I would never want to say that there has never been a case of purely genetic alcoholism, I would honestly have to say I've never seen one. I've been an active part of the recovering community for 22 years. I've counseled some 500 alcoholics and run the Palmer Drug Abuse Program in Los Angeles for four years, having been a consultant to that program for ten years prior to that. In all those years, I've never seen anyone who did not have abandonment issues and internalized shame, along with their physical addiction. My guess is that the same is true for other depressant drugs, like tranquilizers and sleeping pills, likewise for stimulants, hallucinogens, nicotine and caffeine. I believe...that addiction is more than one single identifiable "disease."[22]

These are especially instructive remarks, not least because they highlight the symbolic and moral criteria guiding Bradshaw's discourse. It is, of course, not clear how even someone with "22 years" as a member of the "recovering community" could know "a case of purely genetic alcoholism" on sight, as Bradshaw suggests is possible ("I've never seen one"). Nor is it clear how one can conclude—without some careful effort to sort out cause and effect—that abandonment and shame precede, rather than follow from, years of addiction-related episodes. But the point here is not that Bradshaw's comments are specious. Rather, what is significant is the extent to which these comments reveal that the analogy between alcoholism and problems in living is the conceptual bridge between the two symbolic systems from which co-dependency was derived and from which the co-dependency movement was formed. As we have seen, intentionality and cultural repression are the pivotal connections between liberation psychotherapy and conventional addiction discourse. As an adherent to the liberation psychotherapy worldview, Bradshaw assumes that the psychologically healthy self, the true self, is incapable of bad intentions: All problem behaviors are the product of a troubled psyche, and that troubled psyche is, in turn, the product of culturally mandated repression of the self.

These assumptions are especially evident in the way that Bradshaw draws the causal arrows between shame and addiction; because addiction is "bad" behavior and human nature is intrinsically benevolent, he has only one way to interpret cause and effect: Shame cannot be the understandable affective response of someone whose actions have repeatedly harmed others but must, instead, be the cause of those harmful behaviors. So, too, the possibility that some people intend to behave badly, to mistreat others for their own pleasure or gain, is simply not possible, because, for the liberation psychotherapist, as Carl Rogers has said, it is unquestionably true that human nature is intrinsically benevolent.[23] Moreover, not only is the liberation psychotherapist distinguished by his unwavering fidelity to the view that human nature is essentially benevolent, he is also required to define all misconduct as the negative consequence of group control of the individual: Cultural repression *must* be the causal factor in harmful acts. That Bradshaw is bound by this truth rule is unmistakably reflected in his somewhat curious objections to the "genetic data," curious because a genetic link-up, should it ever be proven, would not threaten—indeed, it would support—the benign view of human nature to which co-dependency holds. However, the discovery of genetic markers would render irrelevant the role of cultural repression; thus, Bradshaw disavows genetic data out of hand because, as a liberation psychotherapist at heart, cultural repression is the only causal agent that he is trained or predisposed to recognize.

Process addiction is an explanation for behavior that both obscures liberation psychotherapy's cultural and societal impact and meets liberation psychotherapy's criteria for truth, whereas genetics, in which culture's repressiveness is irrelevant, or human aggressiveness, which runs counter to the presumption of innate benevolence, do not. Process addicts are like alcoholics in that they do not have bad intentions, but the cause of their harmful actions is invariably cultural.

The Two Types of Process Addiction

Although the manifestations of process addiction, as Bradshaw's list of addictive behaviors suggests, seem to run the gamut of possible human behavior, process addicts are "sick" according to liberation psychotherapy standards; they are addicts in the symbolic system of liberation psychotherapy. As such, those who were "wounded as a child," those with terrible feelings about themselves, will gravitate toward either of two general extremes in attitude and conduct as an adult,[24] and the extremes are deviations from the two essential qualities of the self-actualized individual. These qualities, as mentioned earlier in this chapter, issue from two central axioms in liberation psychotherapy: (1) that the psychologically healthy self is the self-actualized individual, and

(2) that self-actualized individuals, because they have been freed from the deleterious influences of mainstream culture, will exhibit the inborn constructiveness of human nature. Correspondingly, process addicts are either (1) those who are inadequately individuated or (2) those whose actions defy the unquestioned assumption that humans are by nature innately positive and constructive beings. As addicts, of whichever ilk, co-dependents are "powerless" over their deviations from these expectations. For purposes of clarity and brevity, I will refer to these categories, respectively, as "repressed co-dependents" and "obsessive co-dependents";[25] in the same vein, I will refer to the standards that each type of co-dependent violates as—again respectively—the "norm of self-realization" and the "norm of benevolence."

The repressed co-dependent more or less corresponds with the original meaning of the term co-dependency, as it was derived from the idea of co-alcoholism. Co-dependency's progressively changing meanings have already been discussed at some length, so a brief recap here should be sufficient. Recall that the discourse gives a liberation psychotherapy twist to the concepts of the addicted family rules ("don't talk, don't trust, don't feel") and roles engendered by those rules (the Enabler, the Scapegoat, the Mascot, the Hero, and the Lost Child), concluding that any social interaction in which the individual is subordinated to external demands causes sickness. This application, as we saw, effectively equates expectations for the denial of self per se with institutional and ultimately societal dysfunctionality. Repressed co-dependents, reflecting this infusion of liberation psychotherapy logic, are people who subordinate themselves to societal expectations, those who do not see the self—themselves—as the more important member in the relationship between self and society. As such, they are not self-actualized, and they violate the norm of self-realization.

Obsessive co-dependents, on the other hand, are people who do *not* subordinate themselves to others. However, although seemingly emancipated from the self-denying demands and stultifying expectations of mainstream culture, the obsessive co-dependent's actions belie the assumption that people are intrinsically trustworthy, constructive, and positive creatures. The presumption that shapes this category of addiction is that, as essentially benign beings, people would not engage in harmful acts unless they were unable to control themselves. Obsessive co-dependents are people whose actions reveal their liberation from conventional proprieties but whose liberated acts cause harm to others *and* self; they violate liberation psychotherapy's norm of benevolence.

It is the category of obsessive co-dependent that most contributes to co-dependency's all but limitless list of addictive behaviors—a list, as already mentioned, that includes not only alcohol and drug misuse but also gambling, sexual behavior, the abuse and molestation of spouses and children, and so on. Drawing upon the overlap in the ways that liberation psychotherapy and conventional addiction discourse conceive of intentionality, co-dependency argues that, although they may behave with little regard for conventional moral proprieties, these obsessive co-dependents are *not* functioning freely, that they are process addicts, powerless to behave in any other way. In what is clearly the furthest-reaching application of this logic, John Bradshaw defines criminality as a form of process addiction. For Bradshaw, "offender behavior," his euphemism for crime, is "unmanageable" conduct reflecting the offenders' unconscious "acting out" of what happened in their pasts; it is "acting out" that they are powerless to control. Thus, Bradshaw placed great emphasis upon what he described as a large number of prison inmates who wrote to him after his first PBS series, saying that "they had recognized themselves" in his remarks and now understood "that they had been acting out what had happened to them in their childhood."[26] The inference to be drawn, here, is that had it not been for mainstream culture's abandonment and abuse, they would not have developed their addiction to crime and would not be writing to Bradshaw from prison.

* * * * *

Just as is true with the discourse's causal narrative, the new theory of addiction imposes a uniformity upon experience, subsuming the diversity of people's lives beneath a single symbolic rubric. CoDA members exhibit the same mastery and improvisational facility in regard to process addiction as they do with abandonment and abuse. This is not to say that members do or do not recognize that process addiction is the basis for their common ground; rather, it is to say that, even if they do not always or explicitly speak of themselves as addicts, the general themes of addiction discourse infuse all of their testimonials. This influence bears itself out in the members' penchant for failing to draw fundamental distinctions between their experiences as children and their conduct as adults. It is not so much that they speak as if nothing has happened since that moment, now frozen in time, in which they were first sentenced, as the discourse tells them, to the eternal repetition of a childhood developmental failure. They readily acknowledge that things happened in those intervening years—they married and divorced, had children, went to work, had affairs, drank too much, ate too much, tried to keep a handle on their lives. But they speak of everything that happened as the inevitable consequence of their "disease." They were, as a synonymous phrase from the argot has it, "living the script."

CoDA members organize their self-talk around fundamental liberation therapy themes: Meetings are filled with references to inadequate individuation and impeded personal growth. But, in and of themselves, these liberation psychotherapy tenets do not logically require group membership and action; as we have seen, if anything, they reflect and foster a powerfully antigroup orientation. The new theory of addiction, though, overrides the steadfast individualism of liberation therapy; as process addicts, group participation and membership are possible. Reflecting this all-important benefit to process addiction, CoDA members go beyond discussions of their lack of maturation, equating virtually any problems they experience with the telltale signs of addiction. Thus, in CoDA, any attitude, any emotion, any quirk, any behavioral tic, becomes a form of addictive behavior. Roy, for example, says that he seeks to control others because his parents placed such a premium upon public decorum, or "impression management":

> I've got to be in control, got to be right...because that means that you're wrong and then I'm better than, smarter than, more okay than somebody else. And that's supposed to be, always has been, my substitute for being okay with myself. My way of being okay is to try to show that somebody else is *not* okay. And that's just sick, you know? And it comes from my family. My parents lived according to that "we're doing better than they are" standard, and that's supposed to mean that they were better people. Always looking good, but totally on the outside, controlling others' impressions—or trying to, anyway. Judging others according to their own weird rules.

Roy's comments indicate that he sees himself as, in effect, addicted to being judgmental—a conclusion that closely follows the logic of process addiction. Guy responded to Roy's remarks with an anecdote of his own, in which the underlying theme was his powerlessness over his desire to control others:

> Yeah. Control. *I've* got to be in control, *I've* got to be right—I know that. And now I know what happened this morning at this donut shop on the way over here. There

were some people standing around, thinking about what kind of donuts they were gonna buy...no real line, or anything. And I'd made up my mind, so I'm getting ready to order, and this punk kid says to me, "I'm next." I'm next. There wasn't a line. I wanted to say, "look, kid, *I'm* next. There's no line, here," you know? I was worked up...fuck, my heart's pounding right now, just talking about it. I was thinking about this, fucking obsessing about it, all the way over here [to the meeting]. "What's going on? why does this bug me so much?", I was asking myself. And what it was, was I wanted to be right, but this punk kid took that away from me. Didn't know he did, I'm sure, but that's what he did. This punk kid that looked like me when I was his age and was a punk kid. Shit, I'm still a punk kid. But this program's helping me to find the ways to grow up.

As different as these two stories are, both men's comments are informed by the tacit understanding that their adult lives have been no more than a continuation of childhood. Seeking control over social situations and over one's own and others' behavior, negative judgments of other people, the need to look good, be right, be perfect—these are all lessons learned years ago and imparted with such force that they are determinative, not simply influential, in the present. Roy and Guy are addicted to their controlling, judgmental attitudes; as such, they share a common problem, speak a common tongue.

All of the members' references to the symptoms of their addiction refer back to childhood experience in ways that link those experiences to powerlessness over their adult behavior. Their frequent complaints about the struggle to live life "on a feeling level," for example, reflect their conviction that one of the rules that they were presumably taught as children was "don't feel." In the same vein, "being out of touch with emotions" is a prominent theme at meetings. When members are out of touch with their emotions, they are "intellectualizing," or "in their heads." Pauline, discussing her relationship with a man who is "quite a bit younger than I am," illustrates the hazards of intellectualizing: "I've really been in my head about it a lot the last few days, thinking about all the ways that this could go wrong; that it's unworkable, that it's impossible, and just on and on, thinking it over and over."

As CoDA members often describe it, "being in their heads" makes it difficult to fully appreciate the here and now; they are too busy trying to control the moment to simply live it and enjoy themselves. For example, because Pauline has been thinking about her relationship so much,

I'm not ever really here in the present moment. And the funny part of it is, there's nothing wrong. The relationship's going along very well, and he's certainly given me no reason to be skeptical or paranoid. He calls when he says he will, he's on time. It's great. But I'm still up there in my head, figuring out all the problems and making more in the process.

An inability to enjoy the present is only one problem involved in "being in one's head." Intellectualizing is part of the more general and serious matter of trust; "don't trust" is another of the dysfunctional family rules, learned in childhood, that continues to dominate action and experience in adulthood. Without the capacity for trust it is impossible to get onto that feeling level and live life in the pure, experiential mode:

> He's called me on the trust issue. He told me, "look, Pauline, if you can't trust me, we can't make this work." And he hasn't given me any reason not to trust him, like I said. So I've been working on doing just that, on learning to trust. If I could just get out of my head! Just let it go. I think I know why I'm in my head about this so much. I think it's because I'm starting to really care, like I haven't since my divorce seven years ago. I've dated, but I never let myself care, because I didn't want to deal with all of that again. But then yesterday morning, I felt myself caring, and that makes it all a lot scarier than just going out on dates. So, I suppose my intellectualizing is a way to stay in control, and not expose myself to pain.

Though not explicitly invoking the term "process addiction," Pauline's remarks about being in her head reveal the discourse's influence and logic. Echoing Bradshaw's discussion about intellectualizing as what he called an "activity addiction," Pauline concludes that she overanalyzes her situation in order to feel as if she is in control of her environment, and this control is a way of avoiding and taking away her "terrible feelings about herself."

Roxie, who introduced herself as "a co-dependent, ACoA, compulsive overeater," responded to Pauline's remarks with a heated polemic against their disease and its consequences:

> Boy, if we could just get out of our fucking heads, huh? Just get out of there and get into what we feel. Whew! Shit. I hear that. We get into our heads and the next thing we know we're into controlling and scheming and doing things like Pauline, worrying about shit that hasn't and might not happen. And why do we care? You know? Why care? Shit, you're having a good time and you're undermining that at the same time, all because we can't let go. You're having a wonderful time but you can't get out of your head! Damn it! What the fuck do you want? We could all be dead tomorrow anyway. Have a good time. Live in the moment! Live in the God damned moment! [She is shaking her fists and literally screaming at this point.] Christ! This damn disease makes it impossible to just do what you want, to just play, have some fun, and fuck everything else, you know? At least we've got these meetings where we can come in and talk about why we keep sabotaging ourselves.

> You're having a lot of fun, maybe for the first time in your life. And you deserve that. Enjoy it, enjoy it. Like we ever had any luck trying to control things anyway.

Although Roxie's observations reflect core liberation psychotherapy premises, they simultaneously underscore the difference between simply being, say, insufficiently autonomous and being co-dependent. As she says, "at least [co-dependents have] these meetings," where they can go to deal with their problems. This ongoing group identification and affiliation is precisely what liberation psychotherapy has been unable to provide and what co-dependency's reformism makes available. Through the new theory of addiction, meetings, groups, and shared symbolic and relational structures become available. And these reforms are the product of the analogy co-dependency draws between all life problems and older forms of addiction. Chapter 5 will examine the full significance of that analogy.

Notes

1. P. Rieff, *The Triumph of the Therapeutic*, 2.
2. Peter L. Berger, *Invitation to Sociology*, 98.
3. Mead, *On Social Psychology*, 204, 226.
4. MacIntyre, *After Virtue*, 221.
5. Eugene Rochberg-Halton, *Meaning and Modernity: Social Theory in the Pragmatic Attitude* (Chicago: University of Chicago Press, 1986), 39, 38.
6. William H. Whyte, *The Organization Man* (New York: Simon and Schuster, 1956); P. Rieff, The Triumph of the Therapeutic. "Modal personality type" is Rieff's term.
7. Carl Frederick, *EST: Playing the Game the New Way* (New York: Delta, 1976), 171, 177, 168, 174, 190, 211ff.; quoted in Paul Vitz, *Psychology as Religion: The Cult of Self-Worship* (Grand Rapids, Mich.: Eerdmans, 1977), 32–33.
8. Abraham Maslow, *Motivation and Personality*, 2d ed. (New York: Harper, 1970); see chapter 11 for Maslow's full discussion of the qualities of the self-actualized person.
9. Rogers, *On Becoming a Person*, 91.
10. Beattie, *Beyond Codependency*, 169, 94, 85, 84, and 16.
11. Wegscheider-Cruse, *Choicemaking*, 10–11, 21.
12. Quoted passage is from the PBS broadcast *Homecoming*, aired 2 and 8 December 1990.
13. All quoted passages in this section are from the PBS broadcast, *Homecoming*. This is a shorthand expression of co-dependency's central causal hypothesis. From the baseline of one's pent-up, indeed "bound," emotions, "you act it out or you act it in."
14. John Bradshaw, *Healing the Shame That Binds You* (Deerfield Beach, Fla.: Health Communications, 1989), 96; Bradshaw explores this theme at length in this book.
15. Bradshaw, *Bradshaw On: The Family*, 172.

16. Schaef develops this theme in her 1987 book *When Society Becomes an Addict.*
17. Schaef, *Co-Dependence,* 24.
18. Bradshaw, *Healing the Shame,* 95.
19. Ibid., 95, 88.
20. Ibid., 103-4.
21. Ibid., 105, 106. Also, note that Bradshaw introduces the concept "life-damaging" consequences as an additional criterion for evaluating activity addictions. This recalls his earlier redefinition of addiction as "a pathological relationship to any mood-altering experience that has life-damaging consequences" (*Bradshaw On: The Family,* 5). Presumably, adding life-damaging consequences to the equation solves the formidable problems that a simple one-to-one correspondence between mood-alteration and addiction otherwise poses, such as the plausible conclusion that adopting a recovering addict identity is itself, by dint of its effect upon one's moods, a form of addiction. If addiction is defined as mood-altering, then emotions cannot be anything *but* addictive. Emotions are, after all, alterations of mood.
22. *Healing the Shame,* 97. It would seem equally plausible, if not more so, that a pattern of addictive behavior could be both a source of profound self-loathing and highly likely to prompt the addicts' loved ones to leave them. AA has long addressed itself to overcoming addicts' self-contempt and repairing their social estrangement after years of addiction-driven transgressions. But in co-dependency, again mirroring the antithetical relationship between conventional addiction truths and those of liberation psychotherapy, the causal relationship is reversed. In liberation psychotherapy, as noted, individual wrongdoing *always* has cultural precipitants.
23. Rogers, *On Becoming a Person,* 91.
24. Quoted passages in this paragraph are from, respectively, Schaef, *Co-Dependence,* 58; Bradshaw, *Bradshaw On: The Family,* 173. Although it may be ironic that such "either/or" thinking is also often mentioned as a symptom of co-dependency, as Stan J. Katz and Aimee E. Liu point out (see Stan J. Katz and Aimee E. Liu, *The Co-Dependency Conspiracy: How to Break the Recovery Habit and Take Charge of Your Life* [New York: Warner Books], 1991), this is not an isolated example of co-dependency's founders' tendency to sweep themselves up in their own epidemiological net. Given its broad cast, they could hardly hope to do otherwise. Moreover, there are some interesting exceptions to this either/or strategy. "Workaholism" is the most noteworthy. Although it is possible to work "too much," and this is a sign of an underlying disease, it is not, apparently, possible to work too little; at least, it is not identified as a problem. The discourse makes no attempt to predict which type of addict a person will become.
25. The co-dependent's double symbolization as either obsessive or repressed was reflected in Bradshaw's comment, in an earlier passage, that the shame-based self either "acts out or acts in" its childhood experiences. Obsessive co-dependents "act out" their shame in ways that reveal their indifference to others and a disdain for conventional mores. Repressed co-dependents "act in" their shame, obsessively subordinating themselves to the demands of others. These dual categories underlie the discourse's recurrent either/or characterizations of co-dependents. For example, Melody Beattie maintains that co-dependents are given to extremes of conduct and attitude, believing, among other things, either that everything is their fault (repressed) or that nothing is their fault (obsessive), and behaving either overly responsibly (repressed) or irresponsibly (obsessive). The characteristics mentioned here are culled from her exhaustive list of co-dependency's

symptoms, as presented in *Codependent No More*, especially 36–45. The same theme of behavioral and attitudinal extremes is replayed in Bradshaw's contention that the disease of co-dependency is indicated in "being perfect [repressed] or being a slob [obsessive]; [t]rying to control everyone [repressed] or living out of control [obsessive]; [b]eing a people-pleaser (nice guy or sweetheart) [repressed] or raging and blaming [obsessive]" (Bradshaw, *Bradshaw On: The Family*, 181).

26. From the PBS broadcast of *Homecoming*, 2 and 8 December 1990.

5

Addiction and Analogy

It is somewhat paradoxical that reformist discourses are often only loosely coupled with the problems that they seek to explain and correct, so their consequences are not always specifically intended, and their diagnoses of the problems they address are off the mark, but they nonetheless engender solutions, of a sort, to those problems. Thus, for example, as we saw in chapter 1, although the relational problems precipitating the Second Great Awakening—the separation of home and workplace, immigration and migration and the accompanying transformation of both city populations and workforce composition—were all products of the rise of industrial capitalism and the decline of the rural household economy, the discourses that emerged in response to those problems (at least, the discourses that proved the most influential) were all but mute on these economic and infrastructural factors. Economic transformations and demographic pressures posed problems with family structure and community order, but, as Mary P. Ryan has pointed out, people "express[ed] their family concerns...in the language and central ideological structure of their time, that is, in an essentially religious mode of thought...[rather than] in economistic terms."[1] In each historical instance, reformers have framed large-scale change in the dominant cultural imagery and motifs of their own era. Though offering a religious interpretation of what were primarily economic, demographic, and technological factors affecting social relationships, revivalist reformers nonetheless helped to restore stability in turbulent times.

Reform, then, should be understood in terms of its social consequences rather than in terms of the veracity or accuracy of the reformist discourse's portrayals of the troubles of its age. The significance of these considerations here is that there is a similar discrepancy between co-dependency's interpretations of current cultural and societal conditions and the reformist impact the discourse produced. I discussed this discrepancy earlier, in terms of the somewhat "vintage" tone of many co-dependency treatises. The "repressive" society to which those treatises refer—and to which the discourse assigns a central causal role in the problems it seeks to explain—is effectively no longer in existence, as I've previously discussed. There may well be afoot, as some would argue, a current retrogressive response to the cultural changes of the past thirty years, but in co-dependency discourse those changes have simply never occurred. Poring over co-dependency treatises leaves the distinct impression that Eisenhower is at the helm, that rock and roll is still in its infancy, that the nuclear family is still the dominant kinship structure, and that Jack Kerouac is just sitting down to chart the life pulse of an emergent Beat movement.

As noted, the reasons for this sizable lacuna are readily apparent: Co-dependency's architects are devotees of the therapeutic culture and worldview. As such, they take their inspiration from works that antedated and precipitated the cultural changes that are so conspicuously absent in co-dependency discourse, changes, it should be emphasized, that provided the context in response to which co-dependency was constructed and embraced. Guided by such works, those who created co-dependency had but the one explanatory mechanism for personal and social disturbance—namely, repression—at their disposal. It is because of these influences and the theoretical resources they provide that co-dependency winds up painting a largely misconstrued portrait of contemporary U.S. life, effectively diagnosing the problems of an all but vanished social and cultural order. The problems the discourse discusses and analyzes are no more the natural products of an unduly repressive, conformist society than the problems growing out of the dawning urban--industrial age were the reflections of a crisis in religious devotion. However, just as revivalism did, co-dependency nonetheless provides a means of reform, a way to bring social relations into line with an underlying moral-symbolic system. Although the discourse's interpretation of the causes and nature of the problems it addresses is well wide of the mark, the result is reformist in character. Co-dependency facilitates the institutionalization of liberation psychotherapy at the level of intimate and primary-group relationships and of the identities that such relationships engender and help to sustain. That it does accomplish this, and how it does so, are the concerns to which we now turn.

The Sick Role, Legitimacy, and Recruitment

The link between all symbolic and relational systems lies in the commitments to specific courses of action that discourses elicit from their adherents. The concept of process addiction was designed to elicit people's commitment to twelve-step membership. The proliferation of twelve-step groups for the wide range of new process addicts testifies to co-dependency's success in securing that commitment.

Co-dependency discourse repeatedly exhorts its readership that becoming a twelve-stepper is the appropriate course of action for process addicts. Indeed, as we have seen, contrary to traditional twelve-step proscriptions against proselytizing, co-dependency advocates—all of whom are members of the subculture and all of whom have eschewed personal anonymity in the interests of spreading the word—engage in aggressive promotional tactics. In part, these tactics are grounded in the treatment industry's logic of "intervention," as previously discussed. Recall that this logic holds that because alcoholics are sick and because "denial" is said to be a primary symptom of that sickness, outside intervention is required if the person is to be cured.[2] Throughout their expositions, the advocates reveal this interventionist spirit, actively lobbying for the merits of twelve-step membership. Robert Subby, for example, says, "If you ask me, the Twelve Steps of AA are still the best treatment program for co-dependents." Melody Beattie takes the claims to a higher plane, arguing that "Twelve Step programs are not merely self-help groups that help people with compulsive disorders stop doing whatever it is they feel compelled to do.... [Rather,] [t]he Twelve Steps are a way of life." Bradshaw, recounting his own experiences, also extols the virtues of twelve-step programs and groups:

> Coming out of hiding was terrifying, but the love and warmth of the group made it bearable. In fact, I couldn't believe it. The more I shared my truest feelings, the more acceptable I was.... This was the first step in recovery. I was accepting my limitations and gathering up my scattered self. I was experiencing being mirrored, and as the group accepted me, I was accepting myself.... Each time I went to a meeting, I felt better. I couldn't understand it. Nothing was really happening. All we did was share our experiences or talk about one of the twelve steps.... It was not only okay to make mistakes, it was a requirement for membership. Everyone was equal. There were no leaders. The group was based on mutual respect, social equality, and rigorous honesty. People were talking about their feelings.[3]

Such pronouncements assure prospective adherents that, because they are (process) addicts, they "qualify" for twelve-step membership. But what is more salient for understanding co-dependency's translation into a veritable movement is that not only do the discourse's adherents qualify to join a twelve-step group, they are effectively required to do so, or, at least, they face powerful incentives for doing so. The reason for this requirement is most clearly understood through a consideration of the cultural status of the addict, especially the alcoholic, as a category of self and, more generally, of the social and cultural meaning of sickness.

Customarily, people that have a disease are granted a conditional absolution from their normal responsibilities, both from what they have done prior to their diagnosis and from their present actions. A banal example, here, is the person laid up with a case of the flu. No one expects normal social performance from someone running a high fever and suffering from chills and nausea. Rather, the expectations run in the other direction, requiring them to do the opposite of what they normally do: to lie abed, to do nothing, and to cooperate with efforts to make them well. Defined as it is by both privileges and obligations, being sick is a socially structured position, a social role, much like any other; and, much like the privileges of any other role, the privileges of the sick role only accrue to those who also meet its obligations, mainly by cooperation with would-be healers. This translates into quite straightforward and not overly demanding expectations. It is difficult to imagine someone with the flu chafing against expectations that they should rest and try to get well. The contingent nature of absolution from conventional demands, however, suggests that the social status of the sick person depends upon more than simple cooperation; it also depends upon the "legitimacy" of the ailment.

The question of legitimacy returns us to the importance of intentionality as a criterion for evaluating people's behavior. Although they are seldom explicitly expressed, judgments about intention play an important role in how people respond to virtually all forms of illness and thus in how the sick person is treated. The usual presumption is that intent is not a pertinent consideration in relation to sickness; there is generally no question about how people get the flu, whether it counts as a disease or not, or what they must do about it. People get sick "innocently"— they did not intend to do so and did not bring it upon themselves willingly. But decisions as to from what, how much, for how long, and even if the sick person is to be absolved from responsibility are often guided by moral criteria: how the disease was contracted, what kind of disease it is, how serious it is, and so on. Venereal disease best illustrates how this moral dimension to sickness and legitimacy works: Gonorrhea, syphilis, and the like have long been stigmatized. But there is nothing in these diseases per se to warrant this stigma; rather, the means of contracting the disease is what elicits the stigma.[4] Absolution from responsibility due to illness, then, is contingent not only upon cooperation with the effort to cure but also upon the legitimacy of the illness, and that legitimacy, in turn, is contingent upon social and moral judgments having little to do with the person's actual biological condition.

Addiction is a special case of the sick role. The disease model of alcoholism, the view that alcoholism is an addiction, has itself achieved the imprimatur of moral legitimacy only in the last two decades, and only after protracted advocacy by the alcoholism movement.[5] Reflecting the wide acceptance, the legitimacy, of the alcoholic sick role, public policy is largely continuous with the disease model logic that alcoholics cannot help themselves; thus, as previously discussed, the passage of national legislation in 1970, which mandated treatment rather than punishment, amounted to official recognition of alcoholism as a legitimate form of sickness.

Despite the official legitimacy of alcoholism, however, the alcoholic does not receive blanket absolution for his or her actions: Certain forms of conduct are still not legitimate. The social vilification and demonization of the drunk driver is only the most obvious example. In this case, the tacit reasoning is apparently that alcoholics had better find a way to control themselves when the decision as to whether or not to drive is the issue. Once behind the wheel of a car, absolution and legitimacy are no longer relevant considerations.[6]

This somewhat muddled stance regarding the moral legitimacy of addiction reflects an underlying ambiguity regarding intentionality. This ambiguity is reflected in a tendency to draw distinctions among, between, and within types of addiction, and evaluations of intent play a central role in drawing those distinctions. The problem drinker's social fate varies with the degree of imputed intention. Thus, the pivotal social difference between alcoholics and, for want of a gentler term, "drunks" rests upon a judgment of intention: Alcoholics cannot help what they do (again, with the exception of deciding to drive); they do not intend to drink too much, too often; and they cannot help what they do when they are drunk. As we have seen, this obviation of intention informs the twelve-step subculture's notion of powerlessness: Yes, people behave badly, but they do not mean to; they cannot help themselves. Because of their disease, it was inevitable that trouble should arise. When assessing the legitimacy of alcohol-related behavior, then, intention is played off against inevitability, and the drinker's story and social fate depend upon which of the two weighs more heavily.

In evaluating the relative weights of intentionality and inevitability, those with substance or, following Schaef, "ingestive" addictions—especially alcoholics—at least have physiology on their side. In these cases, after a certain point, the body indeed develops a dependency upon the drug, and so alcoholics and sufferers from other ingestive addictions cannot be held responsible for their actions; to use the jargon of the twelve-step subculture, their unmanageable conduct is the product of their powerlessness over their drug. Once physically dependent, it is inevitable that unacceptable behavior will at some point ensue; thus, intention is not a salient factor.

As the phrase "once physically dependent" implies, however, exactly how people get addicted in the first place has always been problematic. For the better part of thirty years, AA and its advocates argued that alcoholics had a "predisposition" toward their addiction. The claim was that they were born with an "allergy" to alcohol, and the allergy accounted for why only some drinkers were incapable of moderation. In a clear reflection of the times, AA's "allergic predisposition" has of late become a "genetic predisposition." There is some evidence for a genetic link, but it remains weak and equivocal; by and large a physiological predisposition to addiction has not been adequately demonstrated. Given the equivocal evidence, it is not too much to say that public policy based upon biological factors has reflected what can fairly be called a willing suspension of disbelief. The moral legitimacy of the alcoholic as an addicted person and of addiction as a conditionally legitimate form of sickness have been granted on an "as if" basis.[7] Whether alcoholics could help (that is, whether they intended) becoming alcoholic or not, they are addicted now, and because of that they probably cannot help (do not intend) much of what they currently do. Guided by the premise that, in most cases, alcoholics should be dealt with as if they cannot help themselves, public policy has reflected a primarily humanitarian judgment that these are people in need of treatment rather than punishment.[8]

These qualifications notwithstanding, intention still remains an important part of the alcoholic's fortunes, playing a pivotal role in determining the legitimacy of the disease and, by extension, public response to problem drinkers. The legitimacy of the alcoholic role, as with any sick role, is contingent upon the alcoholics' cooperation with efforts to get them well. If they cooperate with those efforts to help (by seeking treatment, joining a self-help group, or both), a moral bargain, of sorts, is struck; by meeting the obligation to try to get well, alcoholics are accorded some measure of absolution from past wrongdoing—the principal privilege of the role. In effect, by showing their intent to get well, alcoholics receive the benefit of the doubt as to whether they intended to get sick in the first place. And the principal means of demonstrating one's intention to recover is to become a member of a twelve-step group.

The alcoholic version of the sick role, then, is structured in a way that provides very strong incentives for those who adopt the role to become participants and members of the twelve-step subculture. In exchange for becoming a member, and thereby demonstrating good intent, the addict's past indiscretions are forgiven. By drawing an analogy between alcoholism and process addiction, co-dependency emphasizes these incentives, seeking to elicit its adherents' commitments to twelve-step membership.

Legitimating the Analogy

The co-dependency movement—the sudden surge in new members and groups in the twelve-step subculture fueled by and organized around co-dependency discourse—is the product of the analogy that the discourse draws between alcoholism and any and all other life problems. The concept of process addiction expresses that analogy, and the analogy is the means in and through which co-dependency secures people's commitments to membership in the twelve-step subculture. These commitments, in turn, constitute the social embodiment of a reformed version of liberation psychotherapy—one that makes provisions for stable, repeated patterns of social interaction. Like their alcoholic predecessors, those who subscribe to co-dependency are effectively required to cooperate with efforts to make them well, at least if they hope for absolution from responsibility for past indiscretion; in the exchange, they are expected to take responsibility for making things right again. In that expectation lies the basis for commitment to the twelve-step subculture, and from that commitment the co-dependency movement was born.

We have seen the analogical reasoning underlying co-dependency's construction in previous chapters: The dysfunctional family is "like" the alcoholic family, and mainstream culture is "like" both of these family types; social institutions operate "like" systems; the adult child of a dysfunctional family is "like" the adult child of an alcoholic family. So too, co-dependents are "like" addicts and alcoholics, especially in the sense that they do not intend to harm themselves or others. Therefore, all of the behaviors for which the disease of co-dependency is said to be the culprit are like alcoholism.

This analogy between alcoholism and virtually all problems in living is a somewhat fragile rhetorical construction. Throughout the various treatises on co-dependency, particularly in their discussions of the newest categories of process addiction, the advocates appear to recognize this fragility, taking considerable pains to assure that people take seriously the analogy that the discourse draws between the new categories and more conventional, and publicly accepted, forms of addiction. Anne Wilson Schaef, for one, has expressed concern that "sex addiction" and "romance addiction"—the latter was her own creation—will not be treated *as* addictions, and she has adamantly insisted that they must be. In support of her contentions, Schaef draws upon the "progressive and fatal" imagery that, as we have seen, was a central component in alcoholism's moral legitimation: "[Although] some may find it difficult to take romance addiction seriously,... it is progressive and can be fatal to mind, body, and spirit.... As [in this case, romance addiction] progresses, it takes more and more excitement to get the 'fix.'" Schaef pleads the same case in regard to "sexual addiction"—another of co-dependency's obsessive manifestations: "One can become almost voyeuristic and/or judgmental in discussing sexual addiction and lose contact with the reality that sexual addicts are persons who have a progressive, fatal disease and are in a great deal of pain."[9]

Schaef's repeated recourse to the "progressive and fatal" theme is grounded in the analogical project from which co-dependency and process addiction emerged. In essence, the argument is that, like alcoholism, its already legitimated prototype, process addiction is a progressively worsening disease in which inevitability must outweigh intentionality as the relevant criterion for the assessment and handling of the sufferers. Schaef continually sounds this note in her efforts to redefine the therapeutic culture's identity and relationship problems as addictions caused by the repressions of mainstream culture. Offering an anecdote from her files, she discusses Julian, a young man who, she explains, is addicted to sexual fantasies. Although he does not act them out, his fantasies have begun to interfere with his work life. Explicitly using AA terminology, Schaef explains, "[Julian] had now reached a point that he believed that he was *powerless* over his sexual fantasies, and his life had become *unmanageable* because of them" (emphasis added). Moreover, again like alcoholism, sexual addiction follows a fatal course: "[N]ot only did [Julian] fear acting out his fantasies, but he recently had become so involved in his fantasies that he had a serious automobile accident in which he could have been killed or killed someone else."[10]

Regardless of whether one subscribes to this line of argument, Schaef is unmistakably trying to establish an analogy between process addiction and alcoholism and thereby to achieve legitimacy for process addiction on the same grounds as for alcoholism: the inevitability and unintentional nature of people's conduct. The obviation of intent clearly informs Schaef's assertion that "[i]t is important to remember that this is not who romance addicts are, this is their disease"; toward the same end, she stresses that her sexually addicted client, Julian, "is not a bad person. He has a progressive, fatal disease...and he was in the chronic stage."[11] It was inevitable, she contends, that Julian would become addicted to his fantasies; he did not intend to do so, and therefore should not be censured or punished. The same analogical premises and purposes inform Schaef's observation that "addictive patterns are a learned disease." Because process addicts have a "learned disease," they will not be judged on the basis of their intentions: They were merely doing what mainstream culture had taught them to do, and "if we learned it, it is *not* who we are"[12] (emphasis in original).

The overarching significance of the concept of process addiction is that, although it is entirely faithful to core liberation psychotherapy truth rules, it simultaneously makes twelve-step membership possible, desirable, and—given the nature of the alcoholic role on which it was modeled—necessary. Co-dependents are not simply psychologically troubled in some diffuse fashion; they are now, by dint of analogical reasoning, addicts. This is the logic underlying all of the advocates' exhortations urging prospective believers to join a twelve-step group. Because all problems in living are really addictions, Schaef, like her colleagues, "believe[s] that the Twelve Step program is a crucial tool for recovering co-dependents."[13] In and through this logic, co-dependency's creators provided the therapeutic culture with a means of addressing its enduring difficulties in eliciting stable patterns of action and interaction.

E Pluribus Unum: Process Addiction in Co-Dependents Anonymous

Without the new theory of addiction and the concept of process addiction, there would have been no co-dependency movement. Through the analogy that the discourse established between problems in living and alcoholism, co-dependency constructed a rhetorical commonality among a widely divergent array of experiences. Process addiction serves as a unifying principle, providing people with a way of seeing and understanding how their lives have gone as they have and supplying them with a rationale and an institutional venue for coming together in a common cause, as well as a shared set of meanings to articulate that cause.

Although, as I have noted, CoDA members do not often explicitly invoke the term "process addiction," their testimonials are thoroughly suffused with the logic from which that concept derived. One clear manifestation of this is their various uses of the concept of shame and of being "bound" by it. Here, John Bradshaw's influence upon the co-dependency movement is at work. All of the advocates make at least passing reference to shame, but Bradshaw has most exhaustively addressed the topic and has assigned to shame a particularly significant role. Indeed, as we have seen, for Bradshaw, "toxic shame is the core of addiction."[14]

Reflecting the pivotal status that the concept holds in the discourse, CoDA members use "shame" as a form of shorthand, capturing and expressing the many causes, symptoms, and types of process addiction in a single, symbolically loaded image. Shame serves as a synonym for co-dependency and thus is understood as the cause of a wide range of behaviors. In Donna's case, for example, shame/co-dependency was the root cause of her alcoholism—which co-dependency has reframed as an obsessive form of process addiction:[15]

> The way shame has manifested itself in my life is an awareness [of] the way I acted out not being wanted. It was a tremendous awareness for me when I realized I acted out my shame in many, many different ways in my adult life, and then I could go

back and see where those feelings came from and why I did what I did as an adult. I came from a very dysfunctional family. My father died when I was two, and I was the last of eight children, and my mother was forty-two years old. I used to kid a lot about her not wanting me, and then I got in touch with the shame of not being wanted. I acted out that feeling of not being wanted through alcohol. Whenever I was feeling that I was not being wanted, I had to use other substances so that I couldn't feel. I came from another twelve-step program, and one of the biggest shame spirals that I felt as an adult was when I drank after 18 years of sobriety. This was one of the most difficult things that I ever had to go through, and I realized— through Co-Dependents Anonymous—that the reason that I couldn't get sober again was because of my shame. I did not deserve to be sober. I was not wanted. I had no place in the universe. When I got to the place where I could see the shame behind this, the necessity to drink...left me.

It is impossible to tell from what Donna has said here how she was shamed as a child. There is a sudden and unexplained segue in her story; the link between kidding about not being wanted and her later ability to get "in touch with the shame of not being wanted" is obscure. But if these connections are not clear, those she has drawn between cause and consequence are; "through Co-Dependents Anonymous," Donna has learned that she "did what [she] did as an adult" because, despite the uncertainty of whether her mother in fact told her she was unwanted, she did not feel wanted. As a process addict, she "acted out" her shame about this "in many, many different ways," including alcoholism. Using the discourse to reconstruct and characterize her own actions, she sees now that she could not be sober because of her shame.

As Donna's remarks demonstrate, the concept of shame also expresses a distinction between who people really are and what they have done. At one level, this reflects liberation psychotherapy's distinction between the true self and the self created by cultural repression, but the basis of the distinction is the obviation of intent and the imputation of inevitability—the central components of the addict role. As the "core of addiction," shame is the product of being loved only for what we do rather than who we are, and this leads to an adulthood in which what we do is unlovable. But, as Laura's story demonstrates, it is understood that these unlovable acts are not intentional: The disease, not the person, engendered and carried out the unlovable act. "A lot of my shame," Laura said,

takes [the form of] things that I do to myself, like picking at my skin. There are physically abusive things I do to myself because I'm not good enough. When I was a little girl, nothing I did was good enough or right, everything was negative.... I learned to do things like not even be able to ask for things that everyone had in my family. I would just wait until someone gave it to me, and if they didn't give it to me I just figured I didn't deserve it. Many of the things I began to do were abusive to myself, and abusing myself just engendered, just brought up more shame. [Now, I know that although] I am capable of doing things that are harmful, that does not make me a bad person. I am not the things I do, I am not the things that are done to me.

The addict role renders intention irrelevant as a basis for judging past indiscretions: Doing harmful things is not a valid criterion for evaluating personal identity because the harmful acts were the product of a "shame-bound" self; Laura, like Donna, did not really do them. By obviating intention, the various episodes of the co-dependent life are pulled together with the thread of inevitability. At the next level of abstraction, by expanding inevitability across the spectrum of problems and misconduct, the multiple forms of co-dependent lives are pulled together with the thread of process addiction—thereby making Co-Dependents Anonymous possible.

This expansion of addiction to include all behavioral extremes is reflected in what Donna called the "shame spiral." The shame spiral—which was evident in different ways in both Donna's and Laura's stories—is another name for a vicious circle. In Donna's case, for example, shame was the cause of her acting out, which took the form of alcoholism; in turn, the alcohol-related acting out made her still more ashamed; each new episode of acting out deepens the shame, leading to another round of "acting-out," and so on. Because process addiction also entails violating the norm of self-realization, co-dependents may also experience "acting in" shame spirals, which are characteristic of repressed rather than obsessive co-dependents. The "shame-boundedness" of repressed co-dependents takes a different form: They seldom try or they routinely fail to achieve much of anything; each new failure engenders another bout with toxic shame. Peggy describes this "introjection" of shame:

[Sharing] is probably the hardest thing I will ever do in my life, and that's probably because I have been so ashamed my whole life. I grew up in an extremely dysfunctional family where I always felt shame. Shame, to me, meant I wasn't good enough, that I wasn't lovable, and that I wasn't acceptable the way I was. I was ashamed of who I was, I was ashamed of where I lived, I was ashamed of my parents, I was ashamed of my clothes, and I was ashamed of my appearance. I always felt that I just wasn't good enough. I always assumed blame and shame for everything that happened in my family. Somehow I thought that I was in control, or [that it was] my fault for all the physical abuse and emotional abuse and the sexual abuse, spiritual abuse— whatever abuse happened, it was always my fault and therefore I thought that somehow I could stop it. And when I couldn't, I felt ashamed because I had failed again. So I just lived in shame. Shame controlled me to the point that I was afraid to do anything, I was afraid to try anything new, I was afraid to take risks because I was sure that I would fail and then I would feel ashamed again.... I remember being told repeatedly when I was little, "you should be ashamed of yourself," and as a child I was supposed to act like an adult, and I was supposed to know everything. I remember asking questions when I was little, and my mother saying, "what's the matter with you? You don't know that? You should be ashamed of yourself."

What these various stories reveal is that shame is really just a more evocative paraphrase of the original adult-child formula —"don't talk, don't trust, don't feel"—from which it, and co-dependency itself, was derived. Like Adult Children of Alcoholics, Adult Children of Dysfunctional Families internalized conventional culture and society's repressive, self-denying rules and, in doing so, skewed their self-images.

Although framed in the argot of the twelve-step subculture, the logic here is unmistakably that of liberation psychotherapy: Cultural repression begets psychological sickness. This, then, is but another recitation of conventional wisdom. What is really significant is the infusion of addiction into the discursive and symbolic mix. CoDA members are not just "neurotic" or suffering from "defensively organized personalities"; rather, they are addicted to one or another form of conduct, and this theme gives them access to a common set of symbols and an ongoing set of social relationships.

Co-dependency offers a heady mix of ironclad determinism and universal applicability, and from these elements a movement emerged. The adult child is "shame-bound," and the shame-bound inevitably become addicts of some type. The potent strain of determinism informs all of the members' stories, and those stories reveal an extremely broad array of experiences—all reduced to the logic of the discourse.

Randy, for example, has concluded that the decisive factor in his adult relationships with women was his mother's untimely death:

I remember by about sixth grade—I was about twelve—I was really missing my mom. And then a friend of mine told me, I'll never forget this, that Linda Williams liked me, and I went, "Whoa, a girl likes *me?* All right!" And ever since that time, women have been one of the main ways that I've gotten my fix. You know? Missing my mom, and watching how my dad handled that...I see some parallels there, for sure. I still have problems with my relationships with women.

The addictive connotations of Randy's claim that women are a "fix" for him speak for themselves. His troubles with women were inevitable;

like alcoholism, they have taken on a logic of their own. Steve also describes his present unsatisfying relationships as the inevitable consequence of past experience, in his case, his drug-addicted mother's inability to take care of herself:

> So, what I've done all my life is to look for these weak women, so I can take care of them. But I get totally hooked into doing that, and they get totally hooked into letting me do that and so the relationships are pretty safe, but, you know, totally unrewarding, because neither of us really has an identity—she's just going with what's most familiar, and I am too, and there's no growth.

Underscoring the powerful role that the discourse plays in shaping members' self-conceptions, Steve added that

> I always thought, "yeah, this was some pretty bizarre stuff I grew up with," but I wondered why I kept doing the same things in my relationships. Then, I started reading some books on co-dependency and coming to these meetings, and I think I'm starting to understand why that is.... I found a way to avoid dealing with the pain I felt, because it hurt. It's good to have a way of thinking about this.

These remarks clearly illustrate the significance of the concept of process addiction as the unifying principle that made the co-dependency movement possible. Through reading co-dependency treatises, Steve now has "a way of thinking about" and of talking about the events of his life as being preordained. All co-dependents have precisely this same way of thinking, and because they do, the differences among their experiences are overridden; common cause becomes possible in ways that it was not prior to the creation of process addiction.

There is far more at work in all of the foregoing testimonials than the simple premise that childhood is an important influence on adult character. The governing view, although largely only implicit in such notions as the "script," is that childhood "issues" *must* be resolved, or the person will never leave childhood at all. As Ken's comments below demonstrate, this formula is by no means always implied:[16]

> I was...the youngest in my family, and my father died when I was fifteen months old.... He was violent and sexually abusive and I grew up with exactly his patterns of addiction. I believe that it's not just learned behavior, but that it's genetic and that it's carried over from one generation to the next. I walk just like him and I talk just like him, and my mother would tell me, [when I was] six or seven, "you remind me of your dad so much," in a warm, tender way. Then, two days later, she'd go through rage about what he was like, and say, "that no good slob." [Children] don't know how to say, "well, that's about her, that's not about me," you

know? [Children do not know how to say] "I'll maintain my boundaries, here." I didn't know how to do that. What I did know how to do was to take it on, believe it was about me, and continue to add to my sense of shame...[and] I have taken [the lessons] from my childhood and done to others exactly what was done to me, or exactly the opposite.

The correspondence between the life stories that CoDA members tell and the symbolic tools that the discourse provides is not always quite this direct and striking. Ken's closing sentence is almost a verbatim reprise of Bradshaw's claim, to his *Homecoming* audience, that "we do to our children what was done to us, or exactly the opposite."[17] Clearly, there is no small amount of causal overdetermination in Ken's assertion that co-dependency is not just learned but genetic as well. But this double determinism leads him to understand his life as something in which he has had no choice whatsoever. As an addict, Ken's past actions were inevitable rather than intentional; more important, in terms of understanding how co-dependency engendered a movement, as an addict, he has access to a community of like-minded souls:

Co-dependency dictated my career, my friendships, my work situation. It dictated my marriages, who I was going to marry. I used to think I had choices about who I was in a relationship with. Today, I do—in recovery; but not until now. I attracted the same kinds of people, over and over, because "Tim," [which is my name for] that child inside me, was desperately trying to find a place that I could finally call home.... [And] I know today that [all of my acting out] was about..."Tim" trying to find a mom that was finally there for him, that didn't send him away.

Ken's—and other CoDA members'—fidelity to the discourse is striking. Bradshaw has described the obsessed co-dependent's "acting out" as, in essence, "looking for a daddy."[18] The addiction is a surrogate "daddy," or, in Ken's case, "a mom...that didn't send him away." Invoking the same image, Rhonda, a self-described sexual addict, maintains that she has "always been looking for that father, just repeating that over and over and over." Her father surrogates, she explains, were "food, alcohol, [and] men."[19]

When the Analogy Breaks Down

Process addiction rhetorically and symbolically unifies the wide range of problems of the therapeutic culture and reveals co-dependency's reformist inclinations. Through process addiction and the new theory of addiction, liberation therapy becomes more than just a blueprint for the isolated search for self-actualization; it becomes for a basis for ongoing social relationships and for the identities that such relationships can sustain. For the same reasons, CoDA meetings are something other than one more weekly group therapy session. Process addiction transforms the panoply of experiences and problems that co-dependency addresses into a commonly shared condition, calling for the group action and purpose that has proven elusive for many in the wake of the therapeutic revolution.

Perhaps at no time is the significance of the analogy that co-dependency draws between process and conventional addictions more apparent than when the analogy breaks down—as it did for one CoDA group whose meeting I attended. During the course of this meeting, a woman named Sally expressed a number of concerns about the way things had been going in the group. These concerns revolved around what Sally saw as vitally important differences between twelve-step and regular—that is, clinical and academic—therapeutic approaches, but they also provide some insight into process addiction's essential role as a unifying principle and thus as the linchpin of reform. Specifically, she was disturbed that the other group regulars maintained a very limited involvement, a pattern that had, she believed, resulted in a pattern of "meetings where everybody just comes in and 'dumps their stuff' and leaves. The meetings have been getting more and more negative all the time, and I think that's a bad sign."[20]

As Sally explained, she was of the mind that "this program [CoDA and the twelve steps] is supposed to be more than just group therapy, with people coming in once a week to bitch and complain, and never get anywhere." The twelve steps, Sally said, are meant to foster recovery from problems, and as she saw it, as a twelve-step program, CoDA ought to be a forum for discussing the ways in which membership in the group has improved life. The ongoing negativism at this meeting was a concern for her because

> if this is what CoDA's about, then I worry about the program's future—not just this meeting, but the whole program. The thing is, all I ever hear when I come here anymore is all about everything that's wrong in people's lives. I don't hear about recovery, nothing about what works, or about how the twelve steps or CoDA are making positive differences in our lives. Always just about how things suck, how they aren't working. And that's not recovery to me, that's therapy. And that's why, even though I went to therapy for a lot of years, I never got a thing out of it.

> Because group therapy was just a bunch of people talking about their problems. I went to Al-Anon and to AA and to group therapy, and I know co-dependency is my problem. But, we've got to have our own stories about recovery.

As Sally says, in the course of her own efforts to find a satisfactory way of understanding and dealing with her problems, she had reached the conclusion that mainstream psychotherapy was not the answer. Having effectively comparison-shopped among the twelve-step alternatives, she has concluded that "co-dependency is my problem"—her "core addiction," as members often called it. She is concerned, however, that CoDA is at risk of turning into conventional group therapy.

Part of the problem to which Sally refers is almost inevitable: CoDA, after all, *is* group therapy, albeit organized around an analogy to conventional addiction discourse that makes it something more than group therapy, as well. Talking about one's problems in a group setting is the mechanism by which twelve-step members of all stripes—like their counterparts in clinical group therapy—come to grips with their behaviors and try to straighten out their lives. Sally acknowledged this, but she was nonetheless concerned that the discussions never got beyond the level of complaint and, most important, that the common bond among the members was never really established.

Two women, both old hands in the twelve-step subculture, responded to Sally's remarks. Their comments shed some light upon the distinction between an unalloyed liberation psychotherapy approach to life problems and the reformed version that co-dependency, by way of process addiction, offers its adherents. Barb, who had been impatiently shaking her head and looking at her watch while Sally voiced her complaints, observed that she felt "cheated." She said she had come to the meeting hoping to share and listen and instead found herself listening to a list of grievances about the group itself.

> I've been around twelve-step groups for a long, long time. I've been in AA for a lot of years, but I go to Al-Anon, ACoA, and CoDA meetings, too, and I've been to quite a few. And it doesn't happen much, but I always feel cheated when a meeting turns into a long discussion about the mechanics of the group and the meetings, instead of talking about what's really going on in people's lives.

This type of meeting, Barb continued, never really helps anybody, and she believed that the type of issues that Sally was concerned about should not be raised during regular meeting times: "The beauty and the power of these groups comes from people talking about their lives, and you can't ever get to that stuff if you're battling about details."

Barb's comments get to the core of the problems that CoDA faces if the discourse's addiction analogy breaks down. Although the twelve steps provide a common framework for group members, they have historically been applied to single issues, such as alcoholism or narcotic addiction—issues usually dealing with forms of addiction that are biologically grounded, as well. As such, there is a natural focus and a natural commonality of concern among the members of such groups. Process addiction, as we have seen, subsumes an enormous array of general interpersonal problems. The common focus and concern in groups dealing with process addiction are solely the product of co-dependency's analogical reasoning—our problems are "like" alcoholism—and without that analogy, the common ground disappears.

Mary, the second woman to respond to Sally's concerns, echoed Barb's observations but framed her own remarks in terms of tried-and-true subcultural techniques for effecting communal purpose. From her point of view, meetings turn into "bitch sessions" because "[w]e're not using our biggest tool, our best one. How many of you call each other during the week? [None did.] That's exactly the point. I've been around twelve-step groups a long time, too, and one of the things they all do is use the telephone." In older twelve-step groups, those in which the members grapple with a readily identifiable common problem, the members are routinely in contact with one another, both inside and outside of the regular meetings; they are friends. Unlike those other groups, Mary pointed out, at this CoDA meeting,

> the reason that we come in here once a week and just dump our problems is that we're not really a group. We don't see or talk to each other outside of this room, and so we treat each other like strangers because we *are* strangers. We aren't there for each other; we're not involved in one another's lives. We just have a bunch of people hooked together by the common thing that their lives aren't that great. It doesn't work that way, people.

It is one thing to be "hooked together" by a common problem of lives that "aren't that great" and another altogether to have a disease, an addiction. Co-dependency discourse, through the construct of process addiction and the analogy to alcoholism, transforms the wide diversity of "not so great" lives into a single problem that people can confront in and through communal action. When the analogy breaks down, the lack of commonality rears its head. It is this lack of commonality, and the accompanying difficulties with close relationships and identities, that co-dependency seeks to resolve; and this, again, underscores the discourse's fundamentally reformist character.

* * * * *

Bad marriages, overanalyzing and simply having problems with relationships, self-abuse, alcohol abuse, drug addiction, sexual compulsiveness, systematic underachievement, fear of failure, fear of success—there is little common ground among the issues and troubles people bring with them to CoDA. Process addiction imposes a rhetorical uniformity upon substantively diverse experiences, and thereby makes common purpose and action possible. By defining the problems born of a fragmented cultural and social world as addictions born of repression, co-dependency enables people to piece together the fragments: Reframed as addictions, the problems born of liberation psychotherapy's widespread public acceptance and of its anti-institutionalism are transformed into the inevitable manifestations of cultural repression of the self, becoming a ticket to the shared beliefs, stable social relationships, and ongoing social recognition of identity that mainstream culture can no longer provide and that liberation psychotherapy, without reform, never could.

It is perhaps a tribute to the twelve-step format and to the analogy to addiction itself that more CoDA groups do not fragment into unfocused grievance sessions; on the whole, process addiction successfully provides a baseline commonality that tends to override the disparate backgrounds and experiences of CoDA members. Most of the meetings, even if they have a heavily negative tone, neither dwell entirely in that naysaying realm nor devolve into extended discussions of mechanical concerns—discussions that ultimately reveal that the commonalities among CoDA members are rhetorically constructed rather than based on substantively and self-evidently similar experiences. Sally's group appears to be an exception to this general rule, but her group is an important negative case, illustrating what can happen when those funneling mechanisms break down or do not work in the first place. When this happens, the psychotherapeutic roots of co-dependency and the absence of a self-evidently shared problem are fully visible. Process addiction serves a central and unifying purpose in the meetings and in the movement as a whole; without process addiction, co-dependency would simply be another version of liberation psychotherapy and, like liberation therapy, would not be able to forge common cause and action. In and through the groups designed to deal with these new addictions, co-dependency discourse creates the selves, the types of personalities, that are its tangible social manifestations. It is to the creation of these selves in the context of CoDA meetings, selves that both make co-dependency real and make CoDA possible, that chapter 6 will be addressed.

Notes

1. Ryan, *Cradle of the Middle Class*, 65.
2. Co-dependency advocates' promotional efforts—as do the interventionist orientations of the treatment industry—depart from AA's long-standing distinction between "attraction" and "promotion." AA, the prototype for all twelve-step groups, has always attached a great deal of importance to the idea that people must come to and decide to stay with the organization on the basis of their attraction to the twelve-step philosophy rather than because they have been coerced or cajoled into it. Punctuating this importance, AA's eleventh tradition states that "[o]ur public relations policy is based on attraction rather than promotion; we need always maintain personal anonymity at the level of press, radio, and films" (Alcoholics Anonymous, *Twelve Steps and Twelve Traditions*, 180). AA's founders saw the tenet of anonymity as pivotal to the organization's ability to help people with drinking problems. In part, as the wording of the eleventh tradition suggests, they were concerned that personal efforts to promote AA would compromise the promoter's anonymity, thereby interfering both with members' efforts to achieve and maintain sobriety and with the organization's ability to attract people who had problems with alcohol but did not want it to be public knowledge. Thus, the idea was to "publicize [AA's] principles and its work, but not its individual members" (ibid., 182). AA's emphasis upon attraction rather than promotion also reflected the conviction that alcoholics could only be helped if they wanted to be helped: They had to be attracted to the organization and its philosophy. Thus, the "Big Book," AA's bible, advises prospective members that "[i]f you have decided that you want what we have and are willing to go to any length to get it—then you are ready to take certain steps" (the Big Book's official title is *Alcoholics Anonymous: The Story of How Many Thousands of Men and Women Have Recovered from Alcoholism*, 3d ed. [New York: Alcoholics Anonymous World Services, 1976]; quoted passage is from p. 58). Historically, the decision "that you want what we have" has rested upon the person's attraction to what the organization offered.
3. Quotes are from, respectively, Subby, *Lost in the Shuffle*, 128; Beattie, *Codependent No More*, 170; Schaef, *Co-Dependence*, 95; Bradshaw, *Bradshaw On: The Family*, 197.
4. Eliot Freidson's discussion of the nuances of the sick role, upon which my own remarks are based, is still the most thoughtful; see his *Profession of Medicine: A Study of the Sociology of Applied Knowledge* (New York: Harper and Row, 1970), especially part 3, "The Social Construction of Illness." A more striking and contemporary instance of the extent to which social and moral criteria are operable in the categorization of disease is to be found in the natural history of AIDS in the

United States. Consider the category of the "innocent victim," which is a redundant term if one sees the disease from a physiological standpoint. But morally, the unstated assumption is that although everyone with AIDS may be a victim, those making this distinction do not consider all of them are innocent; see Douglas Crimp, ed., *AIDS: Cultural Analysis, Cultural Activism* (Cambridge: MIT Press, 1988).

5. Schneider, "Deviant Drinking as Disease," and Peter M. Conrad and Joseph W. Schneider, *Deviance and Medicalization: From Badness to Sickness* (St. Louis, Mo.: Mosby, 1980), discuss in some detail the struggle to "accomplish" this social legitimacy for the disease model.

6. Once a drunk person drives, she or he is no longer legitimately sick but has become a form of "folk devil." For a thoughtful analysis of the construction of policies regarding and images of the drunk driver, see Joseph M. Gusfield, *The Culture of Public Problems* (Chicago: University of Chicago Press, 1981). On "moral panics" and "folk devils," see Stanley Cohen, *Folk Devils and Moral Panics* (London: MacGibbon and Kee, 1972; New York: St. Martin's Press, 1980); Nachman Ben-Yehuda, *The Politics and Morality of Deviance: Moral Panics, Drug Abuse, Deviant Science, and Reversed Stigmatization* (Albany, N.Y.: State University of New York Press, 1990).

7. For general criticisms of the disease model of alcoholism, see Herbert Fingarette, *Heavy Drinking: The Myth of Alcoholism as a Disease* (Berkeley: University of California Press, 1988); Stanton M. Peele, *Diseasing of America: Addiction Treatment out of Control* (Lexington, Mass.: D. C. Heath, 1989). The criticisms raised in these books echo the results of the two most comprehensive studies of alcohol-related problems, both of which found little support for the disease model; see Don Cahalan, *Problem Drinkers* (San Francisco: Jossey-Bass, 1970); George E. Vaillant, *The Natural History of Alcoholism: Causes, Patterns, and Paths to Recovery* (Cambridge, Mass.: Harvard University Press, 1983). The claim, announced in spring 1990, that researchers had isolated the gene responsible for alcohol problems has since been modified by those who originally made the discovery. As an article in the *Boston Globe* reported, "the known genetic variant... interacts with the primary defect to predispose carriers" (Richard A. Knox, "Gene Linked to Alcoholism Also Tied to Other Disorders," *Boston Globe*, 2 October 1991, A15). This variant, it is now believed, "is acting as a modifying gene," only, "and is not the major cause of [alcoholism]." Other researchers maintain that even this modified claim is unacceptable. Joel Gelertner and his colleagues insist that "the evidence to date suggests that the association [between the genetic variant and alcohol troubles] is weak," at best. The latter findings were based on a study of 112 Caucasians, of whom 44 were alcoholic and 68 were nonalcoholic. On "as-if" reasoning, see Hans Vaihinger, *The Philosophy of As-If: A System of the Theoretical, Practical, and Religious Fictions of Mankind* (London: K. Paul, Trench, Trubner and Co. Ltd; New York: Harcourt, Brace, and Co., 1924).

8. The distinction between help and punishment is not at all as self-evident as advocates of the treatment route recurrently suggest. Sending people to an institution and keeping them there until they cooperate with the staff bears no small resemblance to incarceration and punishment. The treatment facility is, to be sure, a more benign setting than the penitentiary, but the differences between treatment and incarceration would seem to be more in degree than in kind; see Rice, "'A Power Greater Than Ourselves.'"

9. Anne Wilson Schaef, *Escape from Intimacy—Untangling the "Love" Addictions: Sex, Romance, Relationships* (New York: Harper and Row, 1990), 49, 4.

10. Ibid., 20. The hazards of simultaneously operating heavy machinery while "pre-occupied" with the addictive object, Schaef contends, are not limited to the sexually addicted. Indeed, "being distracted by romance fantasies...can also be fatal while driving" (ibid., 49).
11. Ibid., 49, 21.
12. Ibid., 41, 42.
13. Schaef, *Co-Dependence*, 95.
14. Bradshaw, *Healing the Shame*, 97.
15. Donna's remarks, as well as all subsequent member discussions of shame, are taken from a CoDA cassette on shame, recorded during the Mid-Atlantic CoDA Conference, May 1989.
16. Taken from a transcript of a cassette recording of Ken's comments to a gathering of fellow co-dependents at the First Annual Mid-Atlantic CoDA Conference, May 1989.
17. From the PBS broadcast *Homecoming*, 2 and 8 December 1990.
18. Ibid. The phrase is Bradshaw's.
19. Ibid.
20. This is one version of twelve-step argot for simply spewing out all the things that have gone wrong in life; an emotional purging.

6

Becoming Co-Dependent: Conversion, Ritual, and Obligation

As previous chapters have emphasized, liberation psychotherapy's ascent to cultural power engendered a variety of problems in people's closest relationships. These problems, I have argued, are in part the natural, if unfortunate, complement to the demise of what had been established ways of arranging the relations between and among culture, identity, and social institutions; in even larger part, they are also born of the difficulties with institutionalizing liberation psychotherapy, its inability to replace what it encouraged people to reject, particularly those relationships and institutions with which the individual is most intimately connected on a day to day basis: families, neighborhoods, communities, and the like. In modern societies, these mediating or intermediate institutions, as they have been called (because they stand between and mediate the relationship between the individual and the abstract and powerful structures of economy and state), are the ones most directly charged with the task of socialization; it is in and through these institutions that cultures reproduce themselves across time and that identity is "socially bestowed [and] socially sustained."[1] Because they are responsible for passing on culture's symbolic and moral prescriptions and proscriptions, for impressing inherited beliefs and values upon each new generation, and because liberation psychotherapy views these practices as the repressions from which pathology is born, these mediating institutions were the primary targets of liberation psychotherapy's invective: It is in these most direct and intimate relationships that the external imposition of expectations and demands is most readily apparent and keenly felt.

There is certainly more than a little "killing the messenger" involved in liberation psychotherapy's—and, as we have seen, co-dependency's—

broadsides against the mediating institutions. After all, especially in the modern world, these institutions are driven to a significant degree by the prerogatives of economy and the state. The division of moral and practical labor in the now largely defunct "nuclear family," for example, was a product of the requirements of large-scale capitalism, the separation of home and workplace, the death of the household economy, and the rise of huge urban centers.[2] Clinical psychological discourses, of course, are naturally inclined to focus their attentions on the interaction between self and socializing institutions rather than these larger factors. But for all of their ostensible radicalism, it is noteworthy that neither liberation psychotherapy nor its reformist offspring, co-dependency, pay more than lip service to the role that these larger and infinitely more powerful institutions play in shaping the family, community, the self, and so on. Rather, both discourses focus upon the mediating institutions almost exclusively, dwelling at great length upon their repressive practices.[3]

Because of this overarching emphasis upon the socializing institutions, liberation psychotherapy's reversal of the moral priorities in the self-to-society relationship has played itself out primarily on that stage. Political and economic institutions, despite their evident troubles in the past thirty years, have at their core remained largely unaffected by liberation psychotherapy's rise to power. Self-actualizing individuals carved out their autonomous niches through their liberation from intimate relationships, from mediating institutions, and from their normative and moral demands. Moreover, because they are the principal foundations for identity, the ensuing instability of these relationships and institutions carried over to an instability in self-conception. It is at this location on the social and moral map of contemporary American life—at the intersection of identity, intimate relationships, and mediating institutions—that one finds the distinctive problems that people bring with them to CoDA and to which co-dependency refers and responds.

Because of its staunchly anti-institutional orientation, and—equally important—its curiously selective choice of institutional targets, liberation psychotherapy cannot, or has not, engendered its own institutional forms. Rather, what it can do, and has done, is attach itself to what might be called "host institutions"—procedurally entrenched, rule-governed, more or less stably funded, formally-organized, bureaucratic institutions. Liberation psychotherapy's attachment to these host institutions is reflected in ongoing efforts to alter the philosophies and aims of those institutions: calling for modifications, for example, in educational curricula or established religious dogma, seeking, as much as possible, to shift the institutional priorities away from imposed group expectations and toward recognizing and rewarding the prerogatives of the self. But, precisely because they are formal organizations, institutions such as schools and churches can and have weathered the cultural changes of the past three decades. Such organizations can relatively easily be adapted to any of a number of purposes. Friendship, courtship, family, community, or neighborhood are not such formal organizations; beyond shared, unwritten rules for subordinating oneself to the larger interest, there is no clear way to hold these informal institutions together. These, again, are the relationships and institutions that liberation psychotherapy, in and of itself, could not replace or simply attach itself to; these are the relationships and institutions to which CoDA and other, co-dependency-guided twelve-step groups provide an alternative, offering a way to subordinate the individual to communal interests that is ultimately in keeping with liberation psychotherapy's vision of a world. The new twelve-step groups organized around co-dependency's truths, then, represent the institutionalization of liberation psychotherapy at the level of these informal mediating institutions—at the level of intimate and primary-group relationships and at the level of the identities that are both forged and sustained through those relationships. This, too, is a matter of translating the symbolic into its tangible social embodiments. How this articulation is accomplished is the focus of this chapter.

Newcomers

Liberation psychotherapy's profound cultural and social impact effectively translates into "pushes," driving people in search of possibilities for social action and identifications. This push factor takes either or both of two forms. On the one hand, as we have already seen, for many people, older cultural forms are no longer convincing or compelling enough to provide a stable basis for identity or relationships. On the other hand, liberation psychotherapy has not proven to be a viable alternative. Either alone or in combination, these factors push people toward alternative means of accomplishing such tasks. Co-dependency exerts a complementary "pull," offering people, as Melody Beattie put it, "a way of life,"[4] a middle ground, a way to be both a self-actualized and a social

individual; a way to have communal identifications and purposes that—
in keeping with the times—do not seem to require undue self-denial
and that are organized around the pursuit of self-actualization.

These push and pull factors help to engender a substantial walk-in
trade at CoDA meetings. Nearly every meeting is attended by at least
one "newcomer," as they are called, who has come to find out "what
CoDA is all about." At the time of their initial connections, however,
newcomers are not yet assimilated into the mores, folkways, and norms
of the subculture; they are not yet co-dependents. Becoming co-dependent demands that they acquire and cultivate the ability to conceptualize and talk about themselves in the requisite ways, and acquiring that
ability rests, in the first instance, upon deciding that that is the course of
action they want to pursue. As the following episode illustrates, that
decision is predicated upon the ability to "identify with" or "relate to"
what goes on in CoDA.

During the opening proceedings of a CoDA meeting, it is customary
for those in attendance to introduce themselves to the group. Each person gives his or her first name, almost always followed by "and I'm co-
dependent." During this stage of one meeting, a woman introduced
herself, saying, "Hi, I'm Linda, and I'm just here to listen and find out
whether I think this fits me or not." By describing herself as she did,
Linda identified herself as a newcomer. One of the members asked if it
was her first time in attendance. "No, I've been to two or three other
meetings with Susan, there," she said, nodding in the direction of a
woman seated across from her. "She's the one that first told me she
thought I might get something out of this." "Well, welcome," several
people said, more or less simultaneously. The meeting leader added,
"we usually suggest that you come to at least six meetings before you
make up your mind if CoDA's for you, or not." Linda nodded, and the
introductions continued around the circle of people.

The meeting progressed as usual, with members eventually taking
turns telling their stories to the group. As a young woman documented
her efforts to get her "emotionally unavailable" (as we have seen, one
common CoDA synonym for abandonment) husband to "open up" and
her mounting frustrations that he would not, Linda, the newcomer, began nodding her head in apparent agreement. Her nods grew increasingly vehement as the woman continued, and she began to shift about in
her chair. When the young wife finished, the designated group leader

said, "Linda, you seem to have heard something you could relate to."
She responded,

> That's me. What she said, that's me. That's my husband. That's our marriage. God!
> To a "tee." Wow. And I've been muddling along, thinking I was the only one. Well,
> no—I mean I knew I wasn't, all you've got to do is look around. There's a lot of
> people that feel the same way. But, you know? Nobody to really talk to about this
> stuff. Stuck in a lousy relationship, no clue what to do about it. That gets really
> lonely. I mean, if what you've all been saying is what you mean by co-dependency,
> well hell, I'm as co-dependent as it gets. You're going to be seeing me around here
> a lot from here on out, I can tell you that.

By identifying with what one of the members said, by drawing a
connection between the other woman's comments and her own situation, Linda took a first step in the process of becoming co-dependent.
She did not yet talk of her marital woes as an outgrowth of childhood
abandonment and abuse or as the signs of an addiction; these are skills
she and other newcomers must learn.

Whether newcomers do, in fact, go on to learn those skills is determined in large measure by whether they—like Linda—hear something
they can "relate to" or identify with. The odds are quite high that something they hear will strike a responsive chord. Failed marriages, broken
relationships—and their concomitants, single parenthood, isolation, confusion—have become common themes in contemporary U.S. life, and
they are dominant themes in CoDA. Listening to the members discuss
their own, similar woes and seeing the kindness and commiseration with
which such trials are treated, Linda concluded that she would be back:
As she said, if trouble with marriage "is what you all mean by co-
dependency...you're going to be seeing me around here a lot."

As previous chapters have shown, however, trouble with marriage is
only the tip of the iceberg that is "what you all mean by co-dependency."
Co-dependency is a more or less comprehensive symbolic system, and
everyday social experience is filtered, refracted, and refocused by that
system. Newcomers arrive at CoDA's doorstep with stories of unstable
or broken relationships, the absence of reliable ties to others, and the
pain, loneliness, and uncertainty about self and world that grow out of
those circumstances. Being in CoDA, being a member of that group, is
one way of solving those problems. As a member, there is always someone to listen, someone to talk to, someone with whom a lonely and
discouraged person can go get a cup of coffee. CoDA offers people

ongoing contact with friendly, open-minded, and like-minded people who share common meanings, speak a common language, and support one another in their pursuit of a common purpose. But these commonalities come with time and with becoming co-dependent. All CoDA members were at one time newcomers. They become members, and become co-dependents, through a process of conversion.[5]

Conversion, Ritual, and the Co-dependent Role

The co-dependent, the process addict, is a social role, defined by a set of obligations and privileges. As with the sick role, generally, the principal obligation of the co-dependent role is to cooperate with efforts to cure the "disease," to demonstrate one's intention to get well. This, as members refer to it, entails "working on recovery," and recovery, in turn, involves meeting two very general sets of obligations. The first set of obligations are *biographical.* Falling under the twelve-step rubric of "getting out of denial," the biographical obligations entail admitting powerlessness over an addiction and the unmanageability of one's life. At one level, this means acknowledging that one is sick; at another, it entails fitting one's life story with the discourse's symbolic system. In meeting these obligations, the candidate becomes co-dependent: This, essentially, is a matter of conversion. Moreover, conversion is a form of articulation between a symbolic and a relational system: It is in and through the creation of converts that CoDA becomes possible and that co-dependency discourse becomes socially real.

David A. Snow and Richard Machalek maintain that people's adoption of a new "universe of discourse" is the distinguishing feature of conversion.[6] One particularly important advantage to this view is that it eliminates the need for mind-reading. Rather than trying or claiming to know if people have, indeed, converted to a given symbolic system on the basis of what goes on in their heads, from this perspective conversion "should be discernible in converts' speech and reasoning"[7] and can therefore be adduced by the presence of certain "rhetorical indicators," including (1) *biographical reconstruction,* in which adherents retrofit their life stories with their new symbolic system;[8] (2) *the adoption of a master attribution scheme,* by which converts frame all of their life troubles in terms of a model that "authoritatively informs all causal attributions about self, others, and events in the world";[9] and (3) a *suspen-*

sion of analogical reasoning, manifested in believers' literal rather than metaphorical interpretation of the worldview they have adopted.[10]

Simply based on the CoDA testimonials we have heard in previous chapters, it is evident that members' uses of and facility with the discourse all but perfectly mirror the rhetorical indicators of conversion to which Snow and Machalek point. CoDA members have plainly learned a master attribution scheme, readily tracing a wide range of life troubles to the process addictions they suffer as the result of their childhood abandonment and abuse. Moreover, members also invoke a quite literal, not analogical, interpretation of themselves as addicts and their life troubles as addictions. This suspension of analogical reasoning was perhaps most apparent in observations such as Ken's (in chapter 5) that "co-dependency dictated my career, my friendships, my work situation. It dictated my marriages, who I was going to marry."

Conversion is an intrinsically social enterprise in and through which converts acquire a new identity. "Identity is socially bestowed, socially sustained, and socially transformed,"[11] and CoDA provides the symbolic material and the social grounding for identity acquisition and maintenance. Here, again, the reformist inclinations of co-dependency discourse are apparent. Although co-dependency's creators advocate full personal autonomy and individuation as the apex of selfhood, at some level, they also recognize, unlike liberation psychotherapy, the importance of a social foundation to identity. As we have seen, they all encourage newcomers to seek out a relevant group in the twelve-step subculture. Moreover, the groups themselves encourage newcomers, as with Linda at her CoDA meeting, to attend "at least six meetings" before making up their minds if CoDA is for them. This is a significant recommendation, as it facilitates the social transformation and maintenance of identity. In the course of those six meetings, and as long as they continue to attend, newcomers are repeatedly exposed to the biographical obligations of the role and the identity into which they are to be socialized.

CoDA Rituals

Despite the negative connotations that are frequently attached to the term "ritual"—equating ritual with perfunctory actions stripped of their purpose or vitality—the ritual enactment of symbolic meaning is by no means restricted to staged affairs of church and state (the realms perhaps most often linked with the negative associations). To the contrary, as Erving Goffman, perhaps more than any other social theorist, demonstrated repeatedly throughout his scholarly life, even the most banal and unthinking activities comprise a ritual enactment of complex symbolic and cultural meanings. To an observer as astute as Goffman, the simple exchange of a greeting between two people—a mutual hello and handshake or embrace—is a paradigm, epitomizing the ritualized intercourse of symbols that is constitutive of human social life.[12]

A symbolic system's social significance is a function of its embodiment in system of social relations; it must be continually affirmed and maintained, in and through recurrent and structured group practices—such as twelve-step meetings. This embodiment in relational systems is what makes the symbolic socially *real*. Emile Durkheim maintained that herein lay the principal importance of religious rituals in totemic societies: bringing people together, through a regular cycle of ceremonial occasions, to affirm the sacredness of and thereby to perpetuate the social order. So, too, Mary Douglas, the eminent scholar of symbol and ritual, has emphasized precisely this intimate relationship between ritual and reality, observing that "social rituals create a reality which would be nothing without them.... [They are] an attempt to create and maintain a particular culture, a particular set of assumptions by which experience is controlled."[13] To the degree to which ritual successfully controls experience, it serves an integrative function, uniting people within and guiding their actions through recourse to the same symbolic order.[14]

Ritual accomplishes the "control of experience" by providing what Douglas calls a "focussing mechanism," or "frame," which sets off the reality within the frame from the reality outside of it. In part, this framing effect is achieved in space and time: At a specifically designated location and a specifically designated time of the day and week, CoDA members can gather with others for whom co-dependency's symbolic and narrative structures possess an overarching significance. Even more significant than the ritual demarcation of space and time is that *in* those spaces and *at* those times co-dependency constitutes the only reality; its truths, the only truths. Co-dependency's adherents can come together on those carefully circumscribed occasions to put their beliefs into practice, speaking with one another about their lives and, through their use of the discourse, "bringing memory under the control of...external sign[s]," which link past and present together as unified pieces of a coherent whole.

CoDA meetings, then, are really more than "meetings." They are ritual enactments of a symbolic reality that saturates and permeates the members' interactions. Moreover, the rituals exert a powerful influence over *both* the newcomers and the converts, encouraging the former to convert and affirming the wisdom and efficacy of the latter's decision to do so.

CoDA rituals generally run for sixty or ninety minutes. The time is organized so that one aspect of the rite always follows the other, with specific segments of time set aside for various applications and enactments of the discourse's symbolic elements. Every ritual begins with a series of readings that identify both the mechanical requirements of membership and what it means to be a co-dependent.[15] These readings isolate symptoms, identify causes, and make promises, all refracted through the discourse's symbolic structure. Both tacitly and overtly, they instruct newcomers in and remind converts of the benefits of membership and the desirability of renouncing their submission to the demands of the dysfunctional culture, simultaneously outlining the techniques for reconstructing biography in the necessary fashion.

For example, the first reading, the "Preamble," acknowledges CoDA's intellectual debts to Alcoholics Anonymous, identifies "an inability to maintain functional relationships" as "our common problem," and states that "the only requirement for membership is a desire for healthy and fulfilling relationships with others and ourselves." The last statement serves an important rhetorical function, defining membership in catholic and noncontroversial ways: Everyone desires good relationships. However, although the "desire for healthy and fulfilling relationships" may well be the only stated *requirement* for membership (although, as chapter 8 will discuss, that is not quite the case), *being* co-dependent is the only reason for organizing one's life around the themes of co-dependency and CoDA's meeting and social calendars. If people are to be CoDA members, they will learn the co-dependent role and meet the obligations of the role.

The second reading, the "Welcome," continues the project of biographical reconstruction, tracing members' relationship problems to "our sometimes moderately, sometimes extremely dysfunctional family systems" and asserting that, as a result of being raised in such a family, "[w]e attempted to use others—our mates, our friends, and even our children, as our sole source of identity, value, and well-being and as a way of trying to restore within us the emotional losses from our childhood." In addition to outlining and exemplifying the convert's biographical obligations, the "Welcome" also emphasizes the privileges that will ultimately accrue to its members, promising that "in CoDA we are learning to live life" rather than to merely survive it. The ultimate benefit of membership is that by no longer "rely[ing] on others as a power greater than yourself...[you may] instead find...a new strength within to be that which God intended—Precious and Free."

Following the "Welcome," volunteers from among the group usually read either of two passages that also explicitly identify the qualities of co-dependents. These readings foster the fusion of the members' biographies with the discourse's symbolic order, encouraging a repudiation of mainstream culture, both by reframing the past and by interpreting the present as pathological. Potential converts may begin to locate themselves among and to identify with the "Typical Characteristics of a Co-Dependent," which include "assum[ing] responsibility for others' feelings and or behaviors," being "afraid of being hurt or rejected by others," and a tendency to let "[o]ther people's actions and attitudes... determine how I react or respond [and] to put other people's wants and needs first." The alternative reading, the "Patterns of Co-Dependency," describes such symptoms as allowing "[m]y good feelings about who I am [to] stem from being liked by you...[or] from receiving approval from you" and assessing "[t]he quality of my life...in relation to the quality of yours." Filtered through and shaped by co-dependency's symbolism, the common human qualities and concerns to which the "Characteristics" and "Patterns" refer become symptoms of an addiction. Reflecting the discourse's strong articulation with liberation psychotherapy, the readings show newcomers the fundamental significance of individuation as the criterion for psychological health: Too much concern for or about others is an index of sickness.

Slightly modified versions of AA's "Twelve Steps" and "Twelve Traditions" follow the recitations of characteristics and patterns.[16] These readings also convey important information about being co-dependent, emphasizing, for example, the members' "powerlessness" over their lives. This, as we have seen, is a crucial theme, the basis for seeing oneself as a process addict and therefore qualifying for CoDA membership. As such, it is also a theme that newcomers pick up quickly. For example, a woman attending her first meeting introduced herself by saying, "I don't know what I'm powerless over, yet, but…I'm sure I'll find out." The twelve steps and twelve traditions readings also situate CoDA within the long-standing and publicly respected shadow of AA and Al-Anon, imbuing the newer group with a legitimacy that it might not otherwise have, reducing the potential for any confusion as to the obligations of the convert, and providing members with a clear map of action.

CoDA Roles

Following the opening recitations, CoDA rituals proceed to member testimonials, which are somewhat more casual modes of symbolic observance. But these, too, are still highly conventionalized uses of the discourse, socially organizing the members and prospective members into three general "meeting roles": speakers, sharers, and listeners.[17]

There are explicit CoDA conventions for each meeting role. Speakers, for example, talk about their lives for between fifteen and thirty minutes and are advised to (1) address decisive moments from childhood; (2) provide specific examples of their own version of co-dependent behavior and its consequences; (3) explain how they came to recognize themselves as sick and got into recovery; and (4) discuss the ways in which their lives have improved since coming to CoDA and/or the continuing problems they face. Speakers, then, are role models, charged with the tasks of communicating the form and content of co-dependency's truths and representing the organization and membership therein in a positive light. Thus, CoDA also expects speakers to have more longevity in and a greater familiarity with the program than "sharers."[18]

It is striking how thoroughly faithful speakers are to the norms governing their role. Consider, for example, the following example of speaking: Sherry had been asked to speak about her experiences in relation to the twelfth step ("Having had a spiritual awakening as the result of these steps, we tried to carry this message to other Co-Dependents, and to practice these principles in all our affairs"). Abiding by CoDA's admonition that, "[i]f speaking, it is wise not to dwell heavily on early events," Sherry focused almost exclusively on the third responsibility of the speaker role, emphasizing the "qualitative improvements" in her life since converting to CoDA and avoiding "the tendency to share only an 'abuse-alog.'"[19]

Reflecting CoDA's relative newness as an organization, Sherry began with what is a fairly common disclaimer, noting that "I've only
been in the program for about six months, so I haven't had any 'spiritual
awakening' or even really worked through the steps yet."

> But, for me, I think the twelfth step is one you work on all the time anyway; while
> you're working on the other steps. Because the other steps *are* spirituality to me. I
> mean, that's what they all do, is get you in touch with your Higher Power, so it's
> not like you hit the twelfth step and "boom," you've got this spirituality all of a
> sudden. But it's there all along, and the steps just help you to be aware of it.

In these remarks, Sherry has opted to emphasize one of the privileges of the co-dependent role: that converts will establish closer contact with the twelve-step God, the Higher Power. Moreover, because
she is filled with that spirit, she has been able to "carry the message"
by her own example:

> You can carry the message to other co-dependents just by working on your own
> recovery, and that's just trying to work the steps to the best of your ability. And if
> I'm doing that, then I am carrying the message to anybody that wants it—which I
> think is everybody, anyway.

Juxtaposing the obligations and privileges of being co-dependent, Sherry
traces her ability to act as an effective CoDA missionary to the positive
changes in her life since coming to CoDA:

> It's not like my problems have all been solved, or anything, but they've sure gotten
> more manageable since I started in the program. And that, for me, is the main thing
> about carrying the message to other co-dependents. I'd like to tell my friends,
> "look, things are going so crummy for you because you're co-dependent. Come
> with me to some meetings," but I don't have to, you know, because they see changes
> in me, and they ask me [things] like, "gee, Sherry, you're doing so great here lately.
> What'd you do?" And if they ask, I tell them, "well, have you ever heard of CoDA?"
> People figure, "well shoot, if it helps her so much, maybe I should try it." So, even
> though I haven't been in CoDA all that long, I can see the changes in me, and so
> can other people. So I just thank God for this program and for all of you.[20]

Sherry's example, as she sees it, acts as an inspiration and incentive
for friends not yet in the program. Her positive remarks serve in a similar capacity for those attending the ritual, emphasizing the value of CoDA
membership to newcomers and converts alike.

Sharers' roles are similarly but somewhat less strictly norm-governed.
They are expected to limit their comments to between three and five
minutes. (Several of the groups had found it necessary to assign an offi-

cial time-keeper for sharing, in order to ensure everyone an equal chance to talk.) They are also asked to wait until the appropriate time to share. Although this standard is relaxed to some extent for newcomers, there are limits to the indulgences. At one meeting, for example, about half-way through the normal discussions of "group business,"[21] an elderly woman announced that "I don't know how this all works, but I've got some things on my mind that I'd like to talk about." Members patiently explained to her that sharing came later in the meeting. The woman, as if she had not heard their explanations, began to recount her difficulties since her husband had left her. The members again explained that she would have ample time to discuss her concerns. Again, she pursued the topic. Finally, the group leader advised her that, "you can talk about this when we break up into small groups, but we really have to move on, here." The leader then asked the group whether "there [is] any other business before we go on to the treasurer's report," posing the question at some volume in order to be heard over the newcomer, who pressed on for a moment before settling back, apparently disgruntled, in her chair.

The mechanical norms governing such things as when and how long to share are ultimately subordinate to the more important work of learning how to share and what to say when doing so. These latter abilities, which entail applying co-dependency's symbolic order to one's own life, are more important because they are the means for making the passage from newcomer to convert. CoDA brochures designed to introduce newcomers to the group frequently combine these mechanical and substantive elements, not only generally encouraging sharing but also explaining its importance in language that simultaneously delineates key components of the co-dependent role. For example, a pamphlet on sharing instructs the reader that "we encourage people to begin [sharing] slowly and carefully...[because] most of us have been crippled by shame and fear, thus finding speaking among others, especially strangers, a very difficult task." Members are exhorted to share, but to do so at appropriate times, employing themes gleaned from the discourse. They are also warned to avoid certain practices:

> We attempt to share ourselves with "I" statements, avoiding talking about others or to others, using "you" statements. *We discourage "cross-talk" and "feedback" since as co-dependents we are working to achieve our own realities and break away [sic] from dependency upon what others think, feel, or advise....* We [also] make the caution and suggestion that information be communicated in language which is non-shaming, that is, avoids "should, ought to, must, have to," etc., and respects

the person's right to make his or her own choice, for example, "you might want to, what I did was, have you thought about?" etc. (Emphasis in the original)

Here again, technical information—"we discourage 'cross-talk'"— is interwoven with descriptions of what being co-dependent means and requires: "since we are working to...break away from dependency upon...others." Hemmed in by this array of mechanical and substantive injunctions, sharers, just as speakers, occupy a normatively governed position, a role, in a system of social interaction.

Converts must also learn the role of the listener as part of becoming co-dependent. Since most people at a CoDA ritual get to talk about their lives for five or six minutes at most, listening is a valued and necessary skill—not least because it fosters the capacity to identify with what one hears. Thus, newcomer brochures advise that

> [i]n order to listen well, we suggest answering two questions: 1) What is the speaker wanting from me? and, 2) What am I wanting from the speaker? In the first instance, we can sort out if a) the speaker is only wanting a "sounding board" with no response requested, b) he/she would request a sharing of our emotional responses to what was said, c) we might be asked for our opinion or thinking about a matter, or d) we might be asked to take some action. Usually, at meetings we are asked only to serve as "sounding boards" for the speaker or people sharing in discussion groups. Therefore, our concentration can focus on what we might be wanting from the speaker.[22]

CoDA's meeting roles provide a rough chronology (in reverse order from their presentation here) of the passage from newcomer to convert. Newcomers begin by listening, being systematically and repeatedly exposed to a general outline for what conversion to CoDA means and learning, through the example of others, how to frame their own life stories as co-dependents. Over time, those that embrace the convert role meet the biographical obligations of that role, learning to share their experiences in co-dependency's terms, framing their reconstructed life stories in terms of the discourse's master attribution scheme. Speakers, with their longer history as CoDA members, have mastered the uses of the discourse and continue to reconstruct and solidify their identities while at the same time socializing newcomers. Their stories, fully framed by co-dependency's symbolic structure, become the basis for new identifications, testimonials to the therapeutic efficacy of conversion.

* * * * *

To the extent that newcomers begin to actually appropriate CoDA's interpretations of their lives and the normative instructions adumbrated in official literature, they move from their initial curiosity and openness to new ideas toward actually becoming co-dependent. Plainly, not every newcomer *will* make that move. Some, and there is no way of knowing what proportion, will decide that CoDA is not for them. By the same token, some of those who *do* take steps toward becoming co-dependent will reconsider their decision as new evidence comes in; again, I do not know the numbers of these disaffected converts (although I did encounter one—a woman named Marge—in the course of my research, and I have included some of her observations about CoDA in chapter 8). Despite these exceptions, however, it is clear that CoDA, mainly through its modes of ritual enactment of the discourse of co-dependency, has a notable ability to attract and, as indicated by the very existence of the organization and the ways in which its members frame their lives, to convert newcomers. To use again Mary Douglas's concepts, CoDA's ritual enactments "create a reality," based upon and embodying co-dependency's symbolic order, and that reality "would be nothing without [those rituals]."[23]

Although CoDA members, as we have seen in this chapter, *are* subordinated to the biographical obligations that constitute the co-dependent role, as well as to the organization's mechanical and liturgical norms, the ultimate purpose of the group members is to support each other in the pursuit of recovery, and the recovery ethic, as chapter 7 will explain, is simply the ethic of self-actualization by another name. The reality that CoDA rituals symbolically affirm and enact is, at bottom, a liberation psychotherapy reality; the selves they create are in essence the selves of a liberation psychotherapy world.

Notes

1. Berger, *Invitation to Sociology*, 98.
2. The historical record is quite clear about the ways in which the rise of industrial capitalism profoundly affected the shape and function of intermediate institutions; see, for example, Ryan, *Cradle of the Middle Class;* Johnson, *A Shopkeeper's Millennium.*
3. To go beyond the family and other mediating institutions would ultimately be to venture into the realm of social and political, rather than clinical and psychotherapeutic, action. One common way of talking about this issue, characteristic especially of family systems psychotherapies (to which co-dependency owes key aspects of its logic, as we have seen), has been to argue that by treating the family the therapist is simultaneously treating society, as well. This was the implicit point to John Bradshaw's assertion that, from the vantage point of family

systems theory, "[t]he family itself is a symptom of society at large" (*Bradshaw On: The Family*, 27). Working with the same logic, but in a reverse direction, Anne Wilson Schaef has observed that "[w]e need to see that maybe even the political process as we know it is a form of addiction" (*Escape from Intimacy*, 44). Russell Jacoby, in a critique of family systems psychotherapy, has pointed out that, generally, in the course of applying family systems theory, "[t]he facts discovered during the analysis, in suggesting that the family itself is victimized, confess that family therapy is insufficient.... The absurdity of this approach is based on the illusion that the therapist can 'reconvene' the whole network of which the patient is a part, and secondly, even if it could be done, that these numbers of people could be 'treated.' The question, of course, is why stop with thirty-five people, since they are evidently involved with another seventy, and so on. The implicit logic," Jacoby continues, "suggests the project of gathering all the members of society in one room, as if the antagonisms could be ironed out in the give and take of a group discussion. Objective conditions are refined into 'bad vibes.' At times, [family systems therapists suggest] that the entire world is an expanded family group.... Truths adequate for family therapy degenerate into naive political pronouncements on 'East–West relations' passed off as a family tiff" (Russell Jacoby, *Social Amnesia: A Critique of Conformist Psychology from Adler to Laing* [Boston: Beacon Press, 1975], 137–38). In addition to the points Jacoby raises, the net result of ignoring these larger and more powerful institutions is a tendency to define psychological health in terms of their requirements. Melody Beattie, for example, in a discussion about the ways in which co-dependents can focus more attention upon themselves (about which we will see more, in chapter 7), seems to define psychological well-being as a function of the ability to consume. Says Beattie, "If we [co-dependents] have a problem, make its solution our goal.... Do we want something? A new waterbed, a red sweater, longer hair, longer nails? Turn it into a goal. Do we want to go someplace— Europe, South America, the circus? Do we want a loving, healthy relationship? Turn that into a goal. Is there something we've always wanted to do—go to school, work for a particular company, make $40,000 a year? Turn it into a goal" (*Codependent No More*, 157). John Bradshaw has revealed a similar penchant. As David Rieff notes, "Bradshaw writes in *Homecoming: Reclaiming and Championing Your Inner Child* that he found he had to balance the demands of his new celebrity with his obligations to his 'inner child' and so 'chose some things my inner child likes. For the last few years, we always fly first class'" (David Rieff, "Victims, All? Recovery, Co-dependency, and the Art of Blaming Somebody Else," *Harper's*, October 1991, 56). As I will discuss in the conclusion, however, it is possible to make too much out of such comments as Bradshaw's, and in doing so, to miss the more important aspects of co-dependency's creation and selection.

4. Beattie, *Co-Dependent No More*, 170.
5. The phenomenon of conversion can be conceptualized in a variety of different ways. Obviously, it entails radical personal change. But there is a range of possible changes in the self that fall short of what the term "conversion" connotes. Conversion, after all, is only one type of personal change, and an extreme type at that. Thus, scholars of conversion invoke a variety of concepts to distinguish conversion from other, less-encompassing forms of change. Although it is beyond the scope of this study to delve into the nuances of this scholarship, I note here the most significant variations on conversion and refer the reader to the following sources. A. D. Nock, *Conversion* (New York: Oxford University Press,

1933), for one, contrasts conversion with "adhesion," which refers to the use of new beliefs to supplement rather than to supplant old beliefs. Another variant has been called "alternation," which represents anything less than a "complete disruption" in people's prior beliefs; see W. C. Shepherd, "Conversion and Adhesion," in *Religious Change and Continuity: Sociological Perspectives,* ed. H. M. Johnson (San Francisco: Jossey-Bass, 1979), 251–63; R. V. Travisano, "Alternation and Conversion as Qualitatively Different Transformations," in *Social Psychology through Symbolic Interaction,* ed. G. P. Stone and H. A. Farberman (Waltham, Mass.: Ginn-Blaisdell, 1970), 594–606. "Consolidation," which is the adoption of two contradictory worldviews, is discussed in D. F. Gordon, "The Jesus People: An Identity Synthesis," *Urban Life and Culture* 3 (1974): 159–78. Finally, "regeneration" denotes the embrace of a belief system that had been previously denied or not taken seriously; see Nock, *Conversion*; E. T. Clark, *The Psychology of Religious Awakening* (New York: MacMillan, 1929); K. Lang and G. E. Lang, *Collective Dynamics* (New York: Crowell, 1961). My own discussion is grounded in the belief that breaking down personal change into a series of gradations on a conceptual continuum, although undeniably helpful in some ways, unnecessarily confuses the phenomenon of conversion—particularly as it bears upon the co-dependency phenomenon. In a recent summary and synthesis of the plethora of studies on and conceptions of conversion, David A. Snow and Richard Machalek offer an alternative way of thinking about what the phenomenon entails. My discussion follows much of what those authors have to say; see David A. Snow and Richard Machalek, "The Sociology of Conversion," *Annual Review of Sociology* 10 (1984): 167–90, and "The Convert as a Social Type," in *Sociological Theory, 1983,* ed. Randall Collins (San Francisco: Jossey-Bass, 1983), 259–89.

6. See Snow and Machalek, "The Sociology of Conversion."
7. Ibid., 173.
8. Ibid., especially 173. Biographical reconstruction has been long and widely recognized as a central feature of the conversion experience. See also William James, *The Varieties of Religious Experience* (New York: Longman, 1902); Berger, *Invitation to Sociology;* T. Shibutani, *Society and Personality* (Englewood Cliffs, N.J.: Prentice-Hall, 1961); Kenneth Burke, *Permanence and Change* (Indianapolis, Ind.: Bobbs-Merrill, 1965); Berger and Luckmann, *The Social Construction of Reality;* R. K. Jones, "Paradigm Shifts and Identity Theory: Alternation as a Form of Identity Management," in *Identity and Religion,* ed. H. Mol (Beverly Hills, Calif.: Sage, 1978), 59–82; D. F. Gordon, "The Jesus People"; R. V. Travisano, "Alternation and Conversion."
9. Snow and Machalek, "The Sociology of Conversion," 173.
10. Ibid., 174. Among these rhetorical indicators, Snow and Machalek also include what they call *"embracement of the convert role, "* as reflected by the extent to which the universe of discourse "influences the convert's orientation in all interactive situations." I have not incorporated this indicator, principally because it seems to me to entail clarifications where none are really needed. The principal point of clarification, as I see it, is that conceptualizing "embracement of the convert role" as an *indicator* of conversion at least partially conflates indicators and what they indicate: that is, biographical reconstruction, the acquisition of a master attribution scheme, and the suspension of analogical reasoning would in and of themselves seem to be indicators that a person has "embraced the convert role." Certainly this is the case with co-dependency. In fact, in CoDA, these are

the capacities that qualify and define the members *as* co-dependents. A second point of clarification flows from and is interwoven with the first. Snow and Machalek observe that once a person has embraced the convert role, the universe of discourse "influences the convert's orientation in all interactive situations" (ibid.). This overlooks the extent to which the convert's orientation is itself influenced by the "interactive situation." In other words, people learn what it is to be co-dependent, and they *become* co-dependent, in the structured, "interactive situations" that characterize CoDA meetings.

11. Berger, *Invitation to Sociology,* 98. As chapter 4 discussed at some length, Berger's point has been repeatedly affirmed.

12. In many ways, the significance of ritual was a constant theme in Goffman's work, but it is especially well expressed in *The Presentation of Self in Everyday Life* and *Interaction Ritual* (Garden City, N.Y.: Doubleday/Anchor, 1967).

13. Douglas, *Purity and Danger,* 62, 182.

14. Both Steven Lukes and Eric W. Rothenbuhler have argued that those working in the Durkheimian and neo-Durkheimian traditions have overemphasized the integrative functions of ritual at the societal and cultural level and ignored the degree to which ritual also provides coherence and solidarity to subcultural groups that may be opposed to the larger status quo. Lukes, writing nearly twenty years ago, argued that ritual can work *against* integration into conventional society—that it "can serve to integrate and strengthen subordinate social groups" (Steven Lukes, "Political Ritual and Social Integration," 299). More recently, Rothenbuhler, in a study of a turn-of-the-century labor strike in Lawrence, Massachusetts, has argued that conflicts at the larger societal level can produce integration and ritual solidarity among groups protesting conventional practices; see Eric W. Rothenbuhler, "The Liminal Fight: Mass Strikes as Ritual and Interpretation," in *Durkheimian Sociology: Cultural Studies,* ed. Jeffrey C. Alexander (New York: Cambridge University Press, 1988), 66–89.

15. In what follows, all materials are taken from a photocopied "newcomers packet" made available on the literature table at the meetings (Co-Dependent's Anonymous, Inc., Phoenix, Ariz, 1988). The newcomers packets contain all the formalized canonical readings quoted below. These readings have all been reproduced in Appendix B.

16. In official subculture literature, the first letters of these words are almost invariably capitalized. Whether consciously used or not, this is a significant rhetorical flourish that clearly points to the reverence in which members of the subculture hold the twelve-step method, or "The Program." Moreover, among the California CoDA groups (and, in my experience, only there), it is relatively common to simply say "Program," rather than "*The* Program." (For example, a Los Angeles member would say, "my life has become so much better since I came to Program.") It is an instructive usage. Indeed, dropping the article "the" in this way has important implications, suggesting that differentiating the Twelve Steps from other "programs" by calling it *the* program is superfluous, redundant. There is, in this, a connotation of monotheistic religions, which also find the use of the article "the" to be redundant: Saying "The God" is an absurd usage when one believes that there is, after all, only one.

17. CoDA National Service Conference-Approved Literature, "Attending Meetings, Three Aspects of CoDA Meetings" (brochure, copyright 1989), instructs newcomers that "[t]here are three aspects to gaining the most benefit from attending CoDA meetings: speaking, sharing, and listening."

18. "[S]peakers are asked to share how their lives are now—the qualitative improvements, the difficulties they continue to encounter, how the Promises are coming true in their lives, and, perhaps, the dreams and visions for the future that they are now able to build, thanks to their recovery. It is hoped that speakers will have spent enough time in the Program to generally qualify in these areas" (CoDA, "Attending Meetings"). Longevity, of course, is relative: "Old timers" in CoDA can have, at most, five years of experience; most have substantially less. At the meetings this study observes, membership was most often measured in months. The "Promises" to which the brochure refers are the rewards that converts will begin to realize by "working the program." CoDA reprints them directly from pages 83–84 of "The Big Book" (as *Alcoholics Anonymous: The Story of How Many Thousands of Men and Women Have Recovered from Alcoholism,* the main AA text, has been nicknamed): "We are going to know a new freedom and a new happiness. We will not regret the past nor wish to shut the door on it. We will comprehend the word serenity and we will know peace. No matter how far down the scale we have gone, we will see how our experience can benefit others. That feeling of uselessness and self-pity will disappear. We will lose interest in selfish things and gain interest in our fellows. Self-seeking will slip away. Our whole attitude and outlook upon life will change. Fear of people and of economic insecurity will leave us. We will intuitively know how to handle situations which used to baffle us. We will suddenly realize that God is doing for us what we could not do for ourselves. Are these extravagant promises? We think not. They are being fulfilled among us—sometimes quickly, sometimes slowly. They will always materialize if we work for them." (It is worth mentioning that in California meetings, members say "We think not" as a group—a clear expression of solidarity.)

19. Quoted passages are from CoDA, "Attending Meetings."

20. The theme of attracting new members rather than proselytizing is taken from AA's Twelve Traditions, as discussed in chapter 5. See appendix B, "The Twelve Traditions of Co-Dependent's Anonymous," especially traditions 10, 11, and 12.

21. This section is given over to such things as regional and national CoDA-related announcements, the group treasurer's report, and upcoming CoDA events (dances, hikes, picnics, and so on).

22. All of the preceding quoted material, unless otherwise indicated, was from CoDA, "Attending Meetings."

23. Douglas, *Purity and Danger,* 62.

7

Recovery

As we have seen, as a symbolic system, liberation psychotherapy maintains that conventional society and culture's imposition of behavioral norms translates into the standardization of selves and denies each person's unique qualities. This position is difficult to quarrel with, even were one inclined to do so. Social institutions do, indeed, impose normative standards, and these standards do, indeed, proscribe the range of individual preference. These, moreover, are universal phenomena: The observations hold not only for midcentury U.S. culture but for every culture, every society, in every historical epoch.

But what liberation psychotherapy has always overlooked is that social institutions only exist *as* institutions—that is, as *repeated patterns of behavior*—by imposing standardized behavioral expectations. Behavioral regularities born of imposed norms are not what institutions *do*, it is what they *are*. To tell people that the collective imposition of norms upon the self must be rejected, then, is to do away with social institutions altogether, or to suggest that it is possible to do so.

I am not suggesting that this is what liberation psychotherapy had in mind, exactly. I am suggesting, though, that this is the result of its logic as a symbolic system *when one follows that logic all the way to its conclusions;* and liberation psychotherapy has never devoted much theoretical legwork to working out that logic. If abiding by institutional norms becomes entirely a matter of voluntarism, whimsy, or even caprice, the institutions themselves can exist in, at best, a perpetually malleable state, as institutions chiefly in name.

It has never been entirely clear how institutions in a liberation psychotherapy world were to exist at all or how they were to be maintained as stable patterns of conduct—an uncertainty that pertains especially, as I have noted, to such informal, mediating institutions as friendship, kinship, courtship, and community. How might some form of enduring community be possible without violating the ethic of self-actualization? How can mediating institutions be sustained if the subordination of self to communal purpose and understanding is understood as the cause of psychological sickness? How is it possible, given these baseline presuppositions, to sustain a pattern of relatively intimate social relationships?

It is these problems, I have argued, that liberation psychotherapy has heretofore been unable to resolve; the same problems that one hears in CoDA testimonials, infused as they are with such tacit questions as "With whom do I share a common symbolic heritage? With whom can I come together for mutually understood purposes, on a reliable and recurrent basis? With whom do I have enduring social relationships?" These, ultimately, are the problems to which co-dependency, as a reformed version of liberation psychotherapy, offers at least a partial solution.

Co-dependency is a discourse of reform, and so it is chiefly concerned with the imperfect realization of liberation psychotherapy, the symbolic order with which it agrees and from which it was derived. The aim of co-dependency, then, is to resolve relational and identity-related problems in ways that accord with liberation psychotherapy's central premises. The new theory of addiction provides this relational solution, as we have seen. Because the sickness is an "addiction," co-dependents can and do come together in twelve-step groups. But co-dependency's converts must, of course, go beyond the "admission" that they are "sick": They must become well, too, and being well—in the liberation therapy version of reality—is being self-actualized. Recovery is principally a matter of learning and learning to live by the ethic of self-actualization. The solution that co-dependency discourse offers to the dilemmas of liberation psychotherapy, in short, involves making self-actualization itself the purpose of mediating institutions: The common cause uniting CoDA members is their struggle to become self-actualizing individuals, chiefly in the world *outside* of CoDA.

The Recovery Ethic

Throughout the co-dependency corpus, the message that is repeatedly emphasized is that the self must always come first: Individuals must *either* take precedence over restrictive social conventions, *or* they will be "sick." The discourse expresses this message through two complementary notions: that the healthy self is an ever-unfolding entity and that everyone's principal moral responsibility is to themselves. Although it has never before enjoyed the widespread public acceptance it does currently, this "protean" or "impulsive self" nonetheless has a lengthy lineage.[1] Presented in varying degrees of intellectual complexity and sophistication, this conception has threaded its way throughout the history of ideas, appearing at one moment in romanticism, in another, in Friedrich Nietzsche's thought under the rubric of the transvaluation of the self, and again as the self-reliant individual of Ralph Waldo Emerson's essays and Walt Whitman's "Song of Myself." In the 1960s and 1970s, Carl Rogers, Abraham Maslow, and other liberation psychotherapists resurrected the same idea, expressing it in terms of the self as "a process," perpetually moving into and out of fluid and nonbinding social performances.

The widespread existence of such a self requires public acceptance of a conception of moral obligations in which each person must be his or her own principal priority. This, of course, is liberation psychotherapy's understanding of moral obligation. The recovery ethic faithfully echoes this conception, asserting that if process addicts are to recover, they must follow their own moral compasses, irrespective of social expectations and judgments. Subordination to the demands, opinions, and estimations of others is an obstacle to psychological well-being, a foe that must be vanquished.

Reflecting these premises, co-dependency frames psychological health in terms of people's feelings *toward or about themselves:* The quality, the healthiness, of all social relationships depends upon a good "relationship to oneself." In keeping with contemporary therapeutic argot, the discourse describes this relationship to oneself in terms of "high self-esteem" (which is used interchangeably with self-regard, self-worth, self-respect, and self-love). Recovery is geared toward helping co-dependents to create this new relationship to themselves—toward bolstering their self-esteem and getting them in touch with their natural benevolence, their true selves. Co-dependency manuals are packed with prescriptions for accomplishing that goal, and all of the prescriptions emphasize the self's autonomy from cultural and social constraint. Chief among these prescriptions is "detachment." According to Melody Beattie, the notion of detachment "is based on the premises that each person is responsible for himself, that we can't solve problems that aren't ours to solve, and that worrying doesn't help." Recovering process addicts, she goes on, should recognize that they "can't do anything to control... [other] people"; as such, they should simply have "faith—in [them]-selves, in God, in other people, and in the natural order and destiny of things in this world." There will, Beattie allows, inevitably be temptations to turn the focus outward again, but a "good rule of thumb is: You need to detach most when it seems the least likely or possible thing to do." The recovering co-dependent, then, should "[d]etach. Detach in love, or detach in anger, but strive for detachment. I know it's difficult, but it will become easier with practice. If you can't let go completely, try to 'hang on loose.' Relax. Sit back. Now, take a deep breath. The focus is on you."[2]

The premise that the healthy self must cultivate a capacity for detachment is informed by the ethic of self-actualization. "Healthiness," as it must be in a world in which cultural constraint and self-denial are symbolized as the principal causes of psychological sickness, is here a function of individuation and unfettered self-exploration. Thus, as Beattie says, detachment from others implies a concomitant "focus on" oneself. More than simply focusing on themselves, though, recovering co-dependents must learn "to love ourselves and make a commitment to ourselves." Guided by these premises, Beattie sees it as a sign of her own recovery that "I'm starting to think about and consider what *I* want and need" first, before considering others' wants and needs (emphasis in the original).[3] By placing her own wishes ahead of others, she has begun to master the necessary arts of what she calls "self-care"; she has taken the first essential steps toward constituting herself as a normal and moral self in the world that liberation psychotherapy would bring fully into being.

Beattie's reference to "mak[ing] a commitment to ourselves" again highlights both the reversal of ultimate purposes that underlies the "triumph of the therapeutic" in U.S. culture and the degree to which the individual's right to absolute autonomy from external constraint is at the heart of that reversal. It is also important to recognize--for reasons that chapter 8 will explain at some length—that this is not a retreat from morality but a reconceptualization of it. In the cultural shift from the ethic of self-denial to the ethic of self-actualization, the moral language describing the means and techniques of conduct has not changed; such seemingly ascetic themes as commitment and hard work (albeit work on oneself) continue to be invoked. But the goals of such efforts have changed. Indeed, they have been reversed: Moral action is not understood in terms of a commitment that transcends self-interest but, rather, in terms of a commitment *to* self-interest.

It is with these convictions in mind that all of the co-dependency manuals emphasize such attitudes as detachment, self-love, self-care, and commitment to oneself, portraying them as pathways to recovery, the keys to psychological health. For example, Robert Subby tells his readers that "we must stop trying to build up our own self-worth through the caretaking of others" and begin, instead, to focus on "the things that really count, e.g., self-respect, self-esteem, self-worth, and self-love." So, too, Sharon Wegscheider-Cruse maintains that converts must and, in recovery, will learn to "reprogram our out-dated thinking with affirmations, with messages that promote our self-worth." Seconding Beattie's calls for detachment, Wegscheider-Cruse goes on to assure recovering process addicts that, with practice, "[w]e will learn...to move away from relationships that bring us down, that thwart our self-worth."[4]

In what is the clearest expression of the significance that co-dependency accords to establishing a positive relationship to oneself, John Bradshaw explains that "[a]ll true love begins with self-love." Co-dependents, he says, can cultivate this self-love by, among other things, saying, "*I love myself. I will accept myself unconditionally...out loud and often*" (emphasis in the original).[5] Recounting his own initiation into this view, Bradshaw goes on to say that

> [I] remember vividly the first time I truly accepted and loved myself unconditionally. It was awesome! I later read a book by Gay Hendricks where he talked about the same thing. (See *Learning to Love Yourself* by Gay Hendricks.) He described how he would confront people in his workshops with the simple statement, "Will you love yourself for that?"...At first...I was taken aback. Surely there are things that we do that are unworthy of love. As Gay went on and on, asking the person if he could love himself no matter what he did or didn't do, I remember [*sic*] that our love needs to be for who we are, not for what we do. You are lovable, period.... Understanding the distinction between being and doing is one of the great learnings of my life.... Choosing to love yourself is a free choice. It is a simple decision. The alternatives are a shame-based lifestyle with disastrous consequences. I'm encouraging you to say, "I love myself," to proclaim that you love and accept yourself unconditionally. If you act on such a belief repeatedly you will grow more deeply self-loving and self-valuing.... If I love myself, I will live in reality.[6]

As with Melody Beattie's pronouncements, Bradshaw's advice in the foregoing remarks underscores the changes that have taken place in U.S. culture over the past generation. Self-loving will, indeed, help people to "live in reality," as Bradshaw says; but the statement is true principally because the reality itself has changed. Forty years ago, the sentiments Bradshaw expresses in the just-quoted passage would have been more likely to elicit public condemnation than to have spawned a series of best-selling books, special broadcasts on PBS, and—along with his colleagues' like-minded tomes—a national self-help movement. The importance of Bradshaw's remarks, then, is that they so clearly illustrate the depths of recent cultural changes. In a culture in which the ethic of self-actualization has become widely accepted as a moral philosophy, what would have not so long ago been defined as simple selfishness is now not selfishness at all. Rather, it is now the only truly ethical course of action. Self-love, readers are advised, is not a pathological condition, as the old rules would have defined it. To the contrary, self-love engenders a new way of relating to others and a new way of being in the world; it is a way of constituting a moral self.[7]

Despite the magnitude of cultural change, the recovery ethic's conceptualization of the self, and of what it means to be a moral person, skirts close enough to what seems to be a radical, even a potentially dangerous, relativism that even a believer such as Bradshaw acknowledges that "at first, [he] was taken aback" by such ideas. Thus, the advocates take considerable pains to assure their charges (and, one assumes, their critics) that there is ultimately a higher and more noble motive to the self-absorption the recovery ethic calls for. For example, Beattie, outlining these higher aims, explains that "[l]oving and accepting ourselves unconditionally doesn't mean that we negate our need to change or grow. It's how we enable ourselves to change and grow.... If we love ourselves, we become enabled to love others." Appearances notwithstanding, she goes on, "Having a love affair with yourself...isn't narcissistic or indulgent. It's the one thing I can do that most helps me and others too."[8] In such assurances, co-dependency's architects in essence espouse a view of morality that, as noted in earlier chapters, might be called "therapeutic utilitarianism," a curious mixture of the ideas of Jeremy Bentham and Carl Rogers: Each person's pursuit of emotional and experiential self-interest will produce the greatest good for the greatest number of people. Underlying and supporting this moral calculus is liberation psychotherapy's view of human nature. Guided by the assumption of benevolence, co-dependency's architects assume —as Maslow and Rogers assumed in regard to self-actualization—that recovery will produce positive results because the true self is an immanently moral being.

Whether one agrees or disagrees with, celebrates or excoriates, the conception of psychological health that informs this recovery ethic, there can be no mistake about the self that recovery aims to create. The path to normality in co-dependency, as in liberation psychotherapy, is paved with the self's progressive emancipation from social control, its liberation from emotional repression. As the next section demonstrates, the converts fully understand what the ethic requires of them.

Putting the Ethic to Work: Recovery among the Converts

Understood solely in terms of the self's right to autonomy from external demands, the recovery ethic—which is essentially the ethic of self-actualization—engenders something of a zero-sum game, in which the self becomes the only relevant concern, and others' demands or expectations, others' worldviews, become no more and no less than signs of their own sickness. Given such guidelines, it is not hard to understand how CoDA converts conclude that extrication and autonomy from all externally imposed requirements (save those involved in being codependent) are their principal tasks.

That they have indeed arrived at this conclusion is repeatedly evident in the testimonials at CoDA rituals. Converts tend to conceive of their social roles outside of CoDA as moments in an overall process of self-actualization, performances to which they are not bound and in and through which they can satisfy the obligation to become fully self-actualizing. Frequently, this obligation was expressed under the rubric of "doing what's right for me"—as it was in the comments of a convert named Elaine. Describing an impending separation from her husband, Elaine explained,

> This is just a separation, for now, but now that it's happening, all of a sudden he's [her husband] been real sweet to me, again. Which he hasn't been in quite awhile, frankly. But he's doing all these nice things, and I'm like, "well fine, do this stuff if you want to, but don't think it's going to change my mind or anything, because I'm still moving out." It's just something I've got to do for me, right now. I'm just not real happy being married at this point in my life, and I need to be by myself. This is about me, not him.

Elaine's remarks resound with the constitutive themes of the ethic of self-actualization and, as such, reveal the recovery ethic's indebtedness to those themes. They also provide some insight into how liberation psychotherapy has worked against the stability of social relationships and institutions. This impact has been evident from the first attempts, in the countercultural communes of the 1960s and 1970s, to organize social life around liberation psychotherapy's principles. As Rosabeth Moss Kanter concluded, the communes were by and large unsuccessful because the ethic of self-actualization "places the person's own growth above concern for social reform, political and economic change, or the welfare of the community. The person is free to leave when no longer satisfied; his involvement with the group is limited."[9] Although the concept of process addiction partially solves this conundrum, successfully bringing co-dependents together beneath a rhetorically constructed communal purpose, their group purposes are nonetheless steadfastly individualistic and dominated by the drive for full autonomy.

The point here is emphatically not that people should "stay with their marriages" no matter what. Not only do Elaine's comments not provide sufficient information to support such pronouncements, but making them at all is not the purview of a sociological analysis. What is far more important and instructive is to see how profoundly liberation psychotherapy frames people's understandings of what they are doing, what they need to do, and why. Elaine's observations reveal this framing mechanism at work. Her comments invoke the key propositions of the ethic of self-actualization. Being one's own first priority, for example, is reflected in her judgment that, whatever her husband may want or may try to do to set things right between them, "I'm still moving out," because "it's just something I've got to do for me, right now." The same basic principle is echoed in her view that "[t]his is about me, not him." Her statement "I'm just not real happy being married at this point in my life" resonates not only with the obligation to be one's own chief interest but also with the view of the healthy self as a process, moving into and out of social roles as one's sense of well-being dictates: With regard to the first, to continue to perform the social role of "the wife" despite dissatisfactions with that role would place her well-being on a lower priority than her husband's; and with regard to the second, subordinating herself to external expectations would bring the process of self-realization to a halt. According to the recovery ethic, neither of these options is acceptable. Given that Elaine finds marital life dissatisfying and constraining, to stay in her marriage is to stay sick. Further illustrating the same themes, Elaine's report that she is not happy being married "at this point in [her] life" and that the separation is something she needs to do "right now" suggests both that perhaps later she may again be happy to be married and that she had been happy to be married at an earlier point.

Again, the point is neither to praise nor to criticize Elaine or other CoDA members. Rather, what is important is to see that as she and her fellow converts understand the recovery ethic, entering, performing, and exiting social roles are all courses of action whose merits depend exclusively upon their contribution to the individual's continual unfolding and sense of well-being.

Julie, still more explicitly honoring the obligation that each individual must be his or her own main concern, described "where I'm at in recovery," noting that "I'm now to the point where I can honestly say I'm having a love affair with myself, and that's because of this program. I don't feel a lot of shame about things anymore. I'm enough. Every day, I'm enough. And there's so much freedom in that."

Such sentiments resound with the discourse's emphasis on the principles of unconditional self-love and having a positive relationship with oneself; indeed, Julie's self-to-self relationship is so positive that, as she says, she is "having a love affair with myself." Reflecting the fit between liberation psychotherapy's symbolic order and CoDA's group purposes, not only does Julie love herself unconditionally, but, as she went on to say, her friends in the program do, as well. "I've got so many good friends in CoDA who don't judge me and who love me just as I am." The group, then, affirms Julie's new relationship with herself rather than offering suggestions or criticisms, as nonbelievers would, or making demands, as conventional society and culture would.

In her subsequent comments, Julie reveals that she has also embraced the complementary principles of transitory attachment and self-transvaluation:

> I found my mom in the shower with another woman when I was in sixth grade. She tried to tell me that she didn't know the other woman was gay, but even at that age I knew that was bullshit. Now, though, mom admits she's a lesbian, and I'm to the point where I'm okay with that. She says she's just waiting for me to realize that I'm a lesbian, too, but I'm just like, "give me a break." If it turns out that I am gay, it'll be because *I* choose to be, not because my mom's waiting for me to admit it. And right now, today, I choose to be heterosexual.

The processual self, by definition, must be free to act upon its own preferences. Reflecting this correlation, the operative term in Julie's remarks is "choose"; and the act of choosing, when guided by the right to absolute autonomy, is a matter of whatever serves her sense of personal well-being in any given situation: "If it turns out that I am gay, it'll be because *I* chose to be." The significance Julie attaches to this understanding of choice is also clear in her observation that, in recovery, she has mastered the arts of detachment and self-care: "Now I know, because of this program [CoDA], that I can wear what I want, and do what I want, and if that bothers somebody that's not my problem. It's their problem, and they can do whatever they need to do to take care of it."

Kim was inspired by Julie's remarks:

> Wow. Thanks so much, Julie. I really needed to hear that, because I'm not used to talking about sexuality—especially in public—because it's always been a shame-based issue for me. And hearing people talk, like you just did, is helping me to get past that and to open up. I really appreciated what you said about women's attractiveness. I'm not lesbian or anything, but I've always found certain women very desirable and attractive and I always felt so ashamed when I felt that way. But I've always resented not feeling free enough to say that a woman is very sexy or beautiful.

For Kim, just as for Julie, the pivot upon which recovery turns is freedom of choice and the self's right to autonomy from social control. In the past, she has been restrained by the repressive rules of mainstream culture, but

> [n]ow, I reserve the right to choose whether or not I might act on that. Right now, I choose men, and I prefer heterosexual relationships, but I might change my mind in the future. I really want and like that freedom, and I don't want to give that up because "society" [making quotation marks with her fingers] says I have to.

Guided by the ethic of self-actualization, Julie and Kim claim for themselves the prerogatives of unalloyed self-determination and equate self-denial, construed in terms of a submission to external standards, with a repressive ideology from which they are at long last recovering. Since getting into recovery, they now can do what they want to do without so much as a by-your-leave from "society."

Attempting to Bridge the Ethical Divide

The therapeuticization of U.S. culture has played itself out to a significant degree along generational lines. Those who have adopted liberation psychotherapy's truths have embraced principles that all but completely reverse those held by their parents and earlier generations.

It is difficult to imagine, for example, an exchange such as the one we just saw between Kim and Julie taking place forty years ago.

The data documenting these cultural changes, however, reveal trends, and these trends, in turn, reveal probabilities, rather than hard and fast rules: Not all baby boomers have embraced the ethic of self-actualization, not all parents of baby boomers subscribe to an ethic of self-denial. The "generation gap" that seems to underlie the rise of liberation psychotherapy is, at a more fundamental level, a moral and ethical gap separating those who subscribe to the ethic of self-denial and those adhering to the ethic of self-actualization.[10] In light of this gap, and in light of co-dependency's fealty to the ethic of self-actualization, it is not surprising that a number of CoDA members told stories that reveal the difficulties involved in bridging what is essentially an ethical divide.

As we have seen, CoDA promises its adherents healthier and more fulfilling relationships. Many converts, in pursuit of this general goal, attempt to reorganize their pre-CoDA relationships, hoping to align them in accordance with their new understandings. Often, however, these older relationships lie on the opposite side of the ethical divide, where people speak a different tongue and live a different reality. Nowhere is this ethical translation problem more apparent than in the converts' numerous stories of their dealings with their "emotionally unavailable fathers"—a phrase, as we have seen earlier, that in CoDA serves as a synonym for abandonment. Given the limited and largely disciplinary parental role to which the baby boom generation's fathers were usually assigned, they are the ones the members most commonly (though not exclusively) described as "critical," "shaming," and "emotionally unavailable." Some converts attempt to reconstruct father-child interactions in the present, seeking to place those relationships "on a feeling level" and, hence, on what is understood to be a more authentic and moral footing. As Duane, in the following example, discovered, some fathers appear reluctant to engage in these efforts to reconstruct relationships along liberation psychotherapy guidelines.

Introducing himself as "co-dependent and just fucking pissed off," Duane said his life was not going well on several fronts. He was in the midst of a contested and ugly divorce and was also on the verge of losing his business. But these were not the problems that he wanted to share with his fellow converts. As he explained,

I got a call at the office this week telling me that my dad's in the hospital. They're very wary about any kind of optimism for his future. Heart surgery on top of heart surgery. And I haven't been to see him for a couple of weeks, so I felt guilty about that. But, I'm *really* having a hard time with guilt about my feelings about him possibly dying.

Duane went on to describe his father as "a rageaholic, really. Controlling, judgmental. I could never do anything right, you know?" As such, he said, they had always had a troubled and at times hostile relationship. Because of this stormy history, Duane now felt extreme ambivalence about his father's illness: "Part of me doesn't want him to die, and part of me says, 'oh, go ahead and die, you son of a bitch.' And I feel horrible when I say that or think that, but God, we've had such a shitty relationship my whole life."

This ambivalence was only deepened by Duane's efforts, prior to his father's hospitalization, to establish a different foundation for their relationship:

I'd look at him and think, "who *are* you, anyway?" So closed-off, so critical. [So he sat down with his father one day and] went through this long diatribe about what I feel towards him, and what I'd hoped for in our relationship, and wanting to get to be better friends or something. And I get finished saying all of this, and he nods at me, looks at his watch, and says, "oh, the news is on," and turns on the television. And I'm thinking, "well, fuck it," you know? Like I never even opened my mouth. But I still want to get through to the guy! And even if I don't get through to him, I think "you're still my old man. Don't die."

By "getting through" to his father, Duane plainly means reestablishing the basis for their relationship, reorganizing it along lines more in keeping with the convictions and symbolic logic of CoDA and the recovering co-dependent. But his father appears, at best, uninterested. His only acknowledgment, as Duane says, that the project had been put on the table at all was a nod, followed by the non sequitur, "oh, the news is on"—as if he had been politely attending to the concerns of someone speaking in a foreign language or a badly broken English rather than listening to his son. That apparent lack of comprehension runs both ways. Duane, again, looks at his father and thinks, "who *are* you?"

But perhaps "disinterest" is not the right word to describe Duane's father. Given the ethical divide they must bridge, and the alien tongues with which they must speak, it is more accurate to say that Duane and his father are guided by different visions of what men are supposed to be like, of what father-son relationships are all about, and of how people ought to act. Rather than a story about a failure or an unwillingness to communicate, Duane's anecdote is a portrait of two men trying to communicate in an ethical language that only one of them understands. Speaking to one another across an ethical divide, they remain enigmas to one another.

Another instance, in which this ethical Tower of Babel was both cross-cultural and cross-generational, reveals the breadth of the divide and the problems of translation even more clearly. Jamal, a first-generation Arab-American (one of only three non-Caucasian CoDA members I encountered), was "at a point in recovery where I'm trying to understand myself and my past better"; "and I really don't know my father, so I've been trying to get inside of him a little bit—asking him questions about himself and what he thinks. He just doesn't understand, or something. It's like he doesn't know what I'm talking about."

Past conversations with his father, Jamal said, "have been about really superficial stuff...how much money I'm making, how my career or my marriage is going." Faithful to co-dependency's distinction between what people do and who they really are (itself derived from liberation psychotherapy's true self–false self distinction), Jamal views such concerns as something separate from himself, not really about him. Marriage, career, and the like are mainstream cultural roles and, as a recovering co-dependent, Jamal sees such roles as shot full of arbitrary obligations and synonymous with artifice. From the perspective of a convert, then, something must change if their relationship will ever approach an adequate level of healthiness and authenticity. Just as Duane had tried to do, Jamal attempted to break through these barriers:

> I ask him what his and momma's dreams are and were, and it's always "we wanted you [their children] to have good lives, stable careers, happy families, good homes." And I say, "yes, but what about *you*? what did you want?" And he says, "I just told you." And I ask him, "yes, but didn't you have something you wanted just for you? You know—to climb Mount Everest, or go sailing, or something?" And he just looked at me like he really couldn't understand what I was saying. It's like there's nothing really any deeper than that to him.

Although it was only implicit in Duane's portrait of his father, it is all too clear that Jamal's father defines himself and his own well-being in terms of others: His dreams were for good lives for his children. When seen through the lenses of the ethic of self-actualization, this seemingly utter subordination of self to others becomes a sure path to sickness or, at the least, to superficiality: "It's like there's nothing really any deeper than that to him." Nonetheless, Jamal said that he wanted to keep trying, because

> maybe there's more to him than that. Maybe I just haven't asked the right questions or used the right words. I was going to just give up, but then I thought "no, I'm not going to let him off the hook just yet." If it turns out that that is who he really is, so be it. I'm still going to work my program.

As is true for any comprehensive symbolic system, co-dependency (or liberation psychotherapy) provides both a way to see and a way not to see. As an aspiring self-actualized individual, a recovering co-dependent, Jamal wears the conceptual lenses of liberation psychotherapy (in its reformed version). Seeing things from that vantage point determines the meanings he assigns to the world, generally. As I have noted, co-dependency's symbolism tends to engender a zero-sum game, one informed by the false oppositions born of pitting the self *against* society. There is more than a little of this at work in Jamal's comments. Although he sees himself as working at being understanding, there is little effort at genuine understanding involved; nor could there be, given the mechanics of his adopted symbolic system. Jamal describes his father's worldview not as an equally valid symbolic–moral system but as a shallow one. In the same vein, as a co-dependent in recovery, Jamal takes a dim view of the definition of self through others, seeing it not only as lacking depth but, as the discourse requires, as the cause of psychological sickness.

What both Jamal's and Duane's fathers really share, though, is not their shallowness but their fealty to an ethic in which the "father" role is judged by utterly different criteria from those according to which their recovering children now judge them. In all likelihood the reason Duane's and Jamal's fathers seem to look at their children with a fundamental lack of comprehension is because that is exactly the case: They fundamentally do not understand. They define moral conduct in the opposite way, the old way, in which the denial of oneself for others is the foundation of personal worth and the basis for personal identity rather than a symptom of a psychological disease. For those who still adhere to the ethic of self-denial, their sons and daughters now speak in a language they do not comprehend, raising alien topics and concerns.

New Havens in a Heartless World

Co-dependency's conception of recovery clearly highlights its status as a discourse of reform, as an attempt both to affirm the validity of liberation psychotherapy as a symbolic–moral system and to smooth out the relational difficulties that that system engenders and, without reform, cannot correct. Being co-dependent, being a process addict, provides people with a means of rectifying the losses, the uncertainty, and the persistent pattern of broken and troubled relationships that have issued from liberation psychotherapy's rise to cultural dominance. Reflecting the reformist discourse's characteristic loyalty to a more fundamental symbolic–moral system, co-dependency neither acknowledges nor addresses liberation psychotherapy's impact upon contemporary U.S. life. Recast in liberation psychotherapy's terms, child and spouse abuse, drug and alcohol problems, overeating, undereating, estrangement from kin, compulsive gambling, failed marriages, aborted friendships—all are portrayed as indices of emotional repression, as the products of the subordination of the self to collective control.

A close inspection of the convert's stories, however, reveals the impact rather than the absence of liberation psychotherapy in contemporary life. The recurrent underlying motif—the common thread beneath the stories that, as co-dependents, CoDA members are required to tell—is that the ethic of self-actualization has had profound and often painful consequences in their lives, consequences manifested in the instability of their most significant, most intimate relationships. It is and in and through the close relationships that comprise these institutions—families, friendships, neighborhoods, communities—that people's sense of self and well-being, their social identities, are formed.

It is in its provision of alternatives to these mediating institutions that co-dependency's reforms and their significance become most clearly apparent. CoDA members convene in the safety and the sanctity of their weekly meetings in much the same way that people once returned home after a hard day in the often-cold world of work. In this sense, CoDA groups serve in a capacity similar to what Christopher Lasch has argued home and family once did: A co-dependent's weekly group meeting is a "haven in a heartless world."[11] In co-dependency's and, before it, liberation psychotherapy's worldview, however, kin and close relationships have become part of that larger, colder world. Reframed as the sites and sources of repressiveness and endless social demands, it is these relationships and institutions from which CoDA groups now provide solace, respite, a haven. In CoDA, those who seek to become well can gather to commiserate with one another, offering understanding and support and listening to one another tell the stories of their struggles with the coldness and insanity of the outside world and of their struggles to find autonomy, to self-actualize, in that world.

These dynamics are poignantly expressed in CoDA members' penchant for calling fellow members their "family of affiliation" and identifying their regular group as the "home meeting." For example, Lorrie, who was relatively new to CoDA, said that

> I'd be willing to put in the time to really build the meetings up and make this a really great meeting. I've been going around to different meetings trying to find a home meeting, anyway. I'm committed to co-dependency and to CoDA, but I just haven't settled into one I'd like to make home base, yet.

Dan's remarks also resonate with these themes: "I'm sitting here listening to all these relationship problems—kids, marriages, and parents—and I know what I'm doing in CoDA; because I'm in the same boat. I've got *no* relationship with my family, at all." He continued,

> It seems like the meetings are pretty much anti-men a lot of the time. And, I'm not saying that's not legitimate or anything, but, hey, it goes two ways. It's not like women have exactly got it together either, you know? But that just tells me that if it's like this for both men and women, then that's what this program is all about. It's a program about relationships, and if both men and women are having problems, it's gonna be pretty hard to have good relationships with each other.

"I've learned some good stuff in the program about how to make relationships work," Dan says, but he has not yet had occasion to test his new knowledge. "I just hope I get to apply it someday. I hope I have a relationship someday."

Dan's comments underline the significance of CoDA groups as the mediating institutions, the families of affiliation, in a liberation therapy reality. His remarks are reminiscent of the dinner-table musings of a young man discussing possible futures with his family, of a young man preparing himself to find a wife, leave home, and start his own family.

All of the problems and concerns that CoDA members discuss are suffused with these impressions. Members come to CoDA to take stock, to think out loud, to sort through their dealings with the outside world.

Following the discourse's tutelage, and faithful to its symbolic order, their "families of origin" and of marriage are now clearly understood to be part of that outside world, which is itself understood in accordance with co-dependency's truths. The isolation and confusion born of liberation psychotherapy's impact is reduced to the logic of liberation psychotherapy and co-dependency itself. The members have learned to reframe their problems as symptoms of their own "disease" rather than as part of the larger dynamics of cultural and societal changes. The fit between the members' problems and how the discourse defines those problems, however, is often loose, at best. Ron, for example, discussed the problems he has faced since his divorce. He had recently declared bankruptcy, "[b]ut I don't want to talk about that so much. I've been having a hell of a time with my kids since the divorce—which also had something to do with my bankruptcy, too. But, I'm not getting a lot of time with my kids." He explained that both of his sons are young teenagers, both have part-time jobs, and "their jobs are at completely opposite ends of the city. So, I pick them up, take them to work, and go home. Pick them up again a few hours later. Shit. I don't call that top-notch time, do you?" Ron was also confronted with a problem familiar to many divorced parents:

> When they aren't working, my youngest one wants me to be a "Disneyland Dad." You know, "buy me this, buy me that." I love him with all my heart, and it's hard, because he just doesn't understand that I can't afford to do that. I'm broke, and even though I know better, I'm embarrassed about that.

He said that after he had dropped his boys off at their mother's a few nights earlier, he went home in low spirits:

> I walk into my pukey, quiet little apartment, and I turn on the television, and it's one of those 1940s, happy-ending, happy family movies, and I just lost it. Burst out crying—and I don't mean tears down the cheeks. I mean wailing like a baby. I'm sure my neighbors must've heard me, but I don't care. Anyway, I felt better after that cry. Still do. Things'll work out. It's just hard, is all. It *is* hard. I just thank God I've got you all to come babble at. Thanks.

It is not at all clear in what sense Ron should be understood—as co-dependency would have it—as sick, or even as the product of abuse and abandonment at the hands of the dysfunctional culture. He does not invoke those themes himself, even in passing. Given divorce statistics in the United States and the accompanying problems with money and

child custody (to say nothing of loneliness, sadness, and disillusionment), his remarks are better understood as a snapshot of liberation
psychotherapy's impact upon the "social fabric" and of the consequences
of its inability to repair the relational rents it has torn.

That impact is also evident in the members' repeated references to
their difficulties with making informal and intimate social relationships—
parenthood, marriage, and friendships—work. Certainly, such difficulties informed Sandra's remarks: "As most of you that come to this
meeting know, I guess, I'm going through a divorce right now," she
began, going on to explain that, although divorce is always a "painful
and hard" experience, hers is

> even harder, because [my husband] can't afford to move out right now. So, we're
> trying to live in the same house while the divorce is being processed. It's real
> weird. I hate it, but there's nothing else to do right now. Like I say, he can't afford
> to move, and I don't hate him, or anything. We just want to get divorced.

To make what must be an awkward situation even more so, Sandra's
husband "has been having second thoughts" about getting divorced:

> At least, that's what he says. I think he just can't quite figure out how to put his life
> together. So he's been asking me if there's any way that we can work it out and
> maybe stay together, but I don't think that's really what he wants; he's just a little
> lost right now, and he's having trouble with work and, like I said, with money.

In addition to the obvious troubles with their arrangement, Sandra
explains that her husband has also been asking for her advice and help
with his other problems, as well. This makes things doubly complicated:

> I still care about how he's doing and if he's okay, but I know, too, that if I *do* get
> sucked into talking about his problems, that it'd be a real short step from there to
> me trying to fix him, and then I'd be right back into that old stuff.

She has tried to explain to him why she cannot be his confidante, and
"he says he understands, but he doesn't really." The whole situation,
she says, "is just so sad. I guess that's all I wanted to say—just to get
some of my sadness out." She sighed, and concluded that "I'm glad I've
got someplace to come and talk about this stuff."

As Sandra's remarks indicate, co-dependency's public selection was
and is primarily a function of the opportunities for relatively enduring
communal attachment and support that the discourse offers. Unlike her
husband, who "can't quite figure out how to put his life together" when

faced with the loss of his most significant social relationship, Sandra had a community, of sorts, to turn to for support. The overarching significance of this communal aspect is underscored by the recurrent gratitude: "thanks for being here"; "I just thank God you all are here"; "this program has saved my life." In a world in which neither older cultural forms nor the proposed alternative to those forms, liberation psychotherapy, offers enduring communal purposes, "having" co-dependency makes such an offer. But when the nature of the recovery ethic is factored into this equation, it is also clear that these are "new communities." CoDA members' communal purposes center on, are informed by, and are organized around each person's pursuit of self-actualization. This is the essence of co-dependency's reformist impulses: The member's "home meetings" and "families of affiliation" are the mediating institutions of a liberation therapy reality.

Notes

1. See Robert Jay Lifton, "Protean Man," *Partisan Review* 35, no. 1 (1968): 13–27; R. Turner, "The Real Self."
2. Beattie, *Codependent No More*, 56, 59, 57, 58, 59, respectively.
3. Ibid., 116, 156.
4. Quoted passages, respectively, from Subby, *Lost in the Shuffle*, 40, 23; Wegscheider-Cruse, *Choicemaking*, 123, 140.
5. Bradshaw, *Bradshaw On: The Family*, 170; *Healing the Shame*, 158.
6. Bradshaw, ibid., 158, 160. See also C. Gaylord Hendricks, *Learning to Love Yourself: How to Become a Centered Person* (Englewood Cliffs, N.J.: Prentice-Hall), 1982. Hendricks has also recently written a *Learning to Love Yourself Workbook* (Englewood Cliffs, N.J.: Prentice-Hall, 1990).
7. Michel Foucault has also discussed this dimension of ethical systems, noting that "there is another side to…moral prescriptions, which most of the time is not isolated as such but is, I think, very important: the kind of relationship you ought to have with yourself, *rapport à soi*, which I call ethics, and which determines how the individual is supposed to constitute himself as a moral subject of his own actions" ("On the Genealogy of Ethics," 352). The CoDA recovery ethic instructs converts in how to constitute themselves as the moral subject of their own actions in much the fashion that Foucault suggests.
8. Beattie, *Beyond Codependency*, 133, 38. Chapter 11 of *Codependent No More* is entitled "Have a Love Affair with Yourself." The phrase denotes one of her recommendations for recovery, but it is also an apt summary of what recovery means in the post-traditional groups of the twelve-step subculture.
9. Kanter, *Commitment and Community*, 167.
10. This ethical gap is also reflected in a wide variety of hotly contested contemporary public issues, including public funding for the arts, how to construct family policy, the nature of educational curricula, abortion, and so on. James Davison

Hunter has recently argued that the controversy surrounding these issues springs from the opposed moral visions of the combatants. Although Hunter's terms for these opposed visions differ from my own, the substance of the competing belief systems is essentially the same as the distinction I have been drawing between the ethic of self-actualization and the ethic of self-denial; the difference between what Hunter calls the "orthodox" and "progressive" cosmologies lies in where each locates moral authority. Progressives, like those who subscribe to the ethic of self-actualization, believe that the self is and should be the ultimate moral authority; the orthodox, those who adhere to an ethic of self-denial, see morality as a supra-individual code, a set of absolute truths that override individual preferences; see James Davison Hunter, *Culture Wars: The Struggle to Define America* (New York: Basic Books, 1991). A similar ethical polarity is apparent in Kristen Luker, *Abortion and the Politics of Motherhood* (Berkeley: University of California Press, 1984), particularly in Luker's discussion of the worldviews of pro-choice and pro-life advocates.

11. See Christopher Lasch, *Haven in a Heartless World: The Family Besieged* (New York: Basic Books, 1979).

8

The Ironies and Consequences
of Cultural Change

For some readers, it may seem puzzling that, as we saw in chapter 7, co-dependency advises *both* general types of process addicts to follow the same approach to recovery, telling obsessive and repressed co-dependents alike to set themselves free from conventional society and culture's repressive moral demands. Framing recovery in this way seems puzzling because it is tantamount to saying that both the spouse abuser and the abused spouse suffer from the same problems and share the same experiences, that both are the victims of repression. That is precisely what the discourse does say, and, as this chapter will explain, it is really not so puzzling that it does. Rather, it is entirely consistent with the logic of liberation psychotherapy, which holds that, were it not for culture and society's repressive practices, the individual would naturally develop into the "constructive and trustworthy"[1] self it was intended to be. As co-dependency itself demonstrates, it is but a short stretch from that view to the conclusion that repression's consequences can and do run the gamut from inhibition through exhibition, producing both victims and their victimizers.

The logic involved in this aspect of the recovery ethic is part of a quite complex network of relations among and between ideas and their consequences; the logic is interwoven with, and sheds a great deal of light upon, both liberation psychotherapy's impact upon U.S. culture and society and the consequences of becoming co-dependent. I have devoted this separate chapter to a fuller examination of these points because to do these various themes justice separately and to also show clearly how they are interwoven with one another requires a more extensive discussion.

Irony and the Assumption of Benevolence

I have earlier made the point that discourses must be understood in terms of their consequences rather than for their incisive wisdom or unerring accuracy; the results they produce may, and often do, have relatively little to do with what they say or mean to say. There is often, then, no small amount of irony involved in cultural change and in the consequences of a discourse's public selection. For example, it is ironic that, as Max Weber has demonstrated, religious ideals should have paved the way for and later helped to stabilize capitalism, an economic system organized around activities to which religion had historically been profoundly antagonistic.[2] Similarly, it is also ironic that, as Robert Michels has demonstrated, democratically inspired movements tend to become authoritarian and antidemocratic, if they are successful. Nonetheless, that outcome is sufficiently common that Michels called it "the iron law of oligarchy."[3] Reflecting the same irony, the rise of democracy fueled bureaucratization, a form of organization that, despite its meritocratic universalism, is notoriously hostile to the individual. So, too, is it ironic that the thought of Marx and Engels, so humanitarian and ultimately democratic in spirit, should have inspired despotic, totalitarian regimes that bear no resemblance to what Marx and Engels had in mind, repressing (in the more tangible, political sense) the laboring classes they were designed to serve.

Instances of the ironic consequences of cultural change abound, and there is neither room nor reason to rehearse them all here. The salient point about these ironies in this context is that the "triumph of the therapeutic"—with liberation psychotherapy cast in the starring role—replays once again the same disparity between the intentions driving cultural change and the consequences of that cultural change. As we will see, liberation psychotherapy, when its logic is closely examined, was never intended to be a revolutionary discourse.

For the founders of liberation psychotherapy, there were two main reasons why the self, if it is to be psychologically sound, must achieve autonomy from culture.

First, reflecting the impact of two world wars in the first half of the twentieth century, a variety of intellectual disciplines sounded the alarm about the woeful inadequacy and impotence of existing cultural values. Critical Theory and thinkers of the Frankfurt school of sociology (particularly Theodor Adorno, Herbert Marcuse, Max Horkheimer, and Erich Fromm) explored and forged a theoretical linkage between the ideas of Freud and Marx in an effort to uncover the sources of such distorted values. Seeking answers to roughly the same questions, Jean-Paul Sartre and Albert Camus, among others, developed existentialism into a dominant school of philosophy. Abraham Maslow, representing the psychotherapeutic arm of this body of thought, argued that because of "the total collapse of all values outside the individual," as he characterized the moral terrain of the post-World War II era, "there's no place else to turn but inward, to the self, as the locus of values."[4] For Maslow and other liberation psychotherapists, then, the self might be able to serve as an antidote to what many saw as a crisis in cultural and societal values; but in order for this to happen, the individual would have to achieve autonomy from societal and cultural demands.

The second reason the architects of liberation psychotherapy argued for the self's autonomy from culture issued from the conviction that societal and cultural repressions mass-produce a profoundly diminished self—the "defensively organized personality," as Carl Rogers called it.[5] Thus, from the outset, liberation psychotherapy seemed to say that everything that culture would have people become is antithetical to who they really are and that people should be set free from conventional normative and moral demands in order to become self-directing, to pursue self-actualization.

Such assertions as that the self must be the "locus of values" have invited charges that liberation psychotherapy espoused a radical moral relativism. But such charges overlook the importance of the assumption of natural human benevolence from which, as we have seen, the whole of liberation psychotherapy's symbolism derives. The significance of the assumption of benevolence is twofold. First of all, when that assumption is taken into consideration it becomes clear that relativism was never liberation therapy's intention; indeed, it does not call for a new conception of morality, at all, much less one that varies with each and every individual. Rather, liberation psychotherapy simply relocates established conceptions of morality, moving them from culture to the self—which, again, is assumed to possess an inborn appreciation for what turn out to be really quite conventional conceptions of right and wrong.

Recall that revolutionary discourses issue from and express the judgment that *both* the existing symbolic–moral system *and* the existing relational system must be rejected. Understood, in these senses, as a revolutionary discourse, liberation psychotherapy brought about near-revolutionary consequences. But that understanding was wrong; these consequences were not intended, and the assumption of benevolence tells us why. The following excerpt from Wendy Kaminer's recent polemic against co-dependency and the "recovery movement," as she inaccurately calls it,[6] sheds some light on the sources of misunderstanding. The excerpt comes from a section of Kaminer's book devoted to drawing a distinction between co-dependency and Maslow's humanistic therapy. Kaminer's effort to make that distinction is unconvincing, not least because of an evident confusion about Maslow's vision of self-actualization and what it represented. Noting that Maslow's ideas have long invited charges of moral relativism, Kaminer sets out to put the record straight. Maslow's "celebration of subjectivity," Kaminer asserts, "was not relativism, as it is often assumed to be." The reason it was not relativism, Kaminer argues, is that "Maslow did not suggest that all human behavior was healthy, only that all healthy behavior was self-directed."[7]

Although Kaminer is right that Maslow was no relativist, she has missed the point altogether about *why* he was not. Maslow's views were not relativistic because the self-directedness he seems to call for is in fact proscribed by an external moral standard: As Kaminer herself says, for Maslow, the important thing was less that behaviors are "self-directed" than that they are "healthy." To be sure, this is not relativism; but what gets missed, here, is that it is not relativism because Maslow was not really talking about a genuine self-directedness. The criterion of "healthiness" is a supra-individual standard for evaluating the morality of behavior. The self, then, is not really the "source" of values, at all; rather, what Maslow is saying is that the self is to be free because it can be trusted to be constructive and positive—to choose the "correct," the "healthy" values. The assumption of benevolence, in short, is the justification for and a central feature of self-actualization. The individual's right to be "an autonomous self independent of culture" rests upon the assumption that each person possesses an innately "democratic, egalitarian, and humanitarian character structure and values."[8] This same point is even more evident in Maslow's contentions that self-actualized individuals "tend to do right, because that is what they *want* to do, what they *need* to do, what they enjoy, what they approve of doing" (emphasis in the original).[9] Again, the conviction that self-actualized people will "do right" issues from the tacit assumption that "doing right" is part of humanity's ontological makeup. Maslow's point is not that new standards of right and wrong are necessary, but that it is not necessary to impose those standards upon the self because they are already part of the self.

If they are not really about self-directedness, then, how are we to make sense of liberation psychotherapy and the ethic of self-actualization? Its core logic reveals that liberation psychotherapy was itself intended to be a discourse of reform, rather than revolution: As with any reformist discourse, its founders ultimately had a quarrel not with the symbolic–moral system itself but with its imperfect realization in identity and social relationships. Liberation psychotherapy, in short, was not a critique of culture's judgments about right and wrong. Rather, it was a critique of its *methods;* its central point was that, left to their own devices—which is to say, without cultural and social repression—people would naturally choose the right, the healthy, course of action. The ethic of self-actualization represented no more and no less than a suggestion for an alternative, less repressive, way to effect moral conduct.

The assumption of innate human benevolence effectively equates what the liberation psychotherapist believes to be the true self's innate values with those of the conventional culture, values that liberation psychotherapy only superficially rejected. In that therapeutic worldview, what then-conventional culture defined as morality is actually an inborn feature of the self; thus it is not necessary to repress people or to impose morality upon the individual because the individual is already moral and, as it turns out, moral in quite conventional ways.

Although it is essentially a methodological rather than a genuinely moral critique, liberation psychotherapy's consequences, as we have seen, were "revolutionary." This disparity between intention and outcome is in part a matter of liberation therapy's ambiguity: It never stated its aims very clearly, not least because its creators were themselves not very clear, apparently. Certainly there is a fundamental lack of clarity in references to the "democratic" character structure of a self that is autonomous of culture—as if democratic political theory were not itself a cultural development. That even so astute a thinker as Maslow could conceive of *self*-directedness as being free to "do what is right"—thereby calling for and doing away with that self-directedness in a single stroke of the pen—suggests just how difficult it can be to keep these lines of reasoning distinct.

But liberation psychotherapy's inadvertently revolutionary results are the product of more than simple confusion or the difficulty of clearly expressing its nuances. They are also the result of the logic of liberation psychotherapy itself and the ways in which that logic affects how the ethic of self-actualization is to be interpreted and put into practice. As mentioned previously, the ethic comprises two general norms, which reflect the core principles of liberation psychotherapy: The norm of self-determination is essentially the expectation that the self must achieve autonomy from social and cultural constraint. This expectation, of course, reflects the conviction that repression causes psychological sickness. The second norm, the norm of benevolence, reflects the assumption that humans are innately positive, constructive creatures and that, as such, when freed of cultural influence, they will exhibit that natural endowment—thus, Maslow's tautological formula asserting that self-actualized individuals "do what is right," else we know that they are not really self-actualized.

As chapter 4 illustrated, liberation psychotherapy has never placed much emphasis on the norm of benevolence; instead, it heavily stressed the pivotal importance of self-determination. There are two reasons for this imbalance between the ethic of self-actualization's two constitutive norms, both of which issue from and reflect liberation therapy's logic. First of all, because it is assumed that human nature—independent of cultural and societal influences—is essentially benevolent, there is simply no need to emphasize that such benevolence is expected or required: Allowed free reign, the true self will "naturally" exercise "healthy" self-directedness. Second, because repression is its *only* explanation for personal and social problems, liberation psychotherapy itself is effectively forced to avoid even the appearance of repressiveness. To explicitly define benevolence as a norm to be achieved, rather than simply assuming it, would be "repressive"; doing so would effectively impose external standards on the self.

Due to its underlying logic, then, liberation psychotherapy wound up obscuring its own essentially methodological, versus moral, nature. Portrayed and understood as a repudiation of then-conventional morality itself, liberation therapy became in its consequences a discourse of revolution rather than reform.

It is hardly surprising that co-dependency, in its utter fealty to liberation psychotherapy's legitimacy as a symbolic system, should reveal an identical confusion between morality and method, between revolution and reform, in every significant detail. Certainly, this confusion informs Anne Wilson Schaef's discussion of what she calls "romance addiction." In the midst of that discussion, Schaef, one of co-dependency's most strident cultural critics, launches into a mystifyingly spirited defense of "normal social mores" and "accepted behavior":

> Romance addicts also evidence a loss of spirituality and a breakdown of their own personal morality. They move progressively away from reality, truth, and normal social mores and behaviors in the service of their addiction.... At [the most serious level] of [romance addiction] the addict *has no regard for societal mores and accepted behavior.* (Emphasis added)

At first glance, a passage such as this suggests that Schaef has an exceedingly poor grasp of her own ideas. After all, as with all of co-dependency's founders, she devotes an enormous amount of space and effort in her treatises to trenchant repudiations of precisely the same "societal mores and accepted behavior" that she is so fiercely defending here. Indeed, for Schaef, all addictions "are generated by our families *and* our schools, our churches, our political system and our society as a whole" (emphasis in original)[10]—in short, the very purveyors of standards for "accepted behavior." But, armed with the recognition of co-dependency's unswerving fidelity to liberation psychotherapy and to the latter's fundamental lack of clarity about what it really means to say, it becomes clear that Schaef has merely stumbled over the root conception that has always informed liberation psychotherapy's nascent and all but completely unrecognized conservatism. Schaef has merely failed to recognize that liberation psychotherapy was not designed as a moral critique, but as a critique of repression, of the method by which culture passes on its conceptions of morality. Because the assumption of human benevolence ultimately calls for precisely the forms of conduct that mainstream culture called for—and because it is so easy to miss this equivalency between the putatively innate values of the true self and conventional cultural definitions of morality—Schaef winds up advising her readers that cultural "rules" are the reason they are sick, while at the same time telling them that their "[dis]regard for societal mores and accepted behavior" is also a pivotal indicator of their "disease."

The same can be said for Schaef's observation—in the same quoted passage—that addicts violate "their own personal morality." If a genuinely "personal morality" were indeed what liberation psychotherapy and co-dependency called for, then the category of process addiction logically could not exist. If a personal morality were the aim, then co-dependency's claims that the behaviors to which it refers are forms of psychological sickness would be utterly groundless. Just as Maslow was not really calling for genuine self-directedness, neither is it a genuinely personal morality to which Schaef refers; rather, like liberation psycho-therapy, co-dependency simply relocates conventional morality within the self and redefines that morality as an inborn quality of the self.

Schaef's are not isolated confusions. All of her fellow advocates reveal an equal lack of awareness of the fact that they have confused liberation psychotherapy with a genuine moral critique. For one further example consider again John Bradshaw's argument that mainstream cultural morality comprises a "poisonous pedagogy" that "contaminates" the otherwise pure child; this is the rhetoric of a fiery moral critique, a fierce indictment of conventional, "shaming" values. Yet elsewhere Bradshaw reveals that it is not conventional morality or values that has roused his ire, at all. In a discussion of sexual addiction, he asserts that it is "[t]he repression of sexuality [that] sets up *the wild and shameful sexual acting-out.* "[11] In short, Bradshaw is assailing repression, rather than the conventional moral judgment that certain forms of sexual conduct might be characterized as "wild" or "shameful."

Again, as has been evident throughout this analysis, save for the new theory of addiction—and the common social purposes it makes possible—co-dependency's articulation with liberation psychotherapy is total. There is a new terminology, but the logic is identical, even to the point that co-dependency makes the same logical mistakes, suffers the same contradictions, and offers the same equivocations. As such, it is less than surprising that co-dependency defines recovery in the same way for *all* process addicts: In CoDA, the long-suffering, self-abnegating spouse (the repressed co-dependent) works side by side with the compulsive sexual adventurer, the abuser, the criminal, or the drug addict (the obsessed co-dependent)—each struggling to negate conventional proprieties and to seek out their true selves. Guided by the assumption of benevolence, co-dependency arrives at the same conclusions as liberation psychotherapy: True selves are only true if they do not indulge in too much romance, too much sex, too much gambling, drinking, drug use, spending, shopping, child abuse, spouse abuse, eating, working, thinking, reading, and so on. These actions are not "right" or "healthy," therefore they cannot be truly self-directed—which is to say it is taken for granted that they cannot be directed by the true self. In turn, what this formulation reveals is that the true self is ultimately in full accord with conventional culture's conceptions of right and wrong. Once "in touch with" their true selves, recovering process addicts should follow that self's impulses. Because liberation psychotherapists know (that is, they unquestioningly assume) that those impulses will be benevolent, they rest assured that recovering process addicts will naturally choose self-denial if that is what is right.

The depth of the articulation between these two symbolic systems does not end here. Although co-dependency, like its predecessor, frames psychological health in terms of both the self's autonomy and native benevolence, it also—like its predecessor—articulates the norm of benevolence weakly. Although the violation of that norm underlies co-dependency's judgment that obsessed process addicts, in particular, are sick, that judgment (and what it implies about psychological health) is muted beneath the rhetorical force of such evocative and emotionally charged causal concepts as the "abandonment, abuse, and contamination" of children. Given such a conception of the self-to-society relationship, co-dependency—again like liberation psychotherapy—has little choice but to define absolute autonomy from group demands as the key to psychological health. The expectation that self-actualized individuals, the character ideal to which recovering co-dependents are exhorted to aspire, must carefully exercise their liberation is at no time a dominant or featured theme in the discourse. On the rare occasions when that expectation is articulated, it appears as equivocation or contradiction—such as we have seen in Schaef's remarks about "normal social mores."[12] The norm of benevolence, then, is expressed in a quiet voice, and that voice is all but completely drowned out by the causal logic of the discourse, by the inflammatory rhetoric that expresses that logic, and by a repeated and heavy emphasis upon the importance of an unfettered self-realization as the essence of recovery.

Requirements of Memory, Requirements of Membership

One of the major themes throughout this book has been that symbolic systems inform relational systems; cultural structures—such as liberation psychotherapy and the discourse of co-dependency—engender and are embodied in social structures, and they also engender and are embodied in the processes through which those structures are formed and reformed, endure or perish. Understanding liberation psychotherapy and co-dependency as symbolic systems—their structure, their central images, their logics—is, then, not some idle intellectual exercise, not an abstract mind game, not a cynic's self-referential amusement. These discourses have had and continue to have real social consequences, and we would do well to attend carefully to what they have to say in order to understand those consequences. Although, as indicated in the various testimonials I've quoted here, the litany of troubles one hears from CoDA members resonates with liberation psychotherapy's impact upon people's relationships and lives, the discourse of co-dependency defines that impact away, explaining repression and communal control as the causes of the members' troubles. This disappearance of liberation psychotherapy's cultural and social impact is duplicated by the process of conversion to co-dependency. Those who come to CoDA for the stable social relationships and sense of communal identity and purpose that it offers must reframe their life stories if they are to have continued access to those relationships. Being co-dependent, and being a CoDA member, is the means to that end. Simply having, as one member from whom we have heard put it, "someplace to come and talk about this stuff," having access to a group of people to whom one can regularly and reliably turn for commiseration and support, requires learning a particular way of talking about one's life and problems.

Here is one of the most unsettling consequences of co-dependency's symbolic structure. Because conversion *requires* people to reconstruct their biographies in accordance with the discourse, what co-dependency does is not so much capture as structure the converts' accounts of their life events prior to their conversions; those accounts are socially constructed, reassembled in light of the conversion experience.

The socially constructed character of the members' life stories is repeatedly evident in the almost identical terms by which they account for the years between childhood and CoDA membership. Converts, in order to meet the obligations of their role, must work toward making their biographies conform to the life story that co-dependency's symbolic structure requires. Indeed, as Ann's comments in the following passage show, they often refer to these efforts as "history work":

I've done a lot of work on my history—which they talk about in CoDA: "get your history straight." I thought my history was fine, but then I started to work on it, and I realized that I don't have one recollection of my mother or father spending any time with me; there was a lot of abandonment. The abuse was very subtle in my family, because the messages from my father...were that you were the best,...but the way I interpreted them was...that you could always do better, and that somehow what you did gave you your worth. This has caused me many problems.[13]

The biographical obligations of the co-dependent role clearly underlie this "history work." As Ann says, prior to her association with CoDA, she "thought [her] history was fine." Once she "started to work on it," however, once she began adapting her life story to the discourse, she learned to equate abuse with conditional love, with not being loved for "the very one that you are." Underscoring the degree to which abuse is an obligatory feature of a co-dependent life story, Ann says that, even though her father's messages conveyed praise, "the way I interpreted them was...that you could always do better." This interpretation, or something very close to it, is required if Ann is to be co-dependent. If her life story is to conform to co-dependency, she must learn to explain her troubles as an adult as the result of the abuse and abandonment she experienced as a child. By extension, if she is to have ongoing access to the social support that CoDA provides, she must be co-dependent.

This connection between the symbolic foundations and relational embodiments of the discourse is also evident in the members' uses of John Bradshaw's symbolization of shame. We have already seen the various applications of shame as a proxy for the disease of co-dependency. Converts also draw upon the shame concept in order to reconstruct their biographies. Shame readily lends itself to a wholesale reinterpretation of one's past, principally by way of an inference the discourse encourages them to make: If converts have feelings of shame, they must have been abused and abandoned. May, for one, has opted for this approach:

I'm shame-based. I don't want you to know who I am because that hurts. My shame originates with my family of origin. *I didn't know it until just joining CoDA.* I knew from another twelve-step program that I knew how to live with addicted people, but I didn't know why I responded the way I did all my life, and I knew it was more than just the addicted people in my life, that *it had to start from my family of origin, so I started searching back to that. And I came up with emotional incest,* a lot of verbal abuse, not so much directed at me as at my mother and other people in the family. A lot of complex, underneath-type of derogatory remarks. I also felt that my nationality was questioned. I was a minority in a small farming community—I'm Norwegian, by

> the way, full-blooded Norwegian—and somebody once said to me as a child, "oh, you're a Swede turned inside out." I believed that. I didn't know the impression it had on me until CoDA. And being a girl, the last in a family of four, my mother and father were directly from Norway, and they spoke Norwegian when I was small. I didn't understand that. They argued a lot when I was small. I took that on as my responsibility, and I learned to be a people-pleaser; I learned how to smile when I was hurting inside and to laugh a lot. I learned how to be a nice person. Today, I know that they were coping skills to get along in life. (Emphasis added)[14]

Not "until just joining CoDA" did May recognize the enduring significance of her childhood experiences. Once in CoDA, May "knew" that her problems "had to" start with her family of origin. "So," as she says, "I started searching back to that," and, eventually, she "came up with emotional incest."

The point, I would hope it is clear, is not to impugn May but to underscore the significance of her remarks and of co-dependency's influence over the story she now tells of her life: There is nothing in what she has said to suggest incest or to explain what "emotional incest" is. Even the "verbal abuse" to which she refers, if her anecdote about the ethnic insult is what she means by this abuse, took place outside of her family. But whatever May might or might not mean by her comments, what is far more important is that she clearly understands that she is expected to go back into her past and "come up with" something, some incident of abuse, in order to qualify as a bona fide member of the CoDA community.

As May's testimony indicates, converts *use* the discourse in order to satisfy their biographical obligations, as if co-dependency's conceptual order were a tool kit from which they select the right hardware for the job they are expected to do.[15] Employing a comparable analogy, Sue speaks of co-dependency as a "handbook," explaining that in recovery both she and her husband are

> learning that we have buttons that get pushed by each other and by other people if we let those buttons get pushed. My signal for myself is that if I get into having physical discomfort, that definitely is a signal that there is a shame attack going on, that there is some anger there that is unresolved. So what I've learned to do...is when I feel those signals coming on, *I get out my co-dependent's handbook and I look at the patterns and I look at the characteristics and I ask myself which one fits, what's going on with me right now?* (Emphasis added)

There is not even the vaguest hint of irony or duplicity in the converts' uses of concepts such as "history work" or their ready acknowledgments that they consult the "co-dependent's handbook" in order to "come up with" the required biographical credentials. To the contrary, in all of the testimonials I heard over the course of my field observations at CoDA meetings, perhaps the most striking thing about the members' comments was their overarching credulity—a condition that on more than one occasion brought to mind what Samuel Taylor Coleridge referred to as "the willing suspension of disbelief." But Coleridge was talking about the ideal state of mind that an artfully constructed fiction can induce in its readers. In the world of lived experience, that ideal reader's counterpart is, perhaps, the convert. If so, the companion piece to the willing suspension of disbelief is the "suspension of analogical reasoning," which, as chapter 6 discussed, is one of the essential indicators of conversion.

Converts to co-dependency consistently revealed a profound willingness to take the discourse's claims and apply them to their own lives on an entirely literal level. On more than one occasion, this larger pattern of credulity presented itself in an extraordinarily straightforward fashion. For example, Mary, discussing her adult problems with drugs and alcohol, says—as she must, to be co-dependent—that she knows those problems were the product of childhood abuse. Moreover, she knows that this is true even though "I don't have a lot of memories of childhood. I have sporadic memories. I've been told that the reason for that is that they're either too scary or too painful to remember, and that when it's time, the memories will come."

Pat's remarks even more uniquely illustrate the CoDA convert's necessarily literal-minded acceptance of co-dependency's truths: "As some of you know, I know I was abused as a child, I just don't remember it. But I've been working on that in therapy—going back into the past and trying to bring the memories into clearer focus."

On only one occasion did a member's comments directly address the degree to which CoDA and co-dependency structure rather than capture converts' life experiences. A man named Dave, sharing at another CoDA ritual, announced that when he shares at meetings there have been times that "I've said things that, even while I'm saying them, I think to myself, 'Whoa, wait a minute. Did I just say that? Why? It's not true. That never happened'—but I say them anyway." Having briefly stepped outside of the limits of the co-dependent role, however, Dave quickly stepped back in, concluding that the disparity between his own life experiences and the life experiences that his new reality requires of him is a by-product of the role itself: "Part of it is that I'm not used to talking about my life to a group of people, and so I guess I get carried away, or something. I'm still learning how to share, and how to be comfortable doing that."

Part of CoDA converts' life accounts may well be, as Dave says, getting "carried away," but a far larger part of it is that the co-dependent role is shaped by co-dependency's symbolic order and by CoDA's ritual enactments of the reality the discourse describes. Co-dependency provides its converts with a story to tell regardless of failed, nonexistent, or cloudy recollection, and being co-dependent and a CoDA member requires fitting one's life into that story. For this reason, members take the absence of memories of abuse as a sign of denial, and they take an inability to remember the past as a certain indication that it is, as Mary said, "too scary or too painful to remember" rather than as an instance of simple forgetfulness. The preemptive premises upon which the role of the co-dependent rests are that life problems are the signs of a disease, an addiction, and that the addiction is caused by mainstream culture's practices of abuse and abandonment.

* * * * *

Although the discourse serves as a shared symbolic system in and through which the converts can forge new social relationships, new families of origin, and so on, it also has a profound impact on how the converts deal with those on the "outside." We saw some of this in chapter 7's discussion of the discourse's zero-sum game, which makes it more, not less, difficult to connect with outsiders. The socially constructed nature of the converts' life stories, and especially the nature of that construction, only exacerbates these difficulties. Because of the requirements of being co-dependent, they have learned to see their troubles as adults as the product of childhood abuses—hardly a stance to foster mutual understanding.

In the search for their true selves, converts sometimes bring their requisite memories of abuse back to their parents' and families' doorsteps, seeking, through a confrontation, to "get their histories straight" so that they can get a firmer grasp on the inner child they must unconditionally love as part of their recovery. These confrontations, as one might imagine, are seldom pleasant scenes. Tempers flare when the converts try to discuss events that no one else in the family remembers. Parents and siblings are ill disposed toward sharing in such memories, and the ugliness of what they are asked to recall only exacerbates their anger.

But from the converts' view—indeed, constitutive of this view and its zero-sum aspect—the other family members are "in denial." Thus, Colleen announced,

> my sister called me the other day and told me that they'd all gotten together and decided that I must be crazy. She said they talked about what I said about dad sexually abusing us, and none of them remembers anything like that. Then she called me a "fucking bitch," and said that if I insisted on talking like this they just didn't want me to come around anymore. It's sad, you know? I mean, I don't know what I expected them to do. I guess I hoped they'd admit it, but I should've known better than that. The only people that believe me are all of you [in the meeting].

The memories of abuse that Colleen now uses to explain her life have driven what would appear to be a permanent wedge between her family of origin and herself. Moreover, she does not find the absence of those memories among her kin especially disturbing or surprising: They are sick, and they will continue to be sick as long as they continue to "deny what really happened." Her fellow converts, whose experiences must also include some version of abuse, are the only ones who understand.

In light of co-dependency's symbolic structure and what it demands of them, many converts simply concluded that renegotiating their relationships in light of their new convictions and obligations was simply an unworkable project, a waste of time and energy. Those who had come to this conclusion divested themselves of relationships in which conventional social roles take precedence over the interests of the true self. The decision to break off relationships with others is not restricted to people from one's presumptively abusive past. The obligations that inhere in being a recovering co-dependent foster a general wariness of those who do not adhere to the ethic of self-actualization, as members understand that ethic. Randy, for example, told his group that "I just broke up with Linda, a woman that I'd been seeing for the last few months, and I'm hurting over that. But, I thought she was really together, and then I gradually found out she's one sick lady." It was not entirely clear upon what basis Randy concluded that Linda is "one sick lady," but his subsequent remarks suggested his apparent meaning.

> She's about thirty-nine, has a teen-aged daughter, lives at home with her parents—who are getting kind of old, and she's taking care of them. She doesn't have a program, and it just got clearer to me that she uses her job to get all her good feelings about herself, and she's not really in touch with herself all that well. And finally, well, I told her that I needed to end it. I can't afford to get sidetracked from my program.

Randy's comments illustrate the principle of detachment that, as we have seen, is an integral component of recovery. They also, again, reveal the zero-sum game in operation: Either people are "in recovery" or they are "in denial"; thus, because Linda is not a member of the new twelve-step subculture ("she doesn't have a program"), she is "not really in touch with herself" and "uses her job" and other social and institutional roles "to get all her good feelings about herself." She has sacrificed her true self to meeting the demands of family and work and is thus neither "in process" nor her own top priority; as such, she is "one sick lady." Using the norm of self-realization as his only guide, Randy described his decision to break this relationship off as an indicator of his progress in recovery: "I'm glad I can see my mistakes now, before they happen. Not all the time, but it's getting better. In the past, I would've hung in there, trying to fix it [the relationship], trying to fix her, and now I don't have to do that anymore. I'm just glad I've got this program."

For the most part, one can only speculate about how these unilateral decisions to break off a relationship affect those on their receiving end. The fieldwork for this study was directed toward understanding how and why the discourse of co-dependency took social form, a focus that demanded observation at CoDA meetings; somewhat regrettably, this focus precluded virtually any contact with newcomers who opted not to become co-dependent or with those who did become co-dependent but subsequently changed their minds. However, during the course of fieldwork both for this and for an earlier and somewhat related research project, a number of people who asked about the research, when they learned what it was about, freely volunteered relevant information from and about their own experiences. One of these persons was a woman named Lilly, whose remarks are presented here with her permission, which she granted because she had suddenly and unexpectedly lost an old friend to CoDA for the reasons I am suggesting and, as she said, wanted "the other side to be heard from." As Lilly explained,

> We've been friends for probably twenty years, and all of a sudden she calls me one day and says she can't see me anymore. When I asked her why, she said that since she joined CoDA she's started to see just how "sick" our relationship is and always was. I was hurt for a while, but now I just think, "well, fine. Have a nice life." Still, I can't quite believe it—that friendship is that disposable.[16]

Under similar conditions to those mentioned above, I also had occasion to speak with one ex-CoDA member, Marge, who also, and for reasons much like Lilly's, gave permission to quote her. Marge's reasons for reconsidering and ultimately terminating her conversion to co-dependency were grounded in her discomfort with the prevailing understanding of psychological health in the group. As she explained,

> There was a young woman at one of the last [CoDA] meetings I went to. And when she shared, she said that she was supposed to be helping her brother move from his apartment that day. She [the young woman] said, "but when I got up this morning, I decided that I really didn't feel like helping him move. A few months ago, I probably would've helped him anyway. But now, since I started coming to CoDA, I know that would've just been 'fixing' him, instead of doing what I needed to do for me. So I called him up and told him that he was going to have to do it himself."

Marge's de-conversion from CoDA ultimately issued from her reactions to this young woman's remarks. Probably because she was considerably older than the vast majority of CoDA members (who, as I have already pointed out, are by and large products of the baby boom generation), Marge's reaction resonates with older conceptions of morality and psychological health and reflects her discomfort with the recovery ethic's conceptions of those same categories. "After [the young woman] got finished," Marge said,

> I just sat there in disbelief. I thought, "that just stinks." I mean, her brother is counting on her help, and this little dumbbell thinks that leaving him in the lurch is some sign that she's in recovery? That was kind of a turning point for me. I went to a couple of other meetings after that, but I just didn't hear anything anybody said in the same way. So I finally just quit going altogether.

Although deeply troubled by the logical and moral implications of CoDA's recovery ethic, Marge's admiration for the original twelve-step philosophy remains unaffected by her CoDA experience. As she told me,

> I love AA, and I'll always have a soft spot for it. But, I don't drink. Can't stand the stuff. I went to AA meetings but I didn't quite fit. So, when CoDA came around, I was pretty excited about that. But, CoDA's not AA. It's not even really a twelve-step program. They use the steps, I guess, but it's really group therapy. I've been to therapists. They just don't get it. Neither does CoDA.

Whatever one's view of Marge's judgments regarding the merits of CoDA, her sense of the differences between CoDA and AA is basically accurate: As she says, "CoDA's not AA." At heart, CoDA is the group practice of liberation psychotherapy organized around an analogy to alcoholism. Unlike AA, however, CoDA is designed to help people adapt

themselves to a world in which the self and its prerogatives have become the dominant moral priorities.

* * * * *

In principle, like the basis for liberation psychotherapy, the basis for
co-dependency's battle with mainstream culture is a matter not of what is
or should be chosen or of what is right but of who gets to make the choice
to do what is right. But, also like liberation psychotherapy, co-dependency barely articulates the norm of benevolence and, in that omission,
replays the former's larger societal and cultural impact. Because the original
exponents of liberation psychotherapy did not explain (or did not recognize) that conventional culture's methods, rather than its conception of
morality, were the focus of its critique, their adherents likewise did not
understand (or did not recognize) that point. Interpreted as a moral rather
than a methodological critique, the ethic of self-actualization issues only
one demand: that the self be allowed an unfettered right to self-determination. The norm of benevolence, in which and through which self-determination is in fact legitimated, drops out of the equation. Without that
norm the ethic elicits the attitudes and conduct that fostered a cultural
"revolution" and the accompanying processes that made co-dependency
and the co-dependency movement both possible and attractive.

Co-dependency's advocates—also because they either do not understand or do not recognize the significance of the norm of benevolence,
and hence, the methodological rather than moral nature of their critique—
invoke principles, under the rubric of recovery, that engender the same
processes that liberation psychotherapy set into motion some thirty years
ago. Co-dependency, then, is a reformed version of liberation psychotherapy, applied as a solution to the problems that liberation psychotherapy did so much to create. Co-dependent/process addicts are
liberation psychotherapy's "defensively organized personalities" with a
new name; so, too, CoDA members, under the new term "recovery," are
pursuing the ethic of self-actualization, and they are pursuing the same
attenuated understanding of that ethic that guided their predecessors.
Unlike their earlier counterparts, however, recovering co-dependents—
courtesy of the new theory of process addiction that the discourse successfully established—struggle for self-actualization in a communal
setting; they have access to the stable relationships and institutional forms
that liberation psychotherapy, however inadvertently, did so much to
undermine and was itself unable to replace.

Notes

1. Rogers, *On Becoming a Person*, 91.
2. Max Weber, *The Protestant Ethic and the Spirit of Capitalism*, trans. Talcott Parsons (New York: Charles Scribner's Sons, 1958). It should be added that Weber's analysis fits into a dialectical model of change. The religious ideals informing the Protestant ethic made possible the particular habits of conduct and temperament that proved hospitable to the formation of large-scale, industrial capitalism, but— as I discussed in chapter 1—once in place, capitalism itself required and engendered changes in the symbolic order; see, for example, Heilbroner, *The Nature and Logic of Capitalism*, especially chapter 5. For a complementary analysis, see Reinhard Bendix, *Work and Authority in Industry* (Berkeley: University of California Press, 1974; originally published in 1956), who provides an exceptionally thoughtful and thorough cross-cultural and historical analysis, tracing changing conceptions of community obligations to the poor and changing conceptions of the appropriate organization of workplace relations. See also Albert Hirschman, *The Passions and the Interests* (Princeton: Princeton University Press, 1977).
3. Robert Michels, *Political Parties: A Sociological Study of Oligarchical Tendencies of Modern Democracy* (New York: Collier, 1962; originally published in 1911).
4. Abraham Maslow, *Toward a Psychology of Being*, (Princeton, N.J.: Van Nostrand Reinhold, 1968), 155.
5. Rogers, *On Becoming a Person*, 91.
6. As we have seen, those twelve-step groups formed after the therapeutic "revolution" could not be any more different from their ostensible predecessors. CoDA bears, at most, a superficial resemblance to AA. Kaminer, though, paints them with the same brush, subsuming all twelve-step groups under the "recovery movement" rubric. Doing so fosters an extremely misleading point of view.
7. Kaminer, *I'm Dysfunctional, You're Dysfunctional*, 57.
8. Maslow, *Motivation and Personality.* See chapter 11 for Maslow's full discussion of the qualities of the self-actualized person.
9. Maslow, quoted in Kaminer, *I'm Dysfunctional, You're Dysfunctional*, 58; the quote is from Maslow, *Toward a Psychology of Being*, 155.
10. Schaef, *Escape from Intimacy*, 49, 51, 6.
11. Bradshaw, *Bradshaw On: The Family*, 167.
12. These dynamics are equally apparent in a rhetoric of rights in which advocates have often framed the co-dependent's recovery. For example, Sharon Wegscheider-Cruse offers a list of "Co-Dependent Rights," including "the right to say no to anything that violates my values; the right to dignity and respect; the right to set my own priorities and say 'No!' to any request that conflicts with my priorities. (This is not a right to total selfishness, it's a right to self-care); the right to stand up for myself; the right to say no (assertion versus aggression); a right and an obligation to show my feelings; the right to say 'I don't care'; the right to change my mind; the right to make mistakes; and, the 'obligation not to violate these rights in anyone else'" (Wegscheider-Cruse, *Choicemaking*, 135–36). In at least three of Wegscheider-Cruse's remarks, she tries to adumbrate a set of responsibilities and to balance rights with duties; such equivocation issues from the effort to balance and make sense of the ethic of self-actualization's conflicting obligations of self-realization and benevolence. Qualifying the more general principle

of self-care, for example, she advises her readers that the right to "say no to anything that violates my priorities" must not be confused with a right to "total selfishness." It is only "a right to self-care." The distinction she draws between assertion and aggression duplicates the struggle to cultivate benevolent self-determination; there is a line between taking care of oneself and harming others, and that line should not be crossed. Finally, in the most sweeping of the rejoinders, she instructs her charges that they also are obliged not to violate others' rights to these same privileges. In struggling to strike an acceptable balance between the norms of benevolence and self-determination, Wegscheider-Cruse—as did Schaef—inevitably offers equivocal advice. For example, followed to its logical conclusions, the full attentiveness to the rights of others that Wegscheider-Cruse calls for requires precisely those "external orientations" by which process addiction is said to reveal its presence in the first place. Her attempt to infuse a sense of social obligation (in keeping with the norm of benevolence), then, is not entirely successful; nor could it be in light of her definition of the right to self-care *as* a moral responsibility (in keeping with the norm of self-realization). Understood in this way, both rights *and* responsibilities become a matter of placing oneself in a position of higher moral priority than others. Responsibility, defined as a moral obligation to see that one's rights are not violated, has something of a hollow ring to it. Conversely, and no less important, it also rings somewhat hollow to define self-determination as essentially the freedom to develop and express one's intrinsic benevolence. Wegscheider-Cruse's insistence that believers must also observe this norm reveals the degree to which the presumption of benevolence limits the freedoms demanded by the norm of self-realization. It is in and through these limitations that the decidedly muted radicalism of the ethic of self-actualization becomes apparent; and, as noted, it is in and through the recognition of this muted radicalism that the disparity between liberation psychotherapy's intentions and its consequences comes fully to the light.

13. Ann's comments are from the proceedings of the First Annual Mid-Atlantic CoDA Conference, May 1989.
14. From an official CoDA cassette tape on "shame," recorded at the May 1989 Mid-Atlantic Conference.
15. The notion of a tool kit is borrowed from Anne Swidler, "Culture in Action: Symbols and Strategies," *American Sociological Review* 51 (1986): 273–86.
16. The earlier study on alcohol treatment to which I refer is presented in Rice, "'A Power Greater Than Ourselves.'" The loss of friends to the twelve-step subculture was the most common theme in these unsolicited observations. There are, of course, sociological reasons for so abruptly severing ties. People cannot indefinitely sustain membership in two conflicting social worlds. This appears to be of little consolation to those who are dismayed by their losses, though. Moreover, for some, the benefits brought about by any twelve-step conversion are not clear. One woman, who also granted permission to quote her, said of her AA-alcoholic ex-husband: "It's pretty hard for me to see much of a difference between when he was drinking and since he joined AA. He was a selfish son of a bitch when he was drinking, and he still is. Before, he wouldn't let anything like his family interfere with his getting drunk. Now, he can't let his family interfere with his recovery. Yeah, he doesn't drink, but he still doesn't give a damn about his kids or anybody but himself, so big deal." The behavior this woman describes, however, does not resemble anything that AA traditionally would have identified as recovery.

Conclusion

A Disease of One's Own

In this book I have tried to take a position somewhere between that of co-dependency's creators and that of its critics. There are several convictions informing this effort: first of all, that co-dependency is a significant phenomenon that warrants careful consideration and understanding; second, that a genuine understanding of co-dependency lies somewhere in this middle ground rather than in an unskeptical credulity or an overly skeptical polemicism; and third, that such an understanding can be reached only if one is asking the right questions. As with the emergence of any new cultural product—any new discourse, belief system, ideology, myth, and so on—the essential question about co-dependency that must be addressed, and that this analysis has addressed, is why this product, rather than another, was selected; why do people choose co-dependency? In turn, the answer to that question required careful consideration of two additional factors. It is necessary to consider (1) the discourse's content—that is, what co-dependency actually says: what its central themes and concepts are, how they are organized in relation to one another, what counts as a true statement in the discourse, what criteria determine those truths, and what the discourse requires of those who believe in it; and (2) the social and cultural context in which the discourse emerged: the conditions in the larger social world that encouraged people to seek out a new system of beliefs.

Co-dependency's selection is not explicable through a literal reading of co-dependency treatises themselves. As earlier chapters have shown, co-dependency advocates maintain that there is an "epidemic" of "process addictions"—caused by the disease of co-dependency, which is itself caused by cultural repression of the individual—coursing through contemporary U.S. life and destroying the soul of the nation. But this interpretation of events ignores the larger cultural changes that have been so thoroughly documented and conflates people's compliance with CoDA's membership expectations with the discourse's portrayal of society and culture as immutable forces of repression. Converts talk as they do *because* they are converts. Being a member of the new twelve-step groups is a solution to the variety of problems stemming from liberation psychotherapy's anti-institutionalism. Being a co-dependent—and talking as co-dependents must—is the price of membership.

At the same time, co-dependency's critics by and large generated a good deal more heat than light. I have said little about the critics up to now, largely because of my pursuit of the aforementioned middle ground. Nonetheless, a brief overview of the critical commentary about co-dependency seems in order, if for no other reason than to show why a better and more balanced approach is warranted.

All of those who have written analyses and critiques of co-dependency have gravitated to the discourse's soft underbelly, taking its emergence and public selection as an occasion to display their own critical acumen rather than as a phenomenon calling for serious consideration in its own right. Certainly, there are any number of ways in which the discourse is vulnerable to criticism. Some critics, for example, objected to the self-indulgence and apparent selfishness that co-dependency defines as the apex of psychological well-being, charging that it encourages people's neglect of larger problems, that properly political and public issues are vanishing into the vortex of self-absorption.[1] Feminists also weighed in on the topic, arguing, on the one hand, that the concept obscures the political nature of gender roles and, on the other hand, that it stigmatizes women's internalization of cultural expectations as pathological.[2] Co-dependency has also been the subject of concern on religious grounds. Here, too, the criticisms come from more than one direction. For some, the concept elicits a fuzzy-headed mysticism that undermines and ignores serious research findings; for others, it obviates personal moral accountability.[3]

The point is not that these and other criticisms are valid or invalid. To the contrary, the critics raised issues that, regardless of whether one agrees or disagrees with them, certainly warrant a public airing. But there is generally a dismissive, even condescending, attitude underlying virtually all of the criticisms, and, what is most important, by dint of this dismissiveness, the important questions about co-dependency have been overlooked.

One manifestation of this off-handedness was reflected in the critics' evaluations of how co-dependency was conceptualized and defined. For example, Edith Lisansky Gomberg, a scholar and researcher who has been writing thoughtful analyses of alcohol-related problems for over two decades now, argued that

> the impact of a deviant member of a family , whether that member is alcoholic, depressed, schizophrenic, phobic, brain-damaged, mentally retarded, delinquent or deviant in any way, has *long* been recognized as a major source of stress and distress within the family. [Moreover,] [t]here are *no* data at all which justify diagnosing family members…as manifesting personality disorder solely on the basis of their family membership. (Emphasis in the original)[4]

For Gomberg the term "co-dependency" was and is used "without any consideration of its meaningfulness or its contribution to theory and practice, so that it encompasses virtually the entire population of the United States."[5]

Gomberg's concerns are not ungrounded. As we have seen, co-dependency's advocates take repeated recourse to a rhetoric marked by excessive and inflammatory imagery, and all exhibit an all-but-total indifference to supporting empirical evidence. But to evaluate co-dependency in terms of its adequacy as a diagnostic category or its epidemiological validity is to fall prey to an uncomprehending literal mindedness. As pointed out in the introduction, the advocates' repeated claims that "96% of the population" suffer from the disease of co-dependency cannot be taken seriously as a diagnosis; it is obviously a critique of what the advocates see as conventional culture and society. Recognizing this does not require any special analytical skill; that none of the critics, all of whom are highly educated and otherwise astute thinkers and writers, came to that conclusion reflects the dismissive stance they took toward their subject matter.

The same comments apply to Wendy Kaminer's assessments of co-dependency's conceptual imprecision. In response to Beattie's definition of a co-dependent as anyone who is "affected by someone else's behavior and obsessed with controlling it," Kaminer dryly retorted, "who isn't?" Similarly, Schaef's definition of co-dependency as "a disease process whose assumptions, beliefs, and lack of spiritual awareness lead to a process of non-living which is progressive" prompted Kaminer to observe: "That some readers think they know what this means is a tribute to what George Orwell considered reduced expectations of language and the substitution of attitudes and feelings for ideas."[6] Kaminer also pointed to a correspondence between the flexible definitions of co-dependency and the sweeping epidemiological claims they allow. The advocates, Kaminer observed, defined "every conceivable form of arguably compulsive behavior...as an addiction," including such things as "the arms race, the oppression of emotion, the accumulation of capital, and enlarging the hole in the ozone layer."[7] In a similar spirit, the noted psychoanalyst Robert Coles remarked:

> I have a feeling we're soon going to have special groups for third cousins of excessive sherry drinkers.... You don't know whether to laugh or cry over some of this stuff.... [Co-dependency has] run amok.... [It is a] typical example of how anything packaged as psychology in this culture seems to have an all too gullible audience.[8]

Elizabeth Kristol, writing in *The American Spectator*, raised essentially the same points about co-dependency's loose definitions and concomitantly broad applications:

> [D]efinitions of codependency are so broad as to be all-encompassing. This sits just fine with Melody Beattie...[for whom co-dependency is] "a dependency on people—on their moods, behaviors, sickness or well-being, and their love." In her sequel she is more catholic still: codependency "is about ways we have been affected by other people and our pasts." Let's not get hung up on definitions: "Whatever codependency is," she notes, "it's a problem, and recovering from it feels better than not."[9]

This dismissiveness was also reflected in frequent accusations impugning co-dependency advocates' "real" motives. Nearly all of the critics suggested that what is most clearly gained by the broad definitions of co-dependency is obvious: money, and a lot of it. In this spirit, Kristol argued that "[t]he rooting out of so-called codependent thought and behavior is the linchpin of the booming Recovery industry, a therapy-cum-publishing phenomenon."[10]

Later in the same piece, she more explicitly addressed the commodified aspects of the twelve-step subculture. Noting the increasingly generic applications of the "adult child" appellation, Kristol quoted "ACoA [Adult Children of Alcoholics] expert Herbert L. Gravitz," focusing specifically on Gravitz's assertion that "'[o]ver 200 million of us are denying our past.... Perhaps 230 million children of all ages in our country!'" In response to Gravitz's comment, Kristol wryly remarked that "[t]wo hundred and thirty million *anything* constitute a hefty market sector" (emphasis in original), and, in support of that observation, she noted the proliferation of recovery products and events, including "national and regional conferences...books, motivational tapes and videos...canoe trips, summer camp, calendars, mugs, [and] T-shirts."[11]

Kaminer also emphasized the economic aspect, observing that "[t]his amorphous disease is a business, generating millions of books sales, countless support groups, and, in September 1989, the First National Conference on Co-dependency in Scottsdale, Ariz. Codependency 'has arrived,' according to a conference report." And

> [t]he publishing industry, which didn't exactly invent codependency, is making sure that millions of Americans discover it.... Sales can fairly be called phenomenal. "Codependent No More" has enjoyed...sales of about 1.5 million copies.... Health Communications, Inc. says that its top book, "Adult Children of Alcoholics" by Janet G. Woititz, has sold 1.1 million copies. Charles L. Whitfield's "Healing the Child Within" has sold more than 500,000 copies, and John Bradshaw's "Bradshaw On: The Family" has sold 350,000 copies. Peter Vegso, the president of Health Communications, said he expects sales for all their books to top three million this year.

"It is enough," Kaminer concluded, to say "that codependency is bad and anyone can have it—which makes this condition seem more like a marketing device."[12]

Seeing co-dependency as a "marketing device" is essentially no different than assailing its diagnostic imprecisions; the two criticisms are linked by a shoot-from-the-hip intellectualism that overlies a condescending attitude toward both those who created and those who have adopted co-dependency. The inevitable results of such a stance are unaddressed questions, missed clues, and, ultimately, an inadequate level of understanding.[13]

The condescending assaults on co-dependency's definitions, concepts, and logic—and, by extension, on those who created and adopted the discourse—raise a variety of interesting questions. One is left, for example, with the nagging impression that what is really driving the critics' unnecessarily caustic and strident reactions to co-dependency is outrage at the advocates' temerity and pretentiousness, at the sheer audacity of encroaching upon the boundaries and prerogatives of "real intellectuals" with "real credentials." Indeed, when viewed from this perspective, one is tempted to conclude that perhaps the title to Stan J. Katz's and Aimee Liu's critique, *The Codependency Conspiracy,* holds a double meaning, connoting both the "hoax" that co-dependency ostensibly foisted upon its unwitting dupes and the advocates' attempt, their "conspiracy," to usurp the cultural authority of those more justly entitled to that authority.[14]

But however interesting these questions and speculations are, what is far more important is that the time, space, and effort devoted to mounting critical broadsides left little room or time for serious consideration. Co-dependency, the critics suggested, is, well, silly; those responsible for creating and disseminating such ideas are intellectually out of their league; they do not know what they are talking about. Such a stance, though, ultimately begs the important questions: Why, if co-dependency should not be taken seriously, did so many people do precisely that? Why did the discourse meet with such an enthusiastic response among the general public (bearing in mind, here, that its public comprises primarily white, middle-class, baby boomers)?

To be fair, some of the critics did acknowledge the significance of co-dependency's evident public appeal. These acknowledgments, though, tend to be limited, speculative, even romantic. The limits, of course, are understandable, and no doubt reflect the genres in which they have been presented—the book review essay, the journalistic human interest piece, the academic journal article. Clearly, with the possible exception of the latter, these are not often the venues for in-depth analysis. But, whatever the reasons, the critics' references to the larger cultural and social conditions underlying co-dependency's public appeal were offered in passing, as if they felt obliged to give at least a perfunctory nod in the direction of "social and cultural influences," however vaguely conceived. Gomberg, for example, asked,

> What are the needs these simplistic concepts speak to? In the case of "codependency," we have suggested that the need is related to substance abuse treatment as a growth industry, an expanding number of facilities [and so on].... In the case of the expansion of the concept of addiction, it is more difficult to say. Perhaps a kind of trendy fashion, keeping in style: a "shrink" or a psychoanalyst for one generation, an Addiction Anonymous group for another? Perhaps a need for belonging and a substitution for religious belief? Perhaps a true *cri de coeur*?[15]

"Members of such [Anonymous] groups," Gomberg noted, "assert that membership in the group has helped them. It probably has, and it is a commentary on the lonely crowd."[16]

Kristol, in an equally impressionistic mode, spoke of co-dependency's adherents as "Those Who Identify" with members of twelve-step groups;

that is, the "amazing number of people" who, although neither necessarily from a family with an addicted member nor themselves addicted, nonetheless "wanted to identify" with the themes and methods of the twelve-step subculture. These more generic adult children included "people who felt they hadn't received enough love or attention as children; people who felt a general sense of malaise or spiritual emptiness."[17]

In this same spirit, Kaminer suggested that "[t]he disease of codependency is probably millennium fever":

> Everybody wants to be reborn, and in recovery, everybody is. No matter how bad you've been in the narcissistic 70's and the acquisitive 80's, no matter how many drugs you've ingested, or sex acts performed, or how much corruption enjoyed, you're still essentially innocent: the divine child inside you is always untouched by the worst of your sins.[18]

Gomberg's *"cri de coeur,"* Kristol's "malaise," Kaminer's "millennium fever," and so on all illustrate exactly what the dismissive stance lacks. To offer key words or catchphrases as conclusions about a phenomenon such as co-dependency is to stop at precisely the point at which a serious analysis should begin: Why should there be a widespread cry from the public's heart? What are the reasons for this malaise, this millennium fever? How does co-dependency respond to the conditions to which these terms loosely refer?

As I hope is clear from the analysis presented in the preceding pages, I am not suggesting that a pollyanna-ish credulity is the appropriate stance toward the co-dependency phenomenon or that it should be immune from criticism. There are undeniably negative implications to the ways in which the discourse has taken on tangible social form. The most obvious of these is the equivalency that co-dependency draws between childhood socialization and "abandonment and abuse," a formula that has almost certainly inflated the rhetoric of abuse that is so prevalent in contemporary U.S. life: Everyone is socialized, thus everyone has been abandoned and abused. Such catholic conceptions of abuse and abandonment make it all but impossible to sort out those who have been beaten from those who were scolded as children.[19] As such, the discourse makes it harder rather than easier to find and help those whose experiences of abuse entail events far more nightmarish than being required to control one's anger as a child.

These objectionable elements notwithstanding, however, I think it is important not to be drawn into a cynical view of the phenomenon of co-dependency as a whole. The critics, as the sampler of their views indicates, for the most part fell into such a cynical stance, characterizing co-dependency's creators as primarily profit-motivated, as psychological carpetbaggers capitalizing on individual hardships. By implication, such assessments also paint converts to co-dependency with much the same brush, implying that they are gullible or self-absorbed or simply naive. These views are, to my mind, not only unnecessarily puerile, they are largely beside the point, doing little to forward an understanding of what the phenomenon of co-dependency is all about.

It is possible to see both co-dependency's creators and converts in a more balanced and more relevant way. John Bradshaw and his compatriots are probably best understood as people guided by a sincere wish to do something positive for the world, to help people with their problems. That their efforts have made them wealthy hardly constitutes evidence of their motives. What is more instructive are the ways in which the advocates' social positions and ideological commitments shape their views—a well-established phenomenon in the sociology of knowledge.[20] As counselors, co-dependency's advocates are predisposed to seeing the world in psychologistic terms. More important, they are bound to and limited by specific explanations for people's problems. As we have seen, as adherents of liberation psychotherapy, the sole causal mechanism that co-dependency's architects have at their disposal is cultural repression of the self. Their creation of co-dependency discourse, then, can in part be understood as a monument to the ways in which any belief system constitutes both a way to see and a way not to see. Confronted with a bewildering array of life problems and bound by the conceptual and theoretical commitments of the liberation psychotherapist, they constructed an explanation for those problems that fits with their already established worldview.

Co-dependency's advocates are hardly alone in their enthusiasm for the ethic of self-actualization. Indeed, liberation psychotherapy—the chief distributor of that ethic—has become the dominant symbolism in U.S. life for understanding human behavior and social life and for conducting one's affairs; this dominance is reflected, as we have seen, in educational statistics, in the public's embrace of therapeutic ideals and its recourse to psychological approaches—both formal and informal—to life problems, in surveys of changing public attitudes, and in the institutional instability growing out of those changed beliefs. All of the available evidence, then, indicates the existence of a "master trend," a "silent revolution," a fundamental "culture shift" away from an ethic of self-denial and toward an ethic of self-actualization. The values and actions of the baby boom generation in particular reveal a reversal in moral priorities, in which the self and its prerogatives outweigh the importance of society and its conventions and norms.[21]

Such a profound change of cultural priorities required a completely redrawn moral and symbolic universe, new conceptions of right and wrong, new categories of normality and deviance. These new moral and conceptual categories are still being created—categories reflecting the primacy of personal, rather than social, experience. Their point of departure is the overarching significance of the inner life; the behaviors and beliefs to be valued and rewarded take the self as the primary reference point. Lionel Trilling described the emergence of one such new category over two decades ago, just as these cultural transformations began to take their full effect. Trilling maintained that "authenticity" (in essence, the congruence between the prerogatives of a true, inner, self and the person's conduct) had supplanted "sincerity" (the quality of a person's performance of public roles) as the salient element for estimating personal worth. Peter L. Berger, expanding on Trilling's thesis, observed that in our era "honor," an intrinsically social characterization of an individual, has become progressively obsolete and thus has given way to conceptions of each self's intrinsic "dignity."[22] In both cases, the new categories are grounded in and reflect the reversal of the self-to-society relationship.

The shift from an ethic of self-denial to an ethic of self-actualization also logically required new definitions of psychological health and sickness. Under the guidance of liberation psychotherapy's core premises, it is not possible to accept conceptions of psychological health that take adherence to mainstream culture's norms as their benchmark. Indeed, adherence to collective standards—which requires, from this vantage point, the denial of the self—is both a cause and a symptom of sickness. Thus, those who were considered models of psychological health only a generation ago are now models of psychological sickness. Under the aegis of liberation psychotherapy, the individuated self—a self that forty years ago would in all likelihood have been categorized as "immature," "selfish," or "antisocial"—has become the standard to which individuals should aspire. The failure to express oneself and one's emotions has become a symptomatic display. Individuation and autonomy from collective pressures for conformity have become the benchmarks of psychological health.

Co-dependency is plainly one of these new categorical systems. The discourse's symbolic and narrative structure, as we have seen, duplicates and hinges upon precisely the same inversion of moral judgments. Co-dependency's advocates take for granted all of liberation psychotherapy's central tenets, portraying mainstream culture's rules for acceptable behavior—rules oriented by the ethic of self-denial—as no more than preparations for and guarantors of mental and behavioral pathology. The lessons imparted by families and other institutions seeking to socialize rather than foster the individuation of the young now constitute a "poisonous pedagogy." Former virtues such as "obedience, orderliness, cleanliness, and the control of emotions and desires" are now symptoms, because they are the manifestations of a self that has capitulated to externally imposed demands.[23] In what is perhaps the most obvious example of the reversal of standards, co-dependency defines families that teach children to control their emotions and actions—literally called "functional families" in the 1950s and early 1960s[24]—as "dysfunctional" families that, in the course of passing on inherited moral demands, "shame" and "abuse" their progeny.

The same moral reversals are apparent in the "symptoms" associated with the "disease" of co-dependency. Whereas believers in an ethic of self-denial would probably understand, for example, "external referenting" as a laudable orientation to the well-being of others and the community, co-dependency sees such orientations as a sign that an individual lacks identity. So, too, an eagerness to attend to others' needs is, in co-dependency, "caretaking"—a pathological intrusiveness, a dysfunctional urge to "fix" others' problems and "control" their behavior. Moreover, co-dependency construes a concern with the general civility of personal conduct and appearance as "impression management," betraying a characterological dishonesty learned at the hands of mainstream culture. Just so, "self-centeredness" is no longer a self-absorbed indifference to others but the diagnosable urge to take undue responsibility for the problems of friends and family.

All that co-dependency discourse takes and espouses as true, then, reflects the rise of liberation psychotherapy to its dominant position in U.S. life; a rise that is both expressed by and requires these inversions in meanings. But as we have seen, co-dependency also goes beyond liberation psychotherapy, responding to its successes (or failures) and reforming it into a more fully social doctrine. The self-actualized individual, through emancipation from familial, filial, religious, neighborhood, and community demands, possesses a historically unprecedented range of personal freedom; but this freedom has been won at the expense of the social relationships and institutions in and through which a coherent identity is formed and maintained.

In and through the new theory of addiction and the concept of process addiction co-dependency reveals the two distinguishing impulses of a reformist discourse: the legitimation of an established symbolic--moral system and the provision of a means of bringing social relations more fully into line with the principles of that symbolic system. The legitimation of liberation psychotherapy is evident in the new theory of addiction, which effectively obscures the consequences of liberation psychotherapy's cultural and societal impact; guided by the assumption that human nature's benevolence precludes harmful intent, co-dependency defines problems that issued from the widespread embrace *of* liberation psychotherapy as new manifestations of the products of cultural repression.

By reconceptualizing the consequences of cultural repression in this way, co-dependency also offered a way of stabilizing social relationships, making new forms of communal purpose and action both possible and necessary. As co-dependents/process addicts, those for whom the larger cultural and societal changes of the past generation have proven painful, disillusioning, and disorienting have access to an alternative course of action. By becoming co-dependent, people are able to restore the linkages among and between identity, culture, and, particularly, mediating institutions—linkages that liberation psychotherapy had broken but could not adequately replace. Through its reforms of the original symbolic system, co-dependency renders liberation psychotherapy amenable to enduring patterns of interaction, organizing selves and social relationships around a commonly held and mutually understood moral and symbolic order, steering behavior into more or less stable and reliable patterns, oriented by and toward shared purposes. The old culture, by dint of liberation psychotherapy's successes, no longer possesses these capacities; liberation psychotherapy, by dint of its staunch anticultural and anti-institutional premises, never did.

Although imposing a communal orientation on its believers, co-dependency does not seek to roll back the cultural clock to the ethic of self-denial; rather, it reforms liberation psychotherapy, modifying it so as to forge a common cause among those who have adopted the view that submission to group expectation thwarts self-realization and causes psychological sickness. By fusing the ethic of self-actualization with the disease model of addiction, co-dependency transformed the nature of group expectation: The common cause that co-dependents share is the pursuit of self-actualization. Members of CoDA are oriented toward a mutual goal of recovery, and recovery entails becoming self-actualized individuals.

A Disease of One's Own

The point of emphasizing that co-dependency is a discursive response to the darker consequences of liberation psychotherapy's dominance in contemporary American life is emphatically *not* that "traditional ways" are "good" or that liberation psychotherapy is "bad"; *not* that "repression" is "good" or that "self-actualization" is "bad." Such single- or simple-mindedness seldom yields much insight. Rather, the point is that, when placed in their historical context, co-dependency and the co-dependency movement have important things to tell us about the current state of U.S. life. Underlying co-dependency's emergence and public selection are cultural and societal conditions that have affected millions of people. Liberation psychotherapy has helped to ring out the old with an efficiency matched only by its inability to ring in the new. U.S. institutions—especially the "mediating institutions," that is, family, community, neighborhood—and the cultural precepts underlying them have dwelled in a state of limbo between what was and what is yet to be for nearly a generation now. The impact of this has nowhere been experienced more keenly than among those whose relationships and institutions have been shaken to their very foundations: among the white middle-class men and women of the post–World War II baby boom, many of whom now find themselves filing into the school basements, church meeting halls, and treatment center conference rooms where the old and new twelve-step groups convene. What they are doing there is no less than an attempt to reinvent the common purposes, the communal orientations, and the stable and reliable social patterns that underlie any meaningful use of the word "society."

Because it is fundamentally grounded in social relationships and the institutions arising from those relationships, identity is also inevitably caught up in these larger cultural changes. However much Americans, particularly those holding liberation psychotherapy convictions, might strain against these reins, the organization of personality is largely a social, cultural, and institutional function; as they go, so goes identity. This is one of co-dependency's most appealing features: It offers a way of putting together an identity, ordering the events of people's lives into a reasonably satisfying and coherent narrative, a story in which their mistakes make sense and are, in a manner of speaking, forgiven. Their recurrent missed connections, their failed relationships, their troubled status as both parents and children—all are accounted for, as the logical and inescapable culmination of a previously unremembered, or "incorrectly" remembered childhood.

Access to a coherent life story in which one's failings are absolved, however, is only part of co-dependency's appeal. Liberation psychotherapy, after all, also tells a story of people's lives, and its model for doing so has been widely available for public consumption for a good many years. But, as we have seen, liberation psychotherapy has always invited, if not incited, the therapeutically liberated self to eschew the setting, the history, the social foundations from which any identity garners it baseline intelligibility. The net result is that following the ethic of self-actualization ultimately undermines the commitments by which social relationships and institutions are sustained; these are the very relationships and institutions in which identity is grounded. An identity is an inordinately difficult thing to sustain completely on one's own; it is also, and intrinsically, a product of social relationships and recognitions. In the limbo between the repudiated ethic of self-denial and the heretofore nonsocial ethic of self-actualization, the necessary institutional, historical, and cultural "conversation partners" possess at most a dramatically attenuated capacity to shape and stabilize identity; that capability has been delegitimated by the same themes that set the individual free.

The dominant themes at CoDA meetings clearly point to these larger processes and dynamics—to nonbinding social attachments and fundamental disruptions in close social relationships. The constant litany of despair, disappointment, and disillusionment expressed in these groups does not disclose the epidemic of abuse, abandonment, and addiction that co-dependency describes; rather, it reveals a pattern of indifference toward normative demands that constrain the individual and a corresponding impermanence and unreliability in social attachments. In the members' accounts both of their own and others' actions, mainstream social roles are most notable for their apparently transitory quality rather than for their status as inescapable prisons.

Whatever one's view of its merits or shortcomings, co-dependency offers people a solution to their problems. The point is neither to praise the discourse for making such a solution available nor to condemn it for how it has construed the problems it aims to solve. What is most important is to recognize that this was plainly an offer that many have wanted or needed to hear. Converts to co-dependency use the discourse not as a response to the heavy burdens of cultural repression but as a way to come to terms with the cultural and social changes issuing from the widespread embrace of liberation psychotherapy and the impact that that has had in their own lives. The socially constructed nature of the converts' life stories indicates that people do not participate in the movement because co-dependency captures the story of their lives; rather, they adapt the story of their lives to the discourse's symbolic and narrative structures *in order to participate in the movement.* Converts use the discourse to qualify for group membership and work to invent a personal history that would make them suitable CoDA members. They want "in" badly enough to search their pasts and "come up with something" that legitimates their conversion and membership status. What they "come up with" is a tale that superficially validates co-dependency's— and liberation psychotherapy's—cultural critique, while solving their own quite different problems with relationships and their own identities, problems born of the public success of liberation psychotherapy; they use the discourse as their entry ticket into a communal life that mainstream culture can no longer provide for them and that liberation psychotherapy never could. Co-dependency offers a way to institutionalize liberation psychotherapy, to translate that symbolic system into a corresponding system of social relations, into new forms of identity, family, faith, and community. This is the principal source of co-dependency's appeal, and that appeal, in turn, is a testimonial to the enduring importance of a genuinely social existence, of communal purpose, shared convictions, stable relationships.

* * * * *

The story of the emergence of co-dependency, then, is not a story of addiction at all. But that was perhaps always the least plausible way of understanding the phenomenon anyway. More important, it is not a story of repression, either. Rather, the co-dependency movement is a story about psychotherapeutic liberation, its cultural and social consequences, and the search for ways to translate liberation psychotherapy into stable institutional form. Over the past thirty years, the tenets of liberation psychotherapy as a new form of moral order have become firmly entrenched; yet it has not lent itself to the creation of stable social relationships, institutions, or identities, and so many have begun to seek out or to create solutions. The project of liberation from emotional repression is to some degree being superseded by efforts to deal with the results of that liberation. In this, too, co-dependency is a barometer of larger cultural phenomena. Although it is well beyond the limits of this analysis to develop this point in any detail, it is clear that on any number of fronts, perhaps the preeminent question on the table has become "What to do now?" Seeking a public answer to this question is a principal source of the unmistakable polarization and contentiousness of U.S. life as we approach the millennium.[25] At bottom, the myriad debates on the U.S. landscape—on, for example, family, crime, education, law, art, music—center around individual liberation and are dominated by two vocally, if not numerically, superior choruses: one calling for a return to the old ways; the other, more instructively, calling for the institutionalization of liberation psychotherapy norms.

For those who subscribe to the ethic of self-actualization, a return to the old ways is anathema. But a return to the ethic of self-denial—at least in its previous forms—does not appear likely to happen: Simply as a function of passing time and the accompanying passage of authority from one generation to the next, the ethic of self-actualization is in all likelihood here to stay, at least well into the foreseeable future. Not only do the members of the baby boom generation, now fully coming into power, overwhelmingly (albeit not entirely) endorse the liberation psychotherapy worldview, but it is also clear that the children of the baby boomers are, if anything, even more favorably inclined toward that worldview.[26] Nonetheless, until the battles between the adherents of these conflicting ethics can be resolved, co-dependency provides an alternative course of action; one in which it appears to be possible to keep what has been gained (or lost, depending upon one's standpoint) in individual freedom while simultaneously forging new foundations for collective purpose. Although by and large predicated upon liberation psychotherapy's principles, by fusing liberationist and adaptational psychologies co-dependency also solves some of the key problems that the ethic of self-actualization has helped to create. "Having" a disease of one's own—believing in co-dependency—gives the convert access to a new set of twelve-step relationships, a new twelve-step "family of affiliation," a new community of souls possessed of a common tradition, a shared symbolic and moral order, and a mutually understood sense of purpose. Co-dependency is an attempt at reform, an effort to create a set of social institutions by which liberation psychotherapy can become that which it has never been: an alternative to all that it rejects.

Notes

1. For example, in a *Washington Post* interview, Stanton M. Peele, a social–clinical psychologist and one of the twelve-step subculture's more acerbic critics (as well as one of the most important "defectors" from the subculture), says of co-dependency: "It's ironic and humorous that the main way people define their problems is that they help others too much. With homelessness and all our other problems, I don't get the feeling that lack of selfishness is a massive culture-wide phenomenon" (quoted in David Streitfeld, "The Addiction Habit: Breaking Step with the Self-Help Movement," *Washington Post*, 28 August 1990, C5). Peele has himself done a great deal of research on addiction and, much like George E. Vaillant, in *The Natural History of Alcoholism*, and Don Cahalan, in *Problem Drinkers*, has concluded that the disease model is a useful metaphor upon which to base humanitarian public policy but is of limited utility beyond that. The sources of Peele's disaffection with the treatment industry are well summed up in the title of his critique: *Diseasing of America: Addiction Treatment out of Control*. Frank Reissman, co-director of the National Self-Help Clearinghouse, in an article that otherwise (and not surprisingly) sings the praises of the self-help movement in general and of twelve-step groups in particular, agreed "that focusing so much on yourself does nothing to change the political or social realities that got you addicted in the first place" (quoted in Streitfeld, ibid.). Interviews with some of Schaef's devotees seem, in part, to bear out these concerns. For example, a woman in attendance at one of Schaef's workshops commented, "I don't want to save the world anymore. I want to save myself." When asked how the world was then going to be saved, she responded, "Who says it needs to?... 'saving' sounds like a disease concept to me." Another woman at the workshop fully agreed, asserting her view that "[i]f we're all taking care of ourselves, then no one needs to worry about being taken care of" (see Streitfeld, ibid.). On the issues of misdirected public policy and the neglect of social problems, Peele observes that "[y]oung people take fewer drugs now, drinking is down, and yet we're saying we've got more addiction. We oversold the problem for middle class people. And the people where [*sic*] addiction is increasing is, of course, in the inner city, and we don't

know how to deal with that. We tell them they have a disease too but that no one gives a damn. They're not getting into the Betty Ford Center" (quoted in Streitfeld, ibid.).

2. Co-dependency, from one feminist viewpoint, is a euphemism for political oppression. Kay Leigh Hagan has argued that *"codependency* [is] a term that is much more acceptable than *internalized oppression"*; indeed, it "is a precise description of the way we are trained to support a dominant/subordinate caste system" (Kay Leigh Hagan, "Co-Dependency and the Myth of Recovery," *Fugitive Information: Essays From a Feminist Hothead* [New York: HarperCollins, 1993],32; emphasis in the original). From a different perspective, some have argued that, particularly when informed by liberation psychotherapy's definition of individuation as the benchmark of the psychologically healthy self, family systems psychotherapy—one of co-dependency's intellectual influences, as we have seen—effectively defines connectedness with and concern for others as a sickness; see, for example, Goldner, "Feminism and Family Therapy"; Luepnitz, *The Family Interpreted.*

3. Peele, for example, argues that the life improvements claimed by Schaef and her devotees are less a testimonial to the miraculous powers of the twelve steps than they are "[a] sign of intellectual poverty. It's not evidence. I could find tens of thousands of people who swear they were cured by the laying-on of hands. Does that mean the government should get into the laying-on of hands? We've replaced systematic evaluation...with religious testimony" (quoted in Streitfeld, "The Addiction Habit," C5). At perhaps the opposite extreme, an article in the 9 December 1988 issue of *Christianity Today* observed that "[f]or Christians, the all-inclusive definition of co-dependency may sound like another way of identifying the universal human problem of sin" (Jim Alsdurf and Phyllis Alsdurf, "The Generic Disease," *Christianity Today* 2 [1988]: 33). The concern here is that individual moral responsibility stands to be subsumed beneath the rubric of addiction. Thus, these authors note that "[w]hat is being crafted in this deterministic outlook is a view of the individual as having no control over choices because of the presence of an insidious disease/addiction/ codependency" (ibid.). This misgiving notwithstanding, the twelve-step subculture and the church have traditionally been in one another's good graces, and CoDA groups often follow in the long-standing AA tradition of meeting in church basements and classrooms. Clearly, these friendly terms rest upon the spirituality, however generic, of the twelve steps.

4. Edith Lisansky Gomberg, "On Terms Used and Abused: The Concept of 'Co-dependency,'" *Drugs and Society: Current Issues in Alcohol and Drug Studies* 3 (1989): 116, 118.

5. Ibid., 115.

6. Kaminer, "Chances Are, You're Co-Dependent, Too," *New York Times Book Review,* 11 February 1990, 1. Kaminer went on to expand her review essay, turning it into her book-length critique *I'm Dysfunctional, You're Dysfunctional.* Although the book also raises some interesting and worthwhile points, for the most part it simply rehearses all of the earlier analysis's points in greater detail; as such, it, too, is marred by a dismissive and polemical stance. Indeed, that stance is suggested by the title alone—a tongue-in-cheek play on Thomas Harris's popular treatise on Transactional Analysis, *I'm Okay, You're Okay* (New York: Harper and Row, 1969).

7. Kaminer, "Chances Are, You're Co-Dependent, Too," 1, 2.

8. Quoted in ibid., 1.

9. Elizabeth Kristol, "Declarations of Codependence: People Who Need People Are the Sickliest People in the World—And That's Just for Starters," *American Spectator,* June 1990, 21.

10. Ibid., 21.

11. Ibid., 23.

12. Kaminer, "Chances Are, You're Co-Dependent, Too," 1. All figures in the Kaminer quote are current only up until 1990; see the introduction for more recent sales data. I have included Kaminer's figures here to illustrate the critics' tendency to impugn the motives of Beattie and her colleagues.

13. For example, one issue left unaddressed is that if co-dependency's definitions are simply money-making strategies, then the same must be said of all of the multiple forms of liberation psychotherapy: The idea that collective subordination of the individual—or, simply, culture—is the cause of virtually all psychological sickness certainly did not originate with co-dependency. Kaminer, who is well aware that co-dependency's architects merely drew upon established psychotherapeutic bromides when putting together their own discourse, nonetheless leaves what would seem to be an important question unasked and unacknowledged. If Beattie and Schaef are engaged in cynical market manipulation, then were not Carl Rogers, Abraham Maslow, Rollo May, Fritz Perls, Arthur Janov, and other, less-well-known proponents of the same ideas—ideas that co-dependency by and large reiterates—also doing the same thing? As we have seen, Kaminer is something of an apologist for Maslow, and she launches into a spirited defense of his ideas.

14. Katz and Liu, *The Codependency Conspiracy.* Revealing a decidedly unironic bent, the authors make no mention of the paradoxes involved in effectively taking charge of people's lives in order to tell them how to take charge of their lives. Indicating the legitimacy of their claims to cultural authority, the liner notes inform the reader that Katz "is a nationally recognized expert in the field of family relations, child abuse, and substance abuse whose past affiliations include the National Institute on Drug Abuse, Children's Hospital in Los Angeles, and the Graduate School of Social Welfare at UCLA. In addition to his private practice, he is clinical director of The Maple Center, Beverly Hills' community mental health center, and is a member of the Expert Panel for the L.A. Superior Court." And Liu, moreover, "was an associate producer of NBC's *Today* show before becoming a full-time journalist. She...has co-authored numerous other books and articles on business and health topics." Among the critics, only Gomberg acknowledges the tensions and struggles over authority between academic and self-help, or folk, psychologies and psychologists (see her "On Terms Used and Abused"). As I noted earlier in this book, the treatment industry operates according to an entirely different credentialing process: The legitimacy of the counselors' authority is closely linked with their life experiences as alcoholics or drug addicts. Thus, as we saw, Bradshaw predicated his own legitimacy upon such credentials as "having been an active part of the recovering community for 22 years" (Bradshaw, *Healing the Shame,* 97). The twelve-step subculture has historically eschewed the significance of credentials altogether.

15. Gomberg, "On Terms Used and Abused," 128.

16. Ibid., 127.

17. Kristol, "Declarations of Codependence," 23.

18. Kaminer, "Chances Are, You're Co-Dependent, Too," 3.

19. Wendy Kaminer has also raised this point. Her principal concern revolves around co-dependency's tendency, because of its indiscriminate conceptions of abuse, to

level the "hierarchy of suffering." Kaminer, though, does not provide evidence to document this pattern among the members; see her *I'm Dysfunctional, You're Dysfunctional.*

20. Although the relationship between social position and a person's beliefs has been an important theme in sociology throughout the history of the discipline, I am specifically drawing upon the work of Karl Mannheim, here; see Karl Mannheim, *Ideology and Utopia* (New York: Harcourt, Brace), 1936. For a more contemporary and particularly well-done example of the analytical stance that Mannheim called for in the sociology of knowledge, see Luker, *Abortion and the Politics of Motherhood.* Luker does not identify herself with Mannheim, but her analysis—particularly her discussion of the worldviews of pro-life and pro-choice activists—epitomizes what Mannheim had in mind.

21. Russell, *The Master Trend;* Inglehart, *The Silent Revolution* and *Culture Shift.*

22. Lionel Trilling, *Sincerity and Authenticity* (Cambridge, Mass.: Harvard University Press, 1974). See also Peter L. Berger, "'Sincerity' and 'Authenticity' in Modern Society" (a review essay on Trilling's book), *The Public Interest* 31 (1973): 81–90, and "On the Obsolescence of the Concept of Honor," *European Journal of Sociology* 11 (1970): 373–80.

23. Bradshaw, *Bradshaw On: The Family,* 7.

24. See, for example, Bales and Parsons, *Family, Socialization, and Interaction Process.*

25. These battles have been recently discussed by, among others, Hunter, *Culture Wars;* and Mary Anne Glendon, *Rights Talk: The Impoverishment of Political Discourse* (New York: Free Press, 1991).

26. Ronald Inglehart maintains that the fundamental "culture shift" that has been transpiring for the past thirty years in advanced industrial societies will become increasingly apparent and more deeply entrenched as the "postmaterialists" (a category that roughly corresponds with the baby boom generation) become the numerically superior and culturally dominant part of the population, in a process of gradual population replacement. In regard to the resurgence of conservatism in the United States in recent decades, he notes that "[t]he intensity with which religious issues have been raised in recent years" does not issue from mass support for a return to traditional religious and cultural norms but, rather, "reflects their advocates' conviction that their most basic values are being rapidly eroded." By dint of their life experiences, the generation now seizing the reins of political power—the baby boomers, or "postmaterialists"—"tend to take physical survival for granted and are relatively tolerant of behavior that deviates from traditional social norms" (Inglehart, *Culture Shift,* 205, 206). In terms of the therapeutic values of the baby boomers' children, see Russell, *The Master Trend.*

Appendix A

Methodology

The analysis and conclusions about co-dependency presented in this book emerged out of the research through a process that was more inductive than deductive. I did not approach the topic with specific preconceived notions or with an explanatory framework already in mind. I did, however, for reasons that the text itself explains, approach co-dependency as a cultural product, a discourse, and, as such, I was oriented toward the processes underlying its creation and public selection—an orientation that required close attention to the content of the discourse and to the social, cultural, and historical context in which it emerged and was publicly embraced.

The first stage of the research focused upon co-dependency's content and structure. These initial efforts comprised a close reading and analysis of the best-known and most influential (at least judging from sales figures) co-dependency treatises in order to establish exactly what claims the discourse makes. The primary sources for this analysis included John Bradshaw's *Bradshaw On: The Family* and *Healing the Shame That Binds You;* Anne Wilson Schaef's *Co-Dependence: Misunderstood, Mistreated* and, to a lesser extent, *When Society Becomes an Addict* and *Escape from Intimacy—Untangling the "Love" Addictions: Sex, Romance, Relationships*; Sharon Wegscheider-Cruse's *Choicemaking: For Co-Dependents, Adult Children, and Spirituality Seekers;* Melody Beattie's *Codependent No More: How to Stop Controlling Others and Caring for Yourself* and *Beyond Codependency and Getting Better All the Time;* Charles Whitfield's *Healing the Child Within;* and Robert Subby's *Lost in the Shuffle: The Co-Dependent Reality.* These materials were supplemented with other readings—some directly cited in the text, some not. I also drew upon a variety of materials that CoDA offers either free or at quite reasonable rates to the general public and to new or prospective members, including cassette tapes of various lecturers and of CoDA members discussing their own problems and CoDA's ways of organizing identity, and brochures describing key aspects of the organization and of membership (Appendix B reproduces key meeting readings; these and other materials are cited in the text). Although I have not incorporated them in the analysis (except for excerpts from Bradshaw's *Homecoming* special on the Public Broadcasting System), I have also examined the transcripts of numerous talk shows on which the advocates appeared to ply and publicly discuss their trade.

As the analysis in chapter 3, in particular, reveals, I paid especially close attention to recurring sets of "binary oppositions" in these various co-dependency treatises, as well as to the tensions between those opposed categories. Such oppositions play an important role in structuring belief systems into distinctive forms. In the course of studying co-dependency, several such conceptual polarities emerged. The most general of these was the putatively antagonistic relationship between, on the one hand, mainstream culture and society and, on the other hand, the individual, a relationship that is portrayed in terms of repression (framed, in co-dependency, as "abandonment and abuse" of the self by society). A series of lesser oppositions issued from and were subsumed beneath this most general conflict. For example, the discourse held that because "traditional" culture is reliant upon "rationalism" as its central value, it demands the repression of emotional experience and expression. This conflict between rationality and free expression of feelings begot yet another binary opposition, marked by the emergence of a "false self" (the co-dependent) that was said to dominate the consciousness and behavior of the "true self" (the inner child). Finally, the discourse espoused a bifurcated characterization of action as a way of accounting for the false self's often destructive behaviors. Here, the polarity was between the intentionality and the inevitability of people's conduct. False selves, co-dependency asserted, do not intend to behave as they do; their actions are the inevitable outcome of mainstream culture's repressive practices and normative demands.

As for the mechanics of this initial stage of the research, I marked examples of these recurrent oppositions as they appeared in co-dependency treatises and in the transcriptions I had made of video or audio presentations of the discourse. I then built "files" for each of the prevalent polarities, sorting the claims according to their correspondence with the categories of "true self-false self," "rationality-feelings," "intentionality-inevitability," and "self-society." By effectively "de-constructing" the discourse in this way, it became much easier to understand the foundation of its appeal to a public, and this gave me a clearer sense of what a belief in co-dependency entailed.

Discourses are ways of conceptualizing, interpreting, knowing, and speaking about the world that are governed by tacit rules for what will and will not be accepted as true. These rules structure a discourse in particular ways. As chapter 2 explains, isolating the structuring elements of co-dependency was an exercise in what Michel Foucault called "archaeology," which is to say that the first stage of the research uncovered, or began to uncover, the unspoken rules guiding the discourse's judgments as to what counts as a true statement about self, social relationships, and the world. I had the good fortune of not starting out this analytical work as a complete neophyte. During earlier research on the rise of the addiction treatment industry and the structure of an adolescent inpatient treatment regimen, I had been immersed in the logic of the disease model of alcoholism and, by attending nearly fifty AA meetings as part of that research, had become familiar with the central truths of the twelve-step philosophy. This was more than simply a fortuitous background for analyzing a new version of the twelve-step philosophy. Because of that experience, it was readily apparent to me that, although co-dependency's advocates repeatedly pay homage to the twelve steps and to AA, the structure of opposed categories in co-dependency and the basis for their oppositions engendered a set of claims that ran directly counter to, rather than continued, the original twelve-step tradition. Other than the intentionality-inevitability polarity, co-dependency's central truths plainly bore little resemblance to those of AA. Co-dependency's truths about culture and about the right relationship between self and society, for example, clearly indicated that it was guided by different rules from those of AA, which takes repeated failures to abide by conventional norms as an indication of sickness. In co-dependency, as the text explains, precisely the opposite is true: Sickness grows out of exposure and adherence to conventional norms. Yet, the "sickness" was nonetheless construed as an addiction.

These apparently contrary convictions required a "genealogical" project, in which a truth system's lineage is traced back across a path of logical contradictions and theoretical discontinuities in and through which new truths emerge. As noted in chapter 2, this project revealed co-dependency's odd admixture of conventional addiction truths with presuppositions imported from the liberation psychotherapy of Carl Rogers and Abraham Maslow. This, it became clear, was not a "true" twelve-step doctrine.

Analyzing co-dependency's structuring polarities and isolating the truths to which it was beholden were not idle intellectual preoccupations. The structure and truths provide more than an ideologically informed map of the current social and cultural landscape. Discourses attribute causes for the crises they portray and seek to elicit their public's commitments to a course of action mapped out by the new truths the discourse espouses. The audience is exhorted to repudiate the conditions of imminent collapse that the discourse describes and to participate in some form of systematic redress of those conditions. Discourses such as co-dependency, then, are essentially narrative forms, and an understanding of their social consequences must attend to the courses of action the narrative prescribes for its followers. The principal mechanism driving co-dependency's narrative was a tension between liberation psychotherapy's "ethic of self-actualization" and mainstream culture's "ethic of self-denial." As discussed in chapters 2 and 3, co-dependents are told they are sick because of mainstream culture's "poisonous" teachings and practices. These are not AA truths; therefore co-dependents' commitments are not those of AA but those of liberation psychotherapy's actualizing self.

This first stage of the research, comprising the analysis of the primary theoretical works on co-dependency, was conducted in 1989–1990. The results of that research guided subsequent observations at CoDA meetings I attended during the last months of 1990 through spring 1991. Over this period of time, I attended twenty CoDA meetings—five in Los Angeles, California; one in central Virginia; two in New Jersey; six in Omaha, Nebraska; and seven in Boston, Massachusetts. The goals of this field work were two: although of no statistically generalizable value, I wanted to get some empirically based indication of who the participants in the co-dependency movement were (see table 1), and I wanted to capture, as accurately as possible, the ways in which the discourse influenced the life stories that co-dependents tell. There were no noteworthy variations in terminology or practice among the regional meetings, and such differences as there were included relatively trivial

TABLE 1
CoDA Meetings by Geographical Location,[1] Meeting Size, Gender, and Institutional Setting

	Total	Male	Female	Setting
Los Angeles				
1	12	12[2]	0	Hospital
2	58	21	37	Church
3	46	20	26	Church
4	39	15	24	Counseling Center (CC)[3]
5	24	9	15	Bookstore[4]
Boston				
1	31	11	20	CC
2	14	2	12	Church
3	15	4	11	CC
4	21	5	16	Church
5	26	9	17	CC
6	29	11	18	CC
Omaha				
1	30	12	18	12-step[5]
2	24	10	14	12-step
3	15	3	12	Library
4	25	11	14	Library
5	14	5	9	Church
6	32	15	17	Church
Central Virginia				
1	7	3	4	Church
New Jersey				
1	46	19	27	Church
2	39	16	23	Church
Total				
20	**547**	**213 (39%)**	**334 (61%)**	

[1]Meetings listed for Los Angeles, Boston, and Omaha refer to the greater metropolitan areas of these cities. I have chosen the "Central Virginia" and "New Jersey" designations in order to guarantee that they are not identifiable.

[2]A "stag" meeting—that is, for men only. Figures not included in summary statistics.

[3]The "Counseling Center" designation refers to meetings held in mental health clinics that were unattached to larger health care facilities.

[4]This meeting was held in a "recovery bookstore," such as I referred to in the introduction.

[5]This designation refers to meetings held in property owned and shared by area twelve-step groups.

variations (such as the California groups' practice of applauding after every testimonial made by the members).

As must always be the case, field research entails finding an adequate balance between practical matters and ethical concerns. I attended only meetings that were open to the general public (there are closed meetings, as well as meetings, such as gay and lesbian meetings, restricted to people with specific interests and concerns) and, with one exception, that were large enough that outside listeners and observers were common and unobtrusive. (The central Virginia meetings, although open to the public and more convenient to my home base at the time, were too small to attend as an unobtrusive observer. Thus, the alternatives were to engage in disguised participant observation—an ethically unsupportable move—or to explain my research goals. This I did, at the one meeting in central Virginia that I attended. Although this surmounted one ethical dilemma, it posed another that ultimately proved unresolvable: The members asked me to leave the room while they voted as to whether I could stay at the meeting or not. They agreed to let me stay, but they were then forced to repeat the vote each time a member arrived late. After the meeting, although they assured me that I was welcome to attend because they were open meetings, we agreed that my presence clearly interfered with the normal course of the meetings, which I could not do in good conscience. I have also not identified the exact location of this meeting because of its small size—in deference to the norm of anonymity.)

Also for ethical reasons, at no time in the course of the fieldwork did I pretend to "be" a member or to "be" co-dependent. During the requisite introductions, I simply said "I am just here to listen, and to find out more about CoDA." Throughout the twelve-step subculture, this is an accepted and familiar occurrence. At many meetings I attended, as noted in chapter 6, there was at least one other person who reported that they, too, were there to listen.

Ethical concerns also shaped the actual "data" gleaned from this fieldwork and presented in this study. CoDA, as is true of all of the twelve-step groups, seeks to be an anonymous group. The wish for anonymity must be respected, not least because it is one of the primary secrets of the twelve-step subculture's successes. As such, throughout this study, data drawn from CoDA meetings are not identified by meeting place. As added precautions, I have changed the names of the members, and, where the nature of their comments seems at all likely to compromise their anonymity, the remarks have been altered to retain their substance without allowing the possibility of betraying someone's identity.

Honoring the norm of anonymity influenced the data-gathering process in another important way, as well. Although the members' comments are crucial to an understanding of co-dependency's cultural significance, strategies such as secretly tape recording were also ethically unconscionable. As such, I landed on what I believe to be a satisfactory compromise. Immediately upon leaving CoDA meetings, I transcribed the members' remarks as fully and accurately as possible. This approach at least partially sacrificed verbatim accuracy to the more important ethical concerns. Nonetheless, the transcription period always immediately followed the meetings, and so the meetings were fresh in memory. I am entirely confident that the quotations presented herein are fully in keeping with the spirit and, in large sections, with the actuality of what was said. The aforementioned earlier research on the alcohol treatment industry had presented me with an almost identical set of research problems, leaving me with some practical experience with this approach.

The analysis of the "data" from the field research—CoDA members' comments, organizational brochures and practices, and meeting structure—mirrored the stages by which I analyzed the advocates' and organization's treatises. After I had recorded their stories, I returned to my field notes and marked any and all comments that corresponded with major conceptual themes in the discourse. As noted in the body of this study, the degree of correspondence was striking: Members frequently spoke of themselves and their lives in terms that almost to the word echoed the advocates' central premises. Following the annotation process, I assigned the members' comments to the "files" mentioned above.

The final stage of research involved placing co-dependency's emergence and its selection by a public in social, cultural, and historical context. This was archival work, examining the history of past episodes of cultural production and community building in the United States. As noted, the best sociological and historical studies demonstrated that peak periods of both the production of alternative meaning systems and social experimentation corresponded with periods of profound social and cultural upheaval.

Moreover, as noted in the text, there is often a disparity between a discourse's rendition of the social conditions to which it responds and the nature of those conditions. During the Second Great Awakening, for example, larger social and cultural changes were framed in religious imagery—the dominant cultural framework of the era. This finding helped to make sense of the repeated disparity between co-dependency's portrait of contemporary mainstream culture and both the converts' uses of the discourse and the wealth of both empirical evidence and theoretical exposition that paints a radically different portrait. Drawing upon the findings from the "archaeological" and "genealogical" findings from earlier stages in the research, it became clear that co-dependency's central premises were all grounded in a cultural critique that antedated and precipitated the far-reaching cultural changes to which the discourse responds. Its only significant differences from those previous doctrines issue from the notion of "process addiction," and that notion engenders communal action and sets explicit moral limits to the actions of the therapeutically liberated self.

* * * * *

There was an additional component to the research that, although I have not used the material in this study, bears mention—not least because it proved to be helpful for checking my own conclusions about the discourse. From the summer of 1990 through the early spring of 1991, I conducted ten interviews with clinicians who treated co-dependency. These interviews were open-ended discussions with clinical mental health professionals who had encountered self-diagnosed co-dependents in their practices (clinical social workers, addiction-treatment specialists, and other licensed practical counselors). The questions I posed to them were constructed with two goals in mind: first, to examine co-dependency's influences at the level of lived, clinical experience, and, second, to further illuminate the ways in which the key themes in the discourse were reflected (or not) in clinical application. I wanted to find out whether co-dependency's central themes represented the problems that the clinicians encountered and whether they used the discourse itself to guide them. In brief, were they talking about the same thing? As it turned out, they were and are—albeit with a great deal more caution and skepticism than either the converts or the advocates. I also posed deliberately naive questions to the clinicians to avoid "steering" their answers in directions they might not otherwise have taken. They were asked, for example, to comment upon whether, in their experience, the emotions play a significant role in co-dependency and, if so, how? I expected this deliberate naiveté to be more fruitful than telling them what I had uncovered in my analysis of the discourse, which might have invited responses that were oriented toward helping me confirm my ideas rather than reflecting what they really thought and did. These interviews were also taped and transcribed. The transcriptions were then reorganized, as with all of the other data, in terms of co-dependency's central theoretical categories. I have not used these materials in this study because in many ways they reiterate themes that have been discussed at length in the body of this study. Moreover, although often very useful and interesting, the interviews were not directly relevant to the central focus in the book: the interplay between co-dependency's content and the larger context in which it appeared, an interplay that led people to select the discourse.

* * * * *

Finally, I should say a few words regarding the style of this study. I sought to engage co-dependency's advocates in an intellectual discussion and to examine the discourse on its own terms, reserving my critical comments for the adequacy of co-dependency's logical structure. The critical engagements are undertaken in good faith; at least, that has been the goal. I have attempted to take what co-dependency says seriously, to familiarize myself as thoroughly as possible with the substance of its arguments, and to present those arguments as accurately as possible in these pages. This is a time-honored form of scholarly exchange. Moreover, as of this writing, it is a courtesy that has not yet been extended to the discourse.

The goal of this study, then, was not, as noted in the conclusion, to set up a "straw man" against which I could exercise and parade my own critical skills. However, neither was it to become an apologist for or a convert to co-dependency's version of the twelve-step philosophy. Beattie, Bradshaw, and their colleagues make a powerful and, for many, a convincing bid for cultural authority. The evidence for their success in this bid is solid, as the material presented herein illustrates. A substantial minority of Americans have begun to organize their lives and social relationships in accordance with the doctrines that co-dependency espouses. Far from not taking the discourse or its expositors and advocates seriously, I took it and them very seriously indeed. Both take it upon themselves to instruct others as to the way they should understand and live their lives. This is to lay a claim to an enormously powerful role in society. That a large number of people follow that advice and thereby validate that claim suggests that the exact nature of counsel not only warrants but demands careful consideration. The historical record would surely seem to bear out that suggestion. Conversely, I did not and do not wish to engage in a polemic. I offer no alternatives and propose no policies, settling for clearer understanding.

Although co-dependency is not guided by a single claim, among the most insistent and consistent of their claims is the unaccountability of power under "traditional" forms of social organization. In their arguments, the discourse and its architects have seized something resembling the moral high ground: They are, they insist, speaking for the underdog; calling for greater tolerance, fewer repressions, better treatment of children, happier people, and help for the addicted and emotionally distraught. This places anyone who seeks to bracket his or her own credulity and to closely examine the claims being pressed in the unenviable role of being misinterpreted as an apologist for the opposite point of view, that is, for less tolerance, worse treatment of children, more addiction, a general increase in unhappiness, and so on. To suggest that this is what those engaging in a critical analysis of therapeutic discourses are proposing is preposterous, to be sure, but it is a common enough interpretation, nonetheless.

If a key premise in co-dependency, though, is the unaccountability of those who lay claim to the individual's life, then surely its own claims must be subject to the opposite standard. It is for these reasons that this study takes co-dependency's ideas seriously and tries to engage it at the level of those ideas; for the same reasons, it is important to assess the discourse critically. Thus, although I do not count myself among the critics per se, there is every chance that this study will be read as such. I hope that this exploration will be understood as an attempt to make sense both of what is clearly a significant cultural product and of the historical, social, and cultural context in which that significance has become possible.

Appendix B

Key CoDA Readings

The Preamble

Co-Dependents Anonymous is a fellowship of men and women whose common problem is an inability to maintain functional relationships. We share with one another in the hopes of solving our common problem and helping others to recover; the only requirement for membership is a desire for healthy and fulfilling relationships with others and ourselves.

CoDA is not allied with any sect, denomination, politics, organization or institution; does not wish to engage in any controversy; neither endorses nor opposes any causes. We rely upon the wisdom, knowledge, Twelve Steps, and Twelve Traditions, as adopted for our purpose from Alcoholics Anonymous, as the principles of our program and guides to living healthy lives. Although separate entities, we should always cooperate with all twelve step recovery programs.

The Welcome

We welcome you to Co-Dependents Anonymous—a program of recovery from co-dependency where each of us may share our experience, strength, and hope in our efforts to find freedom where there has been bondage and peace where there has been turmoil in our relationships with others and ourselves.

Most of us have been searching for ways to overcome the dilemmas of the conflicts in our relationships and our childhoods. Many of us were raised in families where addictions existed—some of us were not. In either case, we have found in each of our lives that co-dependency is a most deeply-rooted, compulsive behavior and that it is born out of our sometimes moderately, sometimes extremely dysfunctional family systems.

229

We have each experienced in our own ways the painful trauma of the emptiness of our childhood and relationships throughout our lives. We attempted to use others—our mates, our friends, and even our children, as our sole source of identity, value, and well being and as a way of trying to restore within us the emotional losses from our childhood. Our histories may include other powerful addictions which at times we have used to cope with our co-dependency.

We have all learned to survive life, but in CoDA we are learning to live life. Through applying the Twelve Steps and principles found in CoDA to our daily life and relationships, both present and past, we can experience a new freedom from self-defeating lifestyles. It is an individual growth process. Each of us is growing at our own pace and will continue to do so as we remain open to God's will for us on a daily basis. Our sharing is our way of identification and helps us to free the emotional bonds of our past and the compulsive control of our present.

No matter how traumatic your past or despairing your present may seem, there is hope for a new day in the program of Co-Dependents Anonymous. No longer do you need to rely on others as a power greater than yourself. May you instead find here a new strength within to be that which God intended—Precious and Free.

Typical Characteristics of a Co-Dependent

- I assume responsibility for others' feelings and/or behaviors.
- I feel overly responsible for others' feelings and/or behaviors.
- I have difficulty in identifying feelings—am I angry? lonely? sad? happy? joyful?
- I have difficulty expressing feelings—I am feeling happy, sad, hurt, joyful.
- I tend to fear and/or worry how others may respond to my feelings.
- I have difficulty in forming or maintaining close relationships.
- I am afraid of being hurt or rejected by others.
- I am perfectionistic and place too many expectations on myself and others.
- I have difficulty in making decisions.
- I tend to minimize, alter, or even deny the truth of how I feel.
- Other people's actions and attitudes tend to determine how I react or respond. I tend to put other people's wants and needs first.
- My fear of others' feelings (anger) determines what I say and do.
- I question or ignore my own values to connect with significant others. I value others' opinions more than my own.

- My self-esteem is bolstered by outer or other influences. I cannot acknowledge good things about myself.
- My serenity and mental attention is determined by how others are feeling and/or behaving.
- I tend to judge everything I do, think, or say harshly, by someone else's standards. Nothing is done, said or thought "Good Enough."
- I do not know or believe that being vulnerable and asking for help is both okay and normal.
- I do not know that it is okay to talk about the problems outside the family, or that feelings just are, and it is better to share them than to deny, minimize or justify them.
- I tend to put other people's wants and needs before my own.
- I am steadfastly loyal—even if the loyalty is unjustified and personally harmful.
- I have to be needed in order to have a relationship with others.

Patterns of Co-Dependency

- My good feelings about who I am stem from being liked by you.
- My good feelings about who I am stem from receiving approval from you.
- Your struggle affects my serenity. My mental attention focuses on solving your problems or relieving your pain.
- My mental attention is focused on pleasing you.
- My mental attention is focused on protecting.
- My mental attention is focused on manipulating you...(to do it my way).
- My self-esteem is bolstered by solving your problems.
- My self-esteem is bolstered by relieving your pain.
- My own hobbies are put aside. My time is spent sharing your interests and hobbies.
- Your clothing and personal appearance are dictated by my desires as I feel you are a reflection of me.
- Your behavior is dictated by my desires as I feel you are a reflection of me.
- I am not aware of how I feel, I am aware of how you feel.
- I am not aware of what I want—I ask what you want. I am not aware I assume.
- The dreams I have for my future are linked to you.
- My fear of rejection determines what I say or do.
- I use giving as a way of feeling safe in our relationship.
- My social circle diminishes as I involve myself with you.
- I put my values aside in order to connect with you.
- I value your opinion and way of doing things more than my own.
- The quality of my life is in relation to the quality of yours.

The Twelve Steps of Co-Dependents Anonymous*

1. We admitted we were powerless over *others*—that our lives had become unmanageable.
2. Came to believe that a power greater than ourselves could restore us to sanity.
3. Made a decision to turn our will and our lives over to the care of God as we understood *God*.
4. Made a searching and fearless moral inventory of ourselves.
5. Admitted to God, to ourselves, and to another human being the exact nature of our wrongs.
6. Were entirely ready to have God remove all these defects of character.
7. Humbly asked *God* to remove our shortcomings.
8. Made a list of all persons we had harmed and became willing to make amends to them all.
9. Made direct amends to such people wherever possible, except when to do so would injure them or others.
10. Continued to take personal inventory and when we were wrong promptly admitted it.
11. Sought through prayer and meditation to improve our conscious contact with God as we understood *God*, praying only for knowledge of *God's* will for us and the power to carry that out.
12. Having had a spiritual awakening as a result of these steps, we tried to carry this message to other Co-Dependents, and to practice these principles in all our affairs.

The Twelve Traditions of Co-Dependents Anonymous

1. Our common welfare should come first; personal recovery depends upon CoDA unity.
2. For our group purpose there is but one ultimate authority—a loving God as expressed to our group conscience. Our leaders are but trusted servants, they do not govern.
3. The only requirement for CoDA membership is a desire for healthy and loving relationships.
4. Each group should remain autonomous except in matters affecting other groups or CoDA as a whole.
5. Each group has but one primary purpose—to carry its message to other Co-Dependents who still suffer.

---

* [Other than the relatively uncomplicated substitution of "co-dependents" for "alcoholics" in the twelfth step, there are two significant differences between the AA and the CoDA wordings: the object over which one is powerless, and the de-gendered God-concept. I have identified these changes in italics here.]

6. A CoDA group ought never endorse, finance or lend the CoDA name to any related facility or outside enterprise, lest problems of money, property or prestige divert us from our primary spiritual aim.
7. Every CoDA group ought to be fully self-supporting, declining outside contributions.
8. Co-Dependents Anonymous should remain forever nonprofessional, but our service centers may employ special workers.
9. CoDA, as such, ought never be organized, but we may create service boards or committees directly responsible to those they serve.
10. CoDA has no opinion on outside issues, hence the CoDA name ought never be drawn into public controversy.
11. Our public relations policy is based on attraction rather than promotion; we need always maintain personal anonymity at the level of press, radio, and films.
12. Anonymity is the spiritual foundation of all our traditions; ever reminding us to place principles before personalities.

* * * * *

Although it is somewhat peculiar to refer to the "traditions" of an organization that has been in existence for well under a decade, the twelve traditions are a set of precepts and suggestions handed down by AA's founders. Their hope in making these provisions was to protect AA's autonomy by avoiding its professionalization and any possible conflicts of interest. In addition to the dubious use of the term "traditions," it is clear that CoDA's fidelity to these principles is also quite problematic. Certainly Bradshaw, Schaef, and their colleagues cannot in any way be said to observe the principle of anonymity. Their frequent appearances on *Oprah, Geraldo,* and other mainstays of the public confessional circuit, directly contradict not only the twelve-step norm of anonymity but also the claim that this program, like AA, is "a program of attraction, rather than promotion." The latter assertion is also called into question by co-dependency's notably incendiary rhetoric and imagery. As the discourse's critics are fond of observing, the rhetoric more closely resembles a marketing strategy than a case of leading the exemplary life and inspiring by example. Moreover, CoDA itself is the product of a set of judgments and opinions regarding outside issues, and these opinions have clearly drawn "the CoDA name...into public controversy."

CoDA members often appear to be well aware of these contradictions, and opinions about the leading advocates seem to divide into two camps. Prior to one meeting, for example, a younger member was extolling the virtues of John Bradshaw's *Homecoming* video. He acknowledged that "some people in the program have a real problem with the guy [Bradshaw], and say that he breaks all the traditions and all that, but I think he's great, myself." A much older man responded, "well, I'm not that familiar with Bradshaw, but I don't think there's much doubt that he does ignore most of the main traditions." This man allowed that Bradshaw "seems to have some worthwhile things to say," but that "personally I don't think he's very good for AA or CoDA."

References

Abercrombie, Nicholas, Stephen Hill, and Bryan S. Turner. *The Dominant Ideology Thesis.* London: George, Allen and Unwin, 1980.

Ackerman, Nathan. *The Psychodynamics of Family Life.* New York: Basic Books, 1958.

———. *Treating the Troubled Family.* New York: Basic Books, 1966.

Alcoholics Anonymous. *Alcoholics Anonymous: The Story of How Many Thousands of Men and Women Have Recovered from Alcoholism.* New York: Alcoholics Anonymous World Services, 1976.

———. *Twelve Steps and Twelve Traditions.* New York: Alcoholics Anonymous World Services, 1985.

Alexander, Jeffrey C. "The Promise of a Cultural Sociology: Technological Discourse and the Sacred and Profane Information Machine." In *Theory of Culture,* edited by Richard Munch and Neil J. Smelser, 292–323. Berkeley: University of California Press, 1992.

Alsdurf, Jim, and Phyllis Alsdurf. "The Generic Disease." *Christianity Today,* 2 (1988): 30–38.

Anderson, Charles, Deborah J. Carter, and Andrew G. Malizio. *Fact Book on Higher Education.* New York: MacMillan (American Council on Education), 1990.

Bales, R. F., and Talcott Parsons. *Family, Socialization, and Interaction Process.* New York: Free Press, 1951.

Barth, Karl. *The Church and the Political Problem of Our Day.* London: Hodder and Stoughton, 1939.

Bateson, Gregory, D. Jackson, J. Haley, and J. Weakland. "Toward a Theory of Schizophrenia." *Behavioral Science* 1 (1956): 251–64.

Beattie, Melody. *Codependent No More: How to Stop Controlling Others and Caring for Yourself.* New York: Harper/Hazelden, 1987.

———. *Beyond Codependency and Getting Better All the Time.* New York: Harper/Hazelden, 1989.

———. *The Language of Letting Go: Daily Meditations for Codependents.* San Francisco: Harper/Hazelden, 1990.

Bellah, Robert N. "Civil Religion in America." In *Beyond Belief: Essays on Religion in a Post-Traditional World.* New York: Harper and Row, 1970.

235

Bellah, Robert N., Richard Madsen, William M. Sullivan, Ann Swidler, and Steven M. Tipton. *Habits of the Heart: Individualism and Commitment in American Life*. New York: Harper and Row, 1985.

Bendix, Reinhard. *Work and Authority in Industry*. Berkeley: University of California Press, 1974; originally published in 1956.

Ben-Yehuda, Nachman. *The Politics and Morality of Deviance: Moral Panics, Drug Abuse, Deviant Science, and Reversed Stigmatization*. Albany, N.Y.: State University of New York Press, 1990.

Berger, Peter L. *Invitation to Sociology: A Humanistic Perspective*. Garden City, N.Y.: Doubleday, 1963.

———. "Identity as a Problem in the Sociology of Knowledge." *Journal of Sociology* 7 (1966): 373–84.

———. "'Sincerity' and 'Authenticity' in Modern Society." *The Public Interest* 31 (Spring 1973): 81–90.

———. "On the Obsolescence of the Concept of Honor." *European Journal of Sociology* 11 (1977): 373–80.

Berger, Peter L., and Thomas Luckmann. *The Social Construction of Reality: A Treatise in the Sociology of Knowledge*. Garden City, N.Y.: Doubleday, 1966.

Bertalanffy, L. von. "An Outline of General Systems Theory." *British Journal of the Philosophy of Science* 1 (1950): 134–65.

Best, Joel. *Threatened Children: Rhetoric and Concern about Child-Victims*. Chicago: University of Chicago Press, 1993.

Bethune, John. "Pens and Needles." *Publisher's Weekly*, 20 July 1990, pp.18–20, 24–28.

Black, Claudia. *It Will Never Happen to Me*. Denver, Colo.: M. A. C., 1981.

———. "Foreword." In *Choicemaking: For Co-Dependents, Adult Children, and Spirituality Seekers*, by Sharon Wegscheider-Cruse, v–vii. Deerfield Beach, Fla.: Health Communications, 1985.

Bodin, Arthur M. "The Interactional View: Family Therapy Approaches of the Mental Research Institute." In *Handbook of Family Therapy*, edited by Alan S. Gurman and David P. Kniskern, 267–309. New York: Brunner/Mazel, 1981.

Bowen, Murray. *Family Therapy in Clinical Practice*. New York: Jason Aronson, 1978.

Boyers, Robert, ed. *Psychological Man*. New York: Harper and Row, 1975.

Bradshaw, John. *Bradshaw On: The Family*. Deerfield Beach, Fla.: Health Communications, 1988.

———. *Healing the Shame That Binds You*. Deerfield Beach, Fla.: Health Communications, 1989.

———. *Homecoming: Reclaiming and Championing Your Inner Child*. New York: Bantam, 1990.

———. *Creating Love: The Next Great Stage of Love*. New York: Bantam, 1992.

Brown, J. David. "The Professional Ex-: An Alternative for Exiting the Deviant Career." *Sociological Quarterly* 32 (1991): 219–30.

Bruner, Jerome. "Life as Narrative." *Social Research* 54 (1987): 11–32.

Burke, Kenneth. *Permanence and Change*. Indianapolis, Ind.: Bobbs-Merrill, 1965.

Cahalan, Don. *Problem Drinkers*. San Francisco: Jossey-Bass, 1970.

Canguilhem, Georges. *On the Normal and the Pathological*, translated by Carolyn R. Fawcett (editorial collaboration by Robert S. Cohen, introduction by Michel Foucault). Dordrecht, Holland, and Boston: D. Reidel Publishing, 1978; originally published in 1966.

Clark, E. T. *The Psychology of Religious Awakening*. New York: MacMillan, 1929.

Co-Dependents Anonymous. "Newcomer's Packet." Phoenix, Ariz.: Co-Dependents Anonymous, Inc., 1988.

———. "Attending Meetings: Three Aspects of CoDA Meetings." Phoenix, Ariz.: Co-Dependents Anonymous, Inc., 1989.

Cohen, Stanley. *Folk Devils and Moral Panics*. London: MacGibbon and Kee, 1972; New York: St. Martin's Press, 1980.

Conklin, Edmund S. *Principles of Abnormal Psychology*. Rev. ed. New York: Henry Holt, 1946.

Conrad, Peter M. "The Discovery of Hyperkinesis: Notes on the Medicalization of Deviant Behavior." *Social Problems* 23 (1975): 12–21.

Conrad, Peter M., and Joseph W. Schneider. *Deviance and Medicalization: From Badness to Sickness*. St. Louis, Mo.: Mosby, 1980.

Cowing, Cedric. *The Great Awakening and the American Revolution: Colonial Thought in the 18th Century*. Chicago: Rand McNally, 1971.

Crimp, Douglas, ed. *AIDS: Cultural Analysis, Cultural Activism*. Cambridge, Mass.: MIT Press, 1988.

Cross, Whitney. *The Burned-Over District: The Social and Intellectual History of Enthusiastic Religion in Western New York, 1800–1850*. New York: Harper and Row, 1965; originally published Ithaca, N.Y.: Cornell University Press, 1950.

Danto, Arthur C. *Analytical Philosophy of History*. London: Cambridge University Press, 1968.

Davidson, Arnold I. "Archaeology, Genealogy, Ethics." In *Foucault: A Critical Reader*, edited by David Couzens Hoy, 221–33. Oxford: Basil Blackwell, 1986.

Davis, Kingsley, and W. E. Moore. "Some Principles of Stratification." *American Sociological Review* 10 (1945): 242–49.

Denzin, Norman K. *The Recovering Alcoholic*. Beverly Hills, Calif.: Sage, 1987.

————. *Hollywood Shot by Shot: Alcoholism and the American Cinema.* Chicago: Aldine de Gruyter, 1991.

Douglas, Mary. *Natural Symbols: Explorations in Cosmology.* New York: Pantheon, 1982.

————. *Purity and Danger: An Analysis of the Concepts of Pollution and Taboo.* London, New York: Ark, 1984.

Dreyfus, Hubert L., and Paul Rabinow. *Michel Foucault: Beyond Structuralism and Hermeneutics.* Chicago: University of Chicago Press, 1982.

Durkheim, Emile. *The Rules of the Sociological Method,* translated by Sarah A. Solovay and John H. Mueller, edited by George E. G. Catlin. New York: Free Press, 1938.

————. *The Elementary Forms of the Religious Life.* Translated by Joseph Ward Swain. New York: Free Press, 1965.

————. *The Division of Labor in Society.* Translated by W.D. Halls. New York: Free Press, 1965.

Ehrenreich, Barbara. *The Hearts of Men: American Dreams and the Flight from Commitment.* Garden City, N.Y.: Doubleday/Anchor, 1983.

Fillmore, Kaye Middleton, and Dennis Kelso. "Coercion into Alcoholism Treatment: Meanings for the Disease Concept of Alcoholism." Berkeley, Calif.: Alcohol Research Group, monograph B299, 1986.

Fingarette, Herbert. *Heavy Drinking: The Myth of Alcoholism as a Disease.* Berkeley: University of California Press, 1988.

Fitzgerald, Frances. *Cities on a Hill.* New York: Simon and Schuster, 1987.

Foucault, Michel. *The Archaeology of Knowledge.* New York: Pantheon, 1972.

————. "Truth and Power." Translation of an interview with Alessandro Fontana and Pasquale Pasquino that originally appeared in *Microfisica del Potere.* In *Power/Knowledge: Selected Interviews and Other Writings, 1972–1977,* edited by Colin Gordon, 109–33. New York: Pantheon, 1980.

————. *The History of Sexuality.* Vol. 1. New York: Vintage, 1980.

————. "On the Genealogy of Ethics: An Overview of Work in Progress." In *The Foucault Reader,* edited by Paul Rabinow, 340–72. New York: Pantheon, 1984.

————. "We Other Victorians." In *The Foucault Reader,* edited by Paul Rabinow, 292–300. New York: Pantheon, 1984.

————. "The Repressive Hypothesis." In *The Foucault Reader,* edited by Paul Rabinow, 301–29. New York: Pantheon, 1984.

————. "Nietzsche, Genealogy, History." In *The Foucault Reader,* edited by Paul Rabinow, 76–100. New York: Pantheon, 1984.

Frank, Jerome D. *Persuasion and Healing: A Comparative Study of Psychotherapy.* New York: Schocken Books, 1961.

Frederick, Carl. *EST: Playing the Game the New Way.* New York: Delta, 1976.

Freidson, Eliot. *Profession of Medicine: A Study of the Sociology of Applied Knowledge*. New York: Harper and Row, 1970.

Freud, Sigmund. *Civilization and Its Discontents*. New York: Norton, [1930] 1961.

———. *The History of the Psychoanalytic Movement*. Translated by A. A. Brill. New York: Johnson Reprint Corporation, 1970; originally published in 1917.

Friel, John, and Linda Friel. *Adult Children: The Secrets of Dysfunctional Families*. Deerfield Beach, Fla.: Health Communications, 1988.

Gans, Herbert. "The Positive Functions of Poverty." *American Journal of Sociology*, 78 (1972): 275–89.

Gardner, Hugh. *The Children of Prosperity: Thirteen Modern American Communes*. New York: St. Martin's Press, 1978.

Geertz, Clifford. "The Impact of the Concept of Culture on the Concept of Man." In *The Interpretation of Cultures*, 33–54. New York: Basic Books, 1973.

———. "Ideology as a Cultural System." In *The Interpretation of Cultures*, 193–233. New York: Basic Books, 1973.

Gerson, Kathleen. "Coping with Commitment: Dilemmas and Conflicts of Family Life." In *America at Century's End*, edited by Alan Wolfe, 35–57. Berkeley: University of California Press, 1991.

Glendon, Mary Ann. *Rights Talk: The Impoverishment of Political Discourse*. New York: Free Press, 1991.

Goffman, Erving. *The Presentation of Self in Everyday Life*. Garden City, N.Y.: Doubleday/Anchor, 1959.

———. *Interaction Ritual*. Garden City, N.Y.: Doubleday/Anchor, 1967.

Goldner, Virginia. "Feminism and Family Therapy." *Family Process* 24 (1985): 31–47.

Gomberg, Edith Lisansky. "On Terms Used and Abused: The Concept of 'Codependency.'" *Drugs and Society: Current Issues in Alcohol and Drug Studies* 3 (1989): 114–32.

Gordon, D. F. "The Jesus People: An Identity Synthesis." *Urban Life and Culture* 3 (1974): 159–78.

Gramsci, Antonio. *Selections from the Prison Notebooks*. Edited and translated by Quentin Hoare and Geoffrey Nowell Smith. London: Laurence and Wishart, 1971.

Greenberg, Gary. *The Self on the Shelf: Recovery Books and the Good Life*. Albany: State University of New York Press, 1994.

Greenberg, G. S. "The Family Interactional Perspective: A Study and Examination of the Work of Don D. Jackson." *Family Process* 16 (1977): 385–412.

Gross, Philip. *The Psychological Society*. New York: Random House, 1978.

Gusfield, Joseph M. *The Culture of Public Problems*. Chicago: University of Chicago Press, 1981.

Hagan, Kay Leigh. "Co-Dependency and the Myth of Recovery." In *Fugitive Information: Essays from a Feminist Hothead*. New York: HarperCollins, 1993, 27-39.

Haley, Jay. "Marriage Therapy." *Archives of General Psychiatry* 8 (1963): 213-34.

———. *Strategies of Psychotherapy*. New York: Grune and Stratton, 1963.

Harris, Thomas. *I'm Okay, You're Okay*. New York: Harper and Row, 1969.

Hays, Sharon. "Structure and Agency and the Sticky Problem of Culture." *Sociological Theory* 12, no. 1 (1994): 57-72.

Heilbroner, Robert. *The Nature and Logic of Capitalism*. New York: Norton, 1985.

Hendricks, C. Gaylord. *Learning to Love Yourself: How to Become a Centered Person*. Englewood Cliffs, N.J.: Prentice-Hall, 1982.

———. *Learning to Love Yourself Workbook*. Englewood Cliffs, N.J.: Prentice-Hall, 1990.

Hirschman, Albert. *The Passions and the Interests*. Princeton, N.J.: Princeton University Press, 1977.

Hoy, David Couzens, ed. *Foucault: A Critical Reader*. Oxford: Basil Blackwell, 1986.

Hunter, James Davison. "The Modern Malaise." In *Making Sense of Modern Times*, edited by James Davison Hunter and Stephen C. Ainlay, 76-100. London: Routledge and Kegan Paul, 1986.

———. *Evangelicalism: The Coming Generation*. Chicago: University opf Chicago Press, 1987.

———. *Culture Wars: The Struggle to Define America*. New York: Basic Books, 1991.

Inglehart, Ronald. *The Silent Revolution: Changing Values and Political Styles among Western Publics*. Princeton, N.J.: Princeton University Press, 1977.

———. *Culture Shift in Advanced Industrial Society*. Princeton, N.J.: Princeton University Press, 1990.

Jackson, Don D. "Family Rules: The Marital *Quid Pro Quo*." *Archives of General Psychiatry* 12 (1965): 589-94.

———. "The Myth of Normality." *Medical Opinion and Review* 3, no. 5 (1967): 28-33.

Jacoby, Russell. *Social Amnesia: A Critique of Conformist Psychology from Adler to Laing*. Boston: Beacon Press, 1975.

James, William. *Varieties of Religious Experience*. New York: Longman, 1902.

Jerome, Judson. *Families of Eden: Communes and the New Anarchism*. New York: Seabury Press, 1974.

Johnson, Paul E. *A Shopkeeper's Millennium: Society and Revivals in Roches-ter, New York, 1815–1837.* New York: Hill and Wang, 1978.

Jones, Margaret. "The Rage for Recovery." *Publishers Weekly.* 23 November 1990, pp. 16–24.

Jones, R. K. "Paradigm Shifts and Identity Theory: Alternation as a Form of Identity Management." In *Identity and Religion,* edited by H. Mol, 59–82. Beverly Hills, Calif.: Sage, 1978.

Kahn, Joseph P. "Bradshaw Comes to Town—and, Maybe, to TV." *Boston Globe.* 18 February 1993, pp. 57, 62.

Kaminer, Wendy. "Chances Are, You're Co-Dependent, Too." *New York Times Book Review.* 11 February 1990, pp. 1, 26–27.

———. *I'm Dysfunctional, You're Dysfunctional: The Recovery Movement and Other Self-Help Fashions.* Reading, Mass.: Addison-Wesley, 1992.

Kane, Anne. "Cultural Analysis in Historical Sociology: The Analytic and Con-crete Forms of the Autonomy of Culture." *Sociological Theory* 9, no. 1 (1991): 53–69.

Kanter, Rosabeth Moss. *Commitment and Community: Communes in So-ciological Perspective.* Cambridge, Mass.: Harvard University Press, 1972.

Katz, Stan J., and Aimee E. Liu. *The Co-Dependency Conspiracy: How to Break the Recovery Habit and Take Charge of Your Life.* New York: Warner Books, 1991.

Kirk, Stuart A., and Herb Kutchins. *The Selling of DSM: The Rhetoric of Sci-ence in Psychiatry.* New York: Aldine de Gruyter, 1992.

Knox, Richard A. "Gene Linked to Alcoholism Also Tied to Other Disorders." *Boston Globe.* 2 October 1991, p. A15.

Krier, Beth Ann. "Excess Baggage: People-Pleasers Carry a Suitcase Full of Woes, but That's about All Co-Dependency's Leaders Can Agree On." *Los Angeles Times.* 14 September 1989, pp. 1, 21–22.

Kristol, Elizabeth. "Declarations of Codependence: People Who Need People are the Sickliest People in the World—and That's Just for Starters." *Ameri-can Spectator.* June 1990, pp. 21–23.

Laing, R. D., and A. Esterson. *Sanity, Madness, and the Family.* 2d ed. New York: Basic Books, 1971.

Lang, K., and G. E. Lang. *Collective Dynamics.* New York: Crowell, 1961.

Larsen, Earnie. *Basics of Co-Dependency.* Brooklyn Park, Minn.: E. Larsen Enterprises, 1983.

Lasch, Christopher. *The Culture of Narcissism: American Life in an Age of Diminishing Expectations.* New York: Norton, 1979.

———. *Haven in a Heartless World: The Family Beseiged.* New York: Basic Books, 1979.

Lepenies, Wolf. *Between Literature and Science: The Rise of Sociology.* Translated by R. J. Hollingdale. Cambridge and New York: Cambridge University Press, 1988.

Lévi-Strauss, Claude. *The Savage Mind.* Chicago: University of Chicago Press, 1966.

———. *Structural Anthropology.* Garden City, N.Y.: Doubleday/Anchor, 1967.

———. *The Raw and the Cooked.* New York: Harper and Row, 1969.

Lifton, Robert Jay. "Protean Man." *Partisan Review* 35, no. 1 (1968): 13-27.

Littrell, W. Boyd. "Competition, Bureaucracy, and Hospital Care: Costs in a Midwestern City." In *Bureaucracy as a Social Problem,* edited by W. Boyd Littrell, Gideon Sjoberg, and Louis A. Zurcher, 251-69. Greenwich, Conn.: JAI Press, 1983.

Luepnitz, Deborah Anna. *The Family Interpreted: Feminist Theory in Clinical Practice.* New York: Basic Books, 1988.

Luker, Kristen. *Abortion and the Politics of Motherhood.* Berkeley, Calif.: University of California Press, 1984.

Lukes, Steven. *Individualism.* Oxford: Basil Blackwell, 1973.

———. "Political Ritual and Social Integration." *Sociology* 9 (1975): 289-308.

MacIntyre, Alasdair. *After Virtue.* 2d ed. Notre Dame, Ind.: University of Notre Dame Press, 1984.

McLoughlin, William G. *Revivals, Awakening, and Reform: An Essay on Religion and Social Change in America, 1607-1977.* Chicago: University of Chicago Press, 1978.

Mannheim, Karl. *Ideology and Utopia: An Introduction to the Sociology of Knowledge.* Translated by Louis Wirth and Edward Shils. New York: Harcourt, Brace, 1936.

Martin, Bernice. *A Sociology of Contemporary Cultural Change.* New York: St. Martin's, 1981.

Marx, Karl and Frederick Engels. *The German Ideology.* In *Karl Marx: Selected Writings,* edited by David McLellan. Oxford: Oxford University Press, 1978.

Maslow, Abraham. "Our Maligned Human Nature." *Journal of Psychology* 28 (1949): 273-78.

———. *Toward a Psychology of Being.* Princeton, N.J.: Van Nostrand Reinhold, 1968.

———. *Motivation and Personality.* 2d ed. New York: Harper, 1970.

Matza, David. *Delinquency and Drift.* New York: John Wiley and Sons, 1964.

Mead, George Herbert. *Mind, Self, and Society.* Edited by Charles W. Morris. Chicago: University of Chicago Press, 1934.

———. *On Social Psychology.* Edited by Anselm Strauss. Chicago: University of Chicago Press, 1977.

Michels, Robert. *Political Parties: A Sociological Study of Oligarchical Tendencies of Modern Democracy.* New York: Collier, 1962; originally published in 1911.

Midelfort, C. F. *The Family in Psychotherapy.* New York: McGraw-Hill, 1957.

Miller, Alice. *For Your Own Good: Hidden Cruelty in Child-Rearing and the Roots of Violence.* Translated by Hildegarde and Hunter Hannum. New York: Farrar, Straus, Giroux, 1983.

Minuchin, Salvadore. *Families and Family Therapy.* Cambridge, Mass.: Harvard University Press, 1974.

———. *Family Kaleidoscope: Images of Violence and Healing.* Cambridge, Mass.: Harvard University Press, 1984.

Montagu, Ashley. *On Being Human.* New York: Henry Schuman, 1950.

Morgan, Patricia. "The Political Economy of Drugs and Alcohol." *Journal of Drug Issues* 13 (Winter 1983): 1–7.

Moseley, James G. *A Cultural History of Religion in America.* Westport, Conn.: Greenwood Press, 1981.

National Institute on Drug Abuse and National Institute on Alcohol Abuse and Alcoholism. "Highlights from the 1989 National Drug and Alcoholism Treatment Unit Survey." A thirteen-page early report from the *National Drug and Alcoholism Treatment Unit Survey.* Washington: Government Printing Office, 1990.

Nock, A. D. *Conversion.* New York: Oxford University Press, 1933.

O'Connor, James. *Accumulation Crisis.* New York: Basil Blackwell, 1986.

Parsons, Talcott. *The Social System.* New York: Free Press, 1951.

Peele, Stanton M. *The Meaning of Addiction: Compulsive Experience and Its Intepretation.* Lexington, Mass.: D. C. Heath, 1985.

———. *Diseasing of America: Addiction Treatment out of Control.* Lexington, Mass.: D. C. Heath, 1989.

Reisman, David, Nathan Glazer, and Reuel Denney. *The Lonely Crowd: A Study of the Changing American Character.* New Haven, Conn.: Yale University Press, 1950.

Rice, John Steadman. "'A Power Greater Than Ourselves': The Commodification of Alcoholism." Master's thesis, University of Nebraska at Omaha, 1989.

———. "Discursive Formation, Life Stories, and the Emergence of 'Co-Dependency': 'Power/Knowledge' and the Search for Identity." *Sociological Quarterly* 33, no. 3 (1992): 337–64.

Rieff, David. "Victims, All? Recovery, Co-Dependency, and the Art of Blaming Somebody Else." *Harper's.* October 1991, pp. 49–56.

Rieff, Philip. *The Triumph of the Therapeutic: Uses of Faith after Freud.* 2d ed. Chicago: University of Chicago Press, 1987; originally published 1966.

———. *Freud: The Mind of the Moralist*. 3d ed. Chicago: University of Chicago Press, 1979.

Robertson, Nan. *Getting Better: Inside Alcoholics Anonymous*. New York: Morrow, 1988.

Rochberg-Halton, Eugene. *Meaning and Modernity: Social Theory in the Pragmatic Attitude*. Chicago: University of Chicago Press, 1986.

Rogers, Carl. *On Becoming a Person: A Therapist's View of Psychotherapy*. Boston: Houghton Mifflin, 1961.

Roof, Wade Clark. *A Generation of Seekers: The Spiritual Journeys of the Baby Boom Generation*. New York: HarperCollins, 1993.

Room, Robin. "Treatment-Seeking Populations and Larger Realities." In *Alcoholism Treatment in Transition*, edited by Griffith Edwards and Marcus Grant, 205-24. London: Croom-Helm, 1980.

Rothenbuhler, Eric W. "The Liminal Fight: Mass Strikes as Ritual and Interpretation." In *Durkheimian Sociology: Cultural Studies*, edited by Jeffrey C. Alexander, 66-89. New York: Cambridge University Press, 1988.

Russell, Cheryl. *The Master Trend: How the Baby Boom Generation Is Remaking America*. New York: Plenum, 1993.

Ryan, Mary P. *Cradle of the Middle Class: The Family in Oneida County, New York, 1790-1865*. Cambridge: Cambridge University Press, 1981.

Sahlins, Marshall. *Culture and Practical Reason*. Chicago: University of Chicago Press, 1976.

Satir, Virginia. *Conjoint Family Therapy*. Palo Alto, Calif.: Science and Behavior Books, 1967.

Schaef, Anne Wilson. *Women's Reality: An Emerging Female System in the White Male Society*. San Francisco: Harper, 1985.

———. *Co-Dependence: Misunderstood—Mistreated*. New York: Harper and Row, 1986.

———. *When Society Becomes an Addict*. New York: Harper and Row, 1987.

———. *Escape from Intimacy—Untangling the "Love" Addictions: Sex, Romance, Relationships*. New York: Harper and Row, 1990.

———. *Meditations for Women Who Do Too Much*. San Francisco: Harper/Hazeldon, 1990.

Schneider, Joseph W. "Deviant Drinking as Disease: Alcoholism as a Social Accomplishment." *Social Problems* 25 (1978): 361-72.

Sennett, Richard. *The Fall of Public Man: On the Social Psychology of Capitalism*. New York: Random House, 1978.

Shepherd, W. C. "Conversion and Adhesion." In *Religious Change and Continuity: Sociological Perspectives*, edited by H. M. Johnson, 251-63. San Francisco: Jossey-Bass, 1979.

Shibutani, T. *Society and Personality*. Englewood Cliffs, N.J.: Prentice-Hall, 1961.

Shils, Edward, and Michael Young. "The Meaning of the Coronation." *Sociological Review* 1 (1953): 63-81.

Skocpol, Theda. *States and Social Revolutions.* Cambridge: Cambridge University Press, 1979.

Snow, David A., and Richard Machalek. "The Convert as a Social Type." In *Sociological Theory, 1983,* edited by Randall Collins, 259-89. San Francisco: Jossey-Bass, 1983.

———. "The Sociology of Conversion." *Annual Review of Sociology* 10 (1984): 167-90.

Stacey, Judith. *Brave New Families: Stories of Domestic Upheaval in Late Twentieth-Century America.* New York: Basic Books, 1990.

———. "Backward toward the Postmodern Family: Reflections on Gender, Kinship, and Class in the Silicon Valley." In *America at Century's End,* edited by Alan Wolfe, 17-34. Berkeley: University of California Press, 1991.

Starr, Paul. *The Social Transformation of American Medicine.* New York: Basic Books, 1982.

Streitfeld, David. "The Addiction Habit: Breaking Step with the Self-Help Movement." *Washington Post.* 28 August 1990, p. C5.

Subby, Robert *Lost in the Shuffle: The Co-Dependent Reality.* Deerfield Beach, Fla.: Health Communications, 1987.

———. "Inside the Chemically Dependent Marriage." In *Co-Dependency: An Emerging Issue,* 25-29 (edited, no editors cited). Deerfield Beach, Fla.: Health Communications, 1988.

Swidler, Anne. "Culture in Action: Symbols and Strategies." *American Sociological Review* 51 (1986): 273-86.

Taylor, Charles. *Sources of the Self: The Making of Modern Identity.* Cambridge, Mass.: Harvard University Press, 1990.

Taylor, Michael. "Structure, Culture, and Action in the Explanation of Social Change." *Politics and Society* 17, no. 2 (1989): 115-62.

Travisano, R. V. "Alternation and Conversion as Qualitatively Different Transformations." In *Social Psychology through Symbolic Interaction,* edited by G. P. Stone and H. A. Farberman, 594-606. Waltham, Mass.: Ginn-Blaisdell, 1970.

Trilling, Lionel. *Sincerity and Authenticity.* Cambridge, Mass.: Harvard University Press, 1974.

Turner, Ralph H. "The Real Self: From Institution to Impulse." *American Journal of Sociology* 81, no. 5 (1976): 989-1016.

Turner, Victor. *Dramas, Fields, and Metaphors: Symbolic Action in Human Society.* Ithaca, N.Y.: Cornell University Press, 1974.

———. "Social Dramas and Ritual Metaphors." In *Dramas, Fields, and Metaphors: Symbolic Action in Human Society,* 23-50. Ithaca, N.Y.: Cornell University Press, 1974.

————. "Metaphors of Anti-Structure in Religious Culture." In *Dramas, Fields, and Metaphors: Symbolic Action in Human Society,* 272–99. Ithaca, N.Y.: Cornell University Press, 1974.

————. "Passages, Margins, and Poverty: Religious Symbols of Communitas." In *Dramas, Fields, and Metaphors: Symbolic Action in Human Society,* 231–71. Ithaca, N.Y.: Cornell University Press, 1974.

————. *The Ritual Process: Structure and Anti-Structure.* Ithaca, N.Y.: Cornell University Press, 1977; originally pubished in 1969.

————. *The Forest of Symbols: Aspects of Ndembu Ritual.* Ithaca, N.Y.: Cornell University Press, 1986; originally published in 1967.

Twitchell, Vernon B. "A Psychologist Looks at Psychotherapy." *The American Mercury.* August 1950, pp. 166–75.

U.S. Bureau of the Census. *Statistical Abstracts of the United States.* Washington, D.C.: Government Printing Office, 1984.

————. *Statistical Abstracts of the United States.* Washington, D.C.: Government Printing Office, 1989.

————. *Statistical Abstracts of the United States.* Washington, D.C.: Government Printing Office, 1990.

U.S. Department of Health and Human Services. *Seventh Special Report to the U.S. Congress on Alcohol and Health from the Secretary of Health and Human Services.* Washington, D.C.: U.S. Department of Health and Human Services, 1990.

Vaihinger, Hans. *The Philosophy of As-If: A System of the Theoretical, Practical, and Religious Fictions of Mankind.* London: K. Paul, Trench, Trubner and Co.; New York: Harcourt, Brace and Co., 1924.

Vaillant, George E. *The Natural History of Alcoholism: Causes, Patterns, and Paths to Recovery.* Cambridge, Mass.: Harvard University Press, 1983.

Veroff, Joseph, Elizabeth Douvan, and Richard A. Kulka. *The Inner American: A Self-Portrait from 1957 to 1976.* New York: Basic Books, 1981.

Vitz, Paul. *Psychology as Religion: The Cult of Self-Worship.* Grand Rapids, Mich.: Eerdmans, 1977.

Wallace, Anthony F. C. "Revitalization Movements." *American Anthropologist* 58 (1956): 264–81. Reprinted in *Reader in Comparative Religion: An Anthropological Approach,* edited by William A. Lesser and Evon Z. Vogt. New York: Harper and Row, 1956.

Warner, William Lloyd. "An American Sacred Ceremony." In *American Life: Dream and Reality.* Chicago: University of Chicago Press, 1962, 1–26.

Watzlawick, P. *An Anthology of Human Communication: Text and Tape.* Palo Alto, Calif.: Science and Behavior Books, 1964.

————. *The Language of Change: Elements of Therapeutic Communication.* New York: Basic Books, 1978.

Watzlawick, P., J. H. Beavin, and Don Jackson. *Pragmatics of Human Communication.* New York: Norton, 1967.

Weber, Max. *The Protestant Ethic and the Spirit of Capitalism.* Translated by Talcott Parsons. New York: Charles Scribner's Sons, 1958.

Wegscheider, Sharon. *Another Chance: Hope and Help for the Alcoholic Family.* Palo Alto, Calif.: Science and Behavior Books, 1981.

Wegscheider-Cruse, Sharon. "Co-Dependency: The Therapeutic Void." In *Co-Dependency: An Emerging Issue,* 1–4 (edited—no editors cited). Deerfield Beach, Fla.: Health Communications, 1984.

————. *Choicemaking: For Co-Dependents, Adult Children, and Spirituality Seekers.* Deerfield Beach, Fla.: Health Communications, 1985.

Weisner, Constance M. "The Alcohol Treatment Systems and Social Control: A Study in Institutional Change." *Journal of Drug Issues* (Winter 1983): 117–33.

Weisner, Constance M., and Robin Room. "Financing and Ideology in Alcohol Treatment." *Social Problems* 32 (1984): 167–84.

Whitfield, Charles. *Healing the Child Within.* Baltimore: Charles Whitfield, The Resource Group, 1986.

Whyte, William H. *The Organization Man.* New York: Simon and Schuster, 1956.

Williams, Raymond. *The Long Revolution.* New York: Columbia University Press, 1961.

Woititz, Janet G. *Marriage on the Rocks.* Deerfield Beach, Fla.: Health Communications, 1979.

————. *Adult Children of Alcoholics.* Deerfield Beach, Fla.: Health Communications, 1983.

Wolfe, Alan, ed. *America at Century's End.* Berkeley: University of California Press, 1991.

————. "Introduction." In *America at Century's End,* edited by Alan Wolfe, 1–13. Berkeley: University of California Press, 1991.

————. "Out of the Frying Pan, into . . . What?" In *America at Century's End,* edited by Alan Wolfe, 461–71. Berkeley: University of California Press, 1991.

Wright, Will. *Sixguns and Society: A Structural Study of the Western.* Berkeley: University of California Press, 1977.

Wuthnow, Robert. *Meaning and Moral Order: Explorations in Cultural Analysis.* Berkeley: University of California Press, 1987.

————. *Communities of Discourse: Ideology and Social Structure in the Reformation, the Enlightenment, and European Socialism.* Cambridge, Mass.: Harvard University Press, 1989.

Zablocki, Benjamin. *The Joyful Community.* Baltimore: Penguin Books, 1971.

Zelizer, Viviana. *Pricing the Priceless Child: The Changing Social Value of Children.* New York: Basic Books, 1985.

Zilbergeld, Bernie. *The Shrinking of America.* Boston: Little, Brown and Company, 1983.

Index

Abercrombie, Nicholas (with Stephen Hill and Bryan S. Turner), 39n, 235
Ackerman, Nathan, 70n, 235
Addiction: cultural meanings of, 120; intentionality and, 120-21; moral legitimacy of, 122; powerlessness and, 121-22. *See also* Process addiction, types of.
Adorno, Theodor, 181
Adult Children of Alcoholics, 58, 59-62, 129
Al-Anon, 56-57, 59-62, 66
Ala-Teen, 57, 66
Alcoholics Anonymous, 16n, 49, 52, 66, 102, 115n, 121, 157n, 235; as adaptational psychology, 54-55; conception of intention in, 103; twelve-steps of, 54-55, 103, 119, 148; twelve traditions of, 60, 70n, 136n, 157n
Alcoholism: as legitimate sickness, 121, 136-37n; disease model of, 49, 61, 68n, 102-03; treatment of, 50, 58, 62-63, 70n; *See also* Treatment industry
Alexander, Jeffrey, 40n, 235
Alsdurf, Jim (with Phyllis Alsdurf), 215n, 235
Anderson, Charles (with Deborah Carter and Andrew G. Malizio), 42n, 235
Articulation, 20-21, 25, 35, 37, 73, 75-76, 79, 90-91, 95, 100, 148, 186-87. *See Also* Antonio Gramsci.

Baby Boom Generation, 29-30, 34-35, 95, 100, 169, 204, 207, 210, 213, 217n; expectations of 45n
Bales, R. F. (with Talcott Parsons), 217n, 235
Barth, Karl, 43n, 235

Bateson, Gregory, 71n, 235
Beattie, Melody, 2, 7, 47, 58, 83-84, 93n, 94n, 104, 114n, 115-16n, 119, 136n, 141, 154n, 161-62, 177n, 216n, 219, 224, 235
Beavis, J.H., 71n
Bellah, Robert, 39n, 235; (with Richard Madsen, William Sullivan Anne Swidler, and Steven Tipton), 39n, 42n, 236
Bendix, Reinhard, 197n, 236
Bentham, Jeremy, 164
Ben-Yehuda, Nachman, 137n, 236
Berger, Peter L., 45n, 98, 114n, 153n, 155n, 156n, 207, 217n, 236
Berger, Peter L. (with Thomas Luckmann), 23, 42n, 43n, 74, 92n, 93n, 155n, 236
Bertalanffy, L. von, 70n, 236
Best, Joel, 92n, 236
Bethune, John, 16n, 236
Black, Claudia, 59, 71n, 236
Bodin, Arthur M., 236
Bowen, Murray, 70n, 236
Boyers, Robert, 42n, 236
Bradshaw, John, 3-4, 9, 12n, 58-59, 64-65, 71-72n, 78, 92n, 93n, 94n, 97, 104-05, 106, 108, 114n, 115n, 116n, 119, 126, 136n, 138n, 153n, 154n, 163-164, 177n, 186, 189, 197n, 206, 216n, 217n, 219-20, 224, 233-34, 236-37; on abandonment and abuse, 80-81; on contamination, 81; on "poisonous pedagogy", 79-80; on process addiction, 106-07, 110; on "toxic shame", 82, 104,
Brown, J. David, 69n, 70n, 237
Bruner, Jerome, 45n, 237
Burke, Kenneth, 155n, 237

249